Time
to
Thrive

Chicken Soup for the Soul: Time to Thrive
101 Inspiring Stories about Growth, Wisdom, and Dreams
Amy Newmark, Loren Slocum Lahav.

Published by Chicken Soup for the Soul Publishing, LLC www.chickensoup.com
Copyright © 2015 by Chicken Soup for the Soul Publishing, LLC. All Rights Reserved.

No part of this publication may be reproduced, stored in a retrieval system or transmitted in any form or by any means, electronic, mechanical, photocopying, recording or otherwise, without the written permission of the publisher.

CSS, Chicken Soup for the Soul, and its Logo and Marks are trademarks of Chicken Soup for the Soul Publishing, LLC.

The publisher gratefully acknowledges the many publishers and individuals who granted Chicken Soup for the Soul permission to reprint the cited material.

Front cover photo courtesy of iStockphoto.com/GlobalP (© GlobalP).
Back cover and interior photo courtesy of iStockphoto.com/Alvenge (© Alvenge).
Photo of Loren Slocum Lahav courtesy of Jenna Lee.
Photo of Amy Newmark courtesy of Susan Morrow at SwickPix.

Cover and Interior Design & Layout by Brian Taylor, Pneuma Books, LLC

Distributed to the booktrade by Simon & Schuster. SAN: 200-2442

Publisher's Cataloging-In-Publication Data
(Prepared by The Donohue Group, Inc.)

Chicken soup for the soul : time to thrive : 101 inspiring stories about
  growth, wisdom, and dreams / [compiled by] Amy Newmark [and] Loren
  Slocum Lahav.

  pages ; cm

  ISBN: 978-1-61159-947-3

  1. Self-actualization (Psychology)--Literary collections. 2. Self-actualization (Psychology)--Anecdotes. 3. Self-realization--Literary collections. 4. Self-realization--Anecdotes. 5. Goal (Psychology)--Literary collections. 6. Goal (Psychology)--Anecdotes. 7. Anecdotes. I. Newmark, Amy. II. Slocum, Loren. III. Title: Time to thrive : 101 inspiring stories about growth, wisdom, and dreams

  BF637.S4 C45 2015
  158.1   2015932877

PRINTED IN THE UNITED STATES OF AMERICA
on acid∞free paper

25 24 23 22 21 20 19 18 17 16 15   01 02 03 04 05 06 07 08 09 10 11

Time to Thrive

101 Inspiring Stories about Growth, Wisdom, and Dreams

Amy Newmark
Loren Slocum Lahav

CSS

Chicken Soup for the Soul Publishing, LLC
Cos Cob, CT

Chicken Soup for the Soul

For moments that become stories™

www.chickensoup.com

Contents

Introduction 1

❶
~It's Time to Meet Yourself~

1. Becoming Whole, *Jenni Schaefer* 11
2. Coffee Break, *Lucy Lemay Cellucci* 15
3. A Road Trip to Find Me, *Sheila Wasserman* 19
4. An Object in Motion, *Nicole K. Ross* 23
5. Just Me, *Anna Lucas* 27
6. Five Minutes a Day, *JC Sullivan* 30
7. Enough, *Sandi Staton* 33
8. Positivity in the Wake of Adversity, *Katie Cash* 37
9. Crazy Things, *Ruth Knox* 41
10. The Tango of Life, *Kay L. Campbell* 44
11. Along Came a Spider, *Crystal Thieringer* 47
12. Renewed Strength, *Beth Saadati* 51

❷
~It's Time to Embrace Adventure~

13. Taking Flight, *Marsha Warren Mittman* 59
14. Caged, *Barbara A. Davey* 63
15. Right Back Where I Started From, *Terri Elders* 65
16. Common Ground, *Sue Sanders* 69
17. A Mid-Life Challenge, *Ann Hoffman* 73
18. Mountain Dreams, *Jill Burns* 77
19. Taking a Leap, *Lorri Danzig* 79
20. A Not So Trivial Twosome, *John Forrest* 82
21. Getting Our Groove Back, *Kate Wan* 86

22. My Theory of Relativity, *Benny Wasserman* 89
23. Sweat, Blood and Solitude, *Krystal Klumpp* 92
24. Taught by Teens, *Rhonda K. Maller* 96
25. When in Rome, *Karen Coffee Nicholson* 99

❸

~Thrive on Your Own Path~

26. The Wine Epiphany, *Jennifer Simonetti-Bryan* 105
27. A Man of Letters, *Ryan Kluftinger* 109
28. An Activist Is Born, *Pat Fish* 112
29. A Magical Life of Possibilities, *Mitra Ray* 116
30. Keeping Less, Living More, *Alison P. Martinez* 120
31. They Took My Picture, *Lorraine Cannistra* 123
32. Today Is Your Day, *Neha Gupta* 127
33. The Dream We Didn't Know We Had, *Linda E. Allen* 130
34. Not Giving In, *Lauren Ball* 133

❹

~Make Time for Your Most Important Customer~

35. My Mondays, *Rebecca Hill* 139
36. Guest Treatment, *Paula Klendworth Skory* 143
37. Making My Health a Priority, *Lola Bendana* 146
38. Recharge Rental, *Bonnie L. Beuth* 150
39. Race Against Time, *Angela Wolthuis* 152
40. Walking to a New Me, *Connie Kaseweter Pullen* 155
41. Time Out for Better Time In, *Cortney Fries* 158
42. Just Say No—and Sometimes Yes, *Ann Vitale* 161
43. Solo Gig, *Denise Reich* 164
44. Getting Real, *Michelle Hauser* 168
45. Learning to Fly, *Sage de Beixedon Breslin* 172

❺
~Say Yes to Thriving~

46. The Summer of Yes, *Ericka Kahler* 181
47. It's MY Life! *Marya Morin* 184
48. Perspective, *Heidi FitzGerald* 188
49. Sparked, *Stephanie Jackson* 191
50. Learning to Swim, *Michele Boom* 194
51. Eating to Live, *Connie K. Pombo* 197
52. I Left My Pride on the Beach, *Josephine A. Fitzpatrick* 200
53. On My Own, *Pat Wahler* 204
54. Because I Can, *Sharon Rosenbaum Earls* 207
55. Passing on the Sword, *Sarah LM Klauda* 210
56. The List, *Jean Morris* 212
57. Braver than Superman, *April Knight* 215

❻
~Help the World Thrive~

58. From Living on Change to Changing the World,
    Mike Conrad 223
59. The Future Belongs to Those Who Believe, *Jaki Baskow* 228
60. Reclaiming Myself, *Jane McBride Choate* 231
61. What Diana Ross Taught Me, *Timothy Peterson* 233
62. Take That, Universe! *Courtney Campbell* 236
63. Thriving While Grieving, *Manpreet Dhillon* 239
64. Time to Share, *Denise A. Dewald* 242
65. Now I Know, *Elizabeth Titus* 244
66. Finding a Way, *Judith Fitzsimmons* 248
67. An Open Heart, *Linda M. Johnson* 251
68. A Boost to My Confidence, *Cindy L. Ely* 256
69. Love Is Not Pain, *Berni Xiong* 258

❼

~It's Time to Reinvent Yourself~

70. From Breakdown to Breakthrough, *Kathy Caprino* 265
71. A Future to Step Into, *Sam Georges* 270
72. A Ham Is Born, *Beth Levine* 274
73. Taking a Chance on Me, *Judith Marks-White* 277
74. A Life by Design, *Marcia Castro-Rosenberg* 281
75. Endings Can Be Beginnings, *Brianna Mears* 284
76. Letting Charlie Go, *Alana Marie* 287
77. Nowhere to Go But Up, *Matt Chandler* 289
78. Taking a Chance on Life, *Sallie A. Rodman* 292
79. Countryfied Chick, *Tamara Moran-Smith* 295
80. Small Business Dreams, *Dianna Graveman* 297
81. Dream Life through Freedom, *Andrea Hadhazy* 300

❽

~It's Time to Pursue Your Dreams~

82. 100 Pairs of Shoes, *Dr. Buzz McCarthy* 307
83. A Story of Love and Teeth, *Anjie Reynolds* 311
84. Your Sweater Is Awesome, *Emily Oman* 315
85. Fort, *David Warren* 320
86. But You Were Just a Cop, *Stephen Rusiniak* 323
87. Seeing the World, *Janet Perez Eckles* 326
88. Breaking the Mold, *Denise Marks* 330
89. Music Lessons, *Mary Ann Hayhurst* 333
90. A Student of Life, *Chelsea DuHaime* 337
91. Fear of Falling, *Karen Gray-Keeler* 340
92. My Everest, *Shirley Deck* 344

9
~Make Time for Your Relationships~

93. You Should, *Allyson Ward* 351
94. First Sheep! *Lisa Pawlak* 354
95. The Hourglass, *Deirdre Higgins* 358
96. Fuel, *Kristin Doney* 362
97. The Muscle Car, *Janet Bower* 365
98. A New Kind of Life, *Edie Schmidt* 368
99. The Dad Who Dropped Out, *Geetanjali Krishna* 371
100. The Strength of No, *Loren Slocum Lahav* 374
101. Carving Out Some Work-Life Balance, *Amy Newmark* 377

Meet Our Contributors 381
Meet Amy Newmark 398
Meet Loren Slocum Lahav 400
Thank You 402
About Chicken Soup for the Soul 403

Introduction

We love the little owl on the cover of this book. In many cultures, owls are symbols of wisdom, transition, intelligence, protection and secrets, and this little guy, ready to grow bigger and even wiser, is a great mascot for a book that is all about personal growth, wisdom, and dreams.

The words in the title of our book, "Time to Thrive," have a deliberate double meaning because our stories have two main themes: 1) You need to make time in your busy life to thrive, whether that means putting aside an hour a day for a hobby, or just learning to say no when asked to take on too many responsibilities; and 2) It's time to take charge of your life and pursue your passion, do something you are enthusiastic about, and feel alive! No more putting off those life changes you know you should make.

In this inspiring collection, you'll read stories from regular people who decided it was time for a change. Many of them had been stuck in the same old routine for years, so they can provide you with a roadmap for how you can break out of your own rut and do something new. Some of them found renewed purpose and joy through a new job, a hobby, or volunteer work, and their lives were transformed as a result. Some of them just needed to find balance in lives that were basically okay, but were a little too frenetic and unfocused. Many of our writers say they needed to reacquaint themselves with themselves, going back to their roots and remembering what they had actually intended to do with their lives.

Sometimes we need to take a step back from our busyness and do some self-assessment. In Chapter 1, "It's Time to Meet Yourself," you'll read about Lucy Lemay Cellucci, who took a two-year "sabbatical" to work at Starbucks as a barista, and then found herself ready to go back to her profession as a dance instructor. She says the job "helped me sift through my depressive fog and reconnect with the ability to have fun." You'll also read Sheila Wasserman's story about setting out on a 16,000-mile road trip from Florida to Alaska and back, all by herself! Sheila says she needs to take a break from family obligations and "see if there's any me left in me."

You'll read more about self-discovery in Chapter 2, "It's Time to Embrace Adventure." You'll meet Marsha Warren Mittman, a young widow who surprised her New York relatives by somewhat randomly choosing to move to little Spearfish, South Dakota. She says "I've never regretted my decision to take flight" and, in fact, she says it feels more like she has returned to her true home. In the same chapter, you'll read how Benny Wasserman was discovered by a lookalike talent agency and has made a nice second income as an Albert Einstein lookalike for the past twenty-five years. If you Google him you'll see he really does look like the smartest guy in the world!

Benny talks about how he flourished in his new job post-retirement, and you'll read plenty of stories about new careers in Chapter 3, which is about how to "Thrive on Your Own Path." Jennifer Simonetti-Bryan did this big-time when she quit her six-figure Wall Street job and spent years studying to become one of only four female Masters of Wine in the United States. We've seen her speak about wine and she clearly loves her new job. By the way, she makes more money now than she did before! Jennifer says, "I wake up feeling happy, jazzed every morning, and looking forward to what my workday will bring."

Also in Chapter 3, Dr. Mitra Ray tells us an inspiring story about forging her own path. The child of Indian immigrants, she went to prestigious universities, got her PhD in biochemistry, and even went along with an arranged marriage, all as expected by her parents. But then she raised some eyebrows, both in her professional community and in her Bengali one, by following her heart — getting a divorce, embarking on a new career focused on wellness, and marrying her soul mate. While it was hard, she says that she realized, "I alone was responsible for my happiness." And she's glad she is modeling that outlook for her two teenage daughters now.

No matter how busy we are in business, in our families, or as volunteers, we still need to take care of ourselves. Otherwise we aren't really good for anyone else, either. That's why Chapter 4 is called "Make Time for Your Most Important Customer." Our writers share some great advice about how you can carve out some "me time" to ensure that you remain happy and productive. Sometimes, that just means putting your foot down, as Rebecca Hill does every Monday. Monday is her day off from everything—work, volunteering, and husband. She calls Mondays "My-days" and says they help her maintain a sense of self and help her "to honor myself as an independent person with individual tastes and desires."

Continuing with that theme of self-protection in Chapter 4, you'll read Ann Vitale's important reminder about the power of saying "no." Many of us are very good at what we do, and we become the go-to people at work, in our families, and in volunteer work. Ann finally learned how to say "no" without explaining herself. She says, "I felt light, free, amazed at myself. I'd just said 'No' with no explanation." Try it. You'll like it!

Now that we've taught you how to say "no" we need to address saying "yes" occasionally, too. And that's why Chapter 5, "Say Yes to Thriving," is filled with stories about saying "yes" to all the good things in life—the things you'll have time to do once you master saying "no!" Ericka Kahler tells us about the day she had an epiphany about her life and decided to start saying "yes" to every new experience and adventure that was offered to her. "Yes" became her mantra, and as word got out, her friends invited her to more and more events. Ericka says, "'Yes' literally changed my life." April Knight reports much the same experience in her story about how she decided to ignore her fears and force herself to try new things. She blossomed, changing from a woman afraid of going to the mall to one who travels to Australia alone and rides a wild burro in a rodeo. She says, "I don't want to live a timid, fearful life and I refuse to 'be careful.' I'm running the race!"

Once you have figured out how to thrive in your own life, you may want to spread the word. In Chapter 6, "Help the World Thrive," you'll read about some ordinary people who have become extraordinary people and are helping others thrive as well. Mike Conrad and his brother, for example, were living on food stamps when they realized they could revolutionize the food industry by allowing people to buy food in bulk, straight from their trucks. They started a company called Zaycon Foods that now serves tens of thousands of customers across the U.S., and they are now working on a program to accept food stamps as well. Mike says, "With a little courage and a lot of goodwill, anyone can change the world." We've met him and can attest to the fact that he goes to work every day with a spring in his step!

Jaki Baskow is another mover and shaker whose story will inspire you. After her father was murdered, she moved from New Jersey to Las Vegas, with no prospects and no money. With grit and determination, she has built a huge talent agency there, and has mentored thousands of performers, helping to launch many successful careers. She says, "I'm so grateful that I've been able to live a life of purpose that revolves around helping people help each other."

Mike Conrad and Jaki Baskow talked about how they transformed their lives, following career paths they would have never expected, and we continue in that vein in Chapter 7, "It's Time to Reinvent Yourself." You'll read about Kathy Caprino's winding career path. After eighteen years in publishing and marketing, she realized that she wanted to be a marriage and family therapist. After spending years obtaining a master's degree in the field and having her own therapy practice, Kathy realized that wasn't quite right either. She wasn't afraid to make another change, and now she helps coach working women, helping them stay passionate and purposeful about their own careers and lives. She says, "It wasn't easy by any stretch to reinvent myself (twice)." We love the fact that Kathy wasn't afraid to buck convention and follow her heart.

And that's exactly what Sam Georges did after his wife died. Sam gave up a dream home and a dream job in California and moved to Las Vegas, where he reinvented himself as a champion poker player.

Why did Sam share his personal story with us? He says, "I am a private kind of guy. I decided to share this story because I want anyone who finds themselves in these circumstances to know that life is guided. You unfold the future — the future does not unfold you."

You may not want to become a professional poker player, but you probably do have dreams, and we have plenty of stories that show you how to achieve them. Chapter 8 is called "It's Time to Pursue Your Dreams," because it is! It is *always* time to do that. You just need to make some room in your life for that possibility to manifest itself. Dr. Buzz McCarthy tells us how she chucked it all after a divorce. She closed her business, sold all her possessions, and moved from Australia to London with just a suitcase and a laptop computer. She says, "I'd chosen to launch into the void, and here I was in wonderful London living in total joy."

Stephen Rusiniak tells us how he followed his dream, too. Despite the fact that he was "just a cop" and he had received a C in his freshman writing class in college, Stephen persisted in his writing, and we can tell you with personal knowledge that it is quite good, as he has been published in quite a few Chicken Soup for the Soul books.

We close our book about thriving with a very important chapter, "Make Time for Your Relationships." We loved Lisa Pawlak's story about her family's long, adventurous trip to New Zealand, where they didn't pay attention to the clock or the Internet. They built memories that will bond that family forever, even when the children are grown and raising their own kids. And what a great idea Janet Bower and her husband had when they rented a Camaro while their stodgier car was in the shop. The septuagenarians carefully lowered themselves into those bucket seats and had a great time tooling around San Diego County, attracting amused looks wherever they went. Janet says, "There was the fun, excitement, and challenge that two elderly, long-married people can have but seldom do. There are always routines and schedules, but there are also new opportunities. When those opportunities arise, take them — at any age."

We offer you our own stories at the very end of the book, about how we make sure we stay true to our own needs, protect our most important relationships, and keep ourselves sane. You'll read about saying "no" to some things so that you can say "yes" to others. And more importantly, that will allow you to say "yes" to the people who matter. You'll also learn how to carve out enough "me time" to achieve a work-life balance that allows you to thrive in your own busy life.

We have enjoyed making this book for you and we're almost sorry to be sending it off to the printer already. But it's your turn now to soar like that owl, your time to thrive. We hope through these amazing stories you will find the inspiration, faith, passion and vision to truly live the best life you can make for yourself.

~Amy Newmark and Loren Slocum Lahav

February 17, 2015

Chapter
1

Time
to
Thrive

It's Time to
Meet Yourself

Becoming Whole

If you're brave enough to say goodbye,
life will reward you with a new hello.
~Paulo Coelho

"I am one. Not half of something." I spoke those words from a stage in Duluth, Minnesota, where people had braved the frigid temperatures to attend my presentation and book signing. As a single thirty-something, I have finally learned that I do not need to be part of a couple in order to feel complete. Sure, someday, I would like to be married and have a family, but my life will not start then. I am living happily ever after right now.

I learned the hard way that the most enduring relationship any of us will ever have with a human being is actually the one with ourselves. In the auditorium that evening, I was honored to share my journey of finding myself, which includes, like most people, some failed relationships along the way.

I usually start out by talking about Ed. He controlled my life for nearly twenty years. While I grew to hate the abuse, I could not find the strength to leave for far too long. Ed convinced me that I needed him to cope with life while simultaneously beating me down, yelling things like, "You are fat," and "You messed up—again!"

Countless people in the audience nodded their heads when I spoke about Ed, because they had been in his arms too. No, we did not all date the same guy! But we did all battle eating disorders. In therapy at twenty-two years old, I was taught to call my anorexia and bulimia "Ed," an acronym for "eating disorder." I learned to treat my eating disorder like a relationship rather than an illness or a condition.

Slowly, over time, I began to distinguish Ed's voice from mine and discovered my own unique thoughts and personality. While I did not choose to have an eating disorder, I started to believe that I could, in fact, choose to get better. Sometimes it felt like I had to make that choice over and over again, each and every moment. My favorite quote is the Japanese proverb, "Fall down seven times, stand up eight."

When it comes to Ed, I fell down more like 1,007 times. But that didn't matter, because, with support from both professionals and loved ones, I was able to stand up 1,008 times! Today, even though I have never been married, I consider myself happily divorced—from Ed. But that is not the fairytale ending to the story.

I am fully recovered from an eating disorder but not from life. This was never more evident than when I met Mark at age twenty-seven. It did not take long for me to fall head over heels for this man—a real one, this time. I was so upside down for Mark that I failed to notice that the liquor burning his throat each night was ripping a hole in our relationship. I was blinded by love and even accepted his marriage proposal. The shiny ring on my finger eventually illuminated the truth. After wearing the ring for a few weeks, I came to the frightening realization: I was about to marry a man with whom I could not have a conversation after 7 p.m.

In my opinion, Mark's blackouts from drinking alcohol at night were that bad. (He often couldn't remember discussions, even the really important ones.) The tears I cried in silence and the turmoil we never talked about seemed even worse than the blackouts. Hitting what felt like another rock bottom, I knew that I needed help. Unlike times in the past, I did not turn to Ed. Instead, just like in recovery, I went to therapy, attended support groups, and leaned on family and friends.

It takes two to make a relationship. I had contributed to our downfall, so I needed to go inward and work toward change. But, in the end, Mark refused to get help. I knew from my own recovery that nothing was going to get better if I was putting in more effort than him. Devastated to realize what I needed to do, I wasn't sure that I could. Unlike with Ed, a real wedding was planned with an actual white dress waiting to be worn. Invitations were stamped, but I was grateful they had not been mailed.

At Mark's house one rainy spring day, I handed back the ring with the words, "I love you, but I can't marry you." I will never forget his deer-in-the-headlights look and the ring slipping out of his fingers to the hard floor below.

As I drove away in what turned out to be a downpour, my tears fell even harder. I had hoped for a Hollywood ending, but it wasn't this brokenhearted rain scene that I had wanted. How could the air smell so fresh outside when my life was over?

Of course, that was not the end either. Over time, I did begin to heal. But this is not one of those Cinderella stories where Prince Charming eventually shows up with a glass slipper that just so happens to fit. Someone else has entered the picture though — someone who is here to stay for better or for worse. Her name is Jenni. I am on the magnificent road of falling in love with her, and she is me. I suspect that this road never ends, as I learn something new each and every day. Through sickness and in health, I have made a commitment to cherish myself. I even wrote wedding vows to me! Some of my promises include nourishing my body and soul, dating without losing myself, and simply having more fun. As strange as this might sound, public speaking is when I have some of the most fun.

I closed that talk in the Midwest with a message about never giving up — no matter what roadblocks and hurdles might appear. Often using props to emphasize important points, I held up a stack of over fifty rejections letters addressed to me from publishers for my first book, *Life Without Ed*. And, one by one, I dropped the letters on the stage while reading aloud the reasons why the manuscript had been rejected.

"You are not qualified," someone had thought.

"You will never make it," implied another.

I explained, "I have fallen down in my life far more times than there are letters on this stage. I am here today because I just keep picking myself up."

While those letters all seemed to say a different version of "You aren't good enough," standing there surrounded by that pile of rejection, I knew the truth.

I am enough — imperfections and all. Sure, I have scars from Ed and Mark. And more will come. Even still, I smiled and said with confidence, "I am whole."

~Jenni Schaefer

Coffee Break

A truly happy person is one who can enjoy the
scenery while on a detour.
~Author Unknown

O f all the memorable films to grace the screen in my living room, *American Beauty* is one of the most unforgettable. One of my favorite scenes occurs when Kevin Spacey's character, Lester Burnham, is at a fast food restaurant drive-thru and politely asks for an application, saying, "I'm looking for the least possible amount of responsibility."

This was my own career path between June 2011 and April 2013. This was the stretch when I hid from my career as a dance educator and assumed another identity as a "partner" at Starbucks.

The first thing that struck me was how overwhelming it was to learn the recipes for all the drinks. I actually brought in a journal to make some notes on my bar shifts... something I'm sure was a source of much amusement to all of my co-workers, I mean partners. Those damn caramel macchiatos always threw me off—I often forgot to pour the espresso shots last. Nor did I get the hang of the drinks at the cold bar. For an entire summer I made smoothies with the vanilla bean powder instead of the actual protein powder we were instructed to use; my apologies to anyone who received a smoothie made by me during the summer of 2011. And I can still vividly recall my sense of panic as I watched the cups line up down the bar in my queue. I felt like I was in that episode of *I Love Lucy* where she's a factory worker in charge of wrapping up all the chocolates that pass her by on the conveyor belt—only stuffing all the missed drinks down my blouse to avoid the disapproval of my supervisor wasn't really an option for me.

For all its initial challenges, I still regard my time at Starbucks as my "extended vacation from work." And that's precisely what it was, a break from being responsible for other people. For nearly two years I got to have a job that required no planning prior to showing up for work, no phone calls to make, e-mails to send, no endless search for ideas, music or costumes. I wasn't responsible for anything outside of ensuring that I showed up on time for my shifts and provided courteous and reasonably competent service to customers. Not to mention I actually got to be at home in the evenings to have dinner with my family—a novelty for many of us in the dance industry.

But perhaps the most surprising thing about my stint at Starbucks was how I found myself forming friendships with people who were at a completely different stage of life than I was, being a good decade or two younger. A couple of months into my employment, I found myself receiving invitations to parties where games such as beer pong and *Twister* were played. We had a picnic in the park, a casino night, an evening at a comedy club, a romp at Laser Quest, a karaoke night, and an entertaining evening that involved listening to a very intoxicated Latin-tongued partner recite the works of Dr. Seuss to an audience of co-workers who were only too happy to delight in his difficulties.

On the opposite end of the spectrum, I also had the privilege of interacting with a rather cheeky partner who was in his eighties! Like me, this remarkable gentleman viewed his hours at the store as a break from his own set of personal challenges. Each weekday morning he would check his "baggage" at the door and spend two hours smiling, singing, and pulling out the best parts of himself to make each customer who came through the door feel personally acknowledged. I cannot adequately express the incredible strength, wisdom, and optimism this man possesses but he was an inspiration to us all. I am both humbled and inspired by his courage, and make great efforts to remember the words he left us with at his retirement party: "Just being alive means that you're successful."

The best thing that I took away from my sojourn at Starbucks wasn't the pride I felt when people looked at my gleaming pastry case (I actually miss cleaning that thing… is that weird?), but rather the way it helped me sift through my depressive fog and reconnect with the ability to have fun. It gave me the time to stop and actually reflect on what was happening in my life, allowing me to see the areas where I needed to make some changes.

And, inevitably, change did find me. It started with the occasional appearance of a certain retired professional dancer who, as luck would have it, opened a dance studio in my neighborhood. She came into my store to grab some goodies one day and recognized me. On two separate occasions she offered me a teaching position at her studio. On two separate occasions I politely declined and instead offered to put whipped cream on her beverage. When the spring of 2013 arrived, I turned in my green apron and took some time off to recover from the exhaustion that had been accumulating since the birth of my second child. The end result was improved health, a finished manuscript, and the realization that I deeply missed being a dance teacher—thankfully, I knew of a place where they were looking for one!

Luckily for me, my story ends on a more cheerful note than that of my *American Beauty* counterpart. Lester Burnham never got to enjoy his newfound wisdom when the fog of his midlife crisis began to dissipate. Because I have the good fortune of having neighbors who are kind enough not to shoot me, I can happily move forward with my now healthier sense of self-awareness and construct my life in a way that works for me. By setting firm boundaries for what I can reasonably handle, not only as a teacher, but also a writer and a mother, I can be one of those lucky people who get to do what they love and love what they do.

And I can't think of a more beautiful gift to receive than the knowledge that the life I'm currently living is just that: a beautiful gift.

Thanks for the coffee break, Starbucks.

~Lucy Lemay Cellucci

A Road Trip to Find Me

*As you travel solo, being totally responsible for
yourself, it's inevitable that you will discover just how
capable you are.*
~Author Unknown

I check my rearview mirror to see what I'm leaving behind. Oh
yeah — can't see anything but the camper. It blocks the rear
window plus some. The camper is going to be my home for
the next two months. "Look ahead," I remind myself. "The
adventure is before you."

My passenger seat holds what will be my companion for the
trip: an old milk crate filled with maps, guidebooks and the book
that started this journey, *The Milepost.* It's a mile-by-mile guide along
the Trans-Canada Highway into Alaska, my final destination. I've
planned a solo 16,000-mile round trip from my home in St. Petersburg,
Florida, across to California, north to Alaska, then back home through
Chicago and Toronto where I'll visit family. My compact truck camper
is the most efficient RV for the torturous roads over the far northern
permafrost.

•••

My husband and I loved to wander through the aisles of the RV show every January in Tampa. It's advertised as one of America's biggest. We already have a ten-year-old camper. It's small, but sufficient for two and comfortable for one. We thought we'd find a deal on a new camper or at least some travel knickknacks we couldn't live without. Representatives from state visitors' bureaus filled rows of kiosks offering pamphlets and candies to entice RVers into their states.

I picked up brochures for Alaska, a dream destination. Maps, campgrounds and visitor guide leaflets filled my increasingly heavy bag. Maybe someday. Alaska was too far away and would mean too much time off work. Besides, gas was too expensive.

Further along the aisle, someone was selling last year's *The Milepost* for ten dollars. The current year's book, also for sale, was thirty-five dollars. It's considered the bible for anyone planning a road trip on the Alcan, the Alaska-Canada Highway. The guidebook includes where there's gas or a pull-off, where to watch for bears, and where to get the world's best or biggest cinnamon bun.

I was not ready to spend money on a trip I might never take… but it was a dream that wouldn't let go. I heard my mother's voice in my head. Before dying too young, she stressed the urgency of following your dreams while you could. Things happen to stop you if you let them. When you're at the end of your life, you don't want to look back at opportunities lost.

Several months earlier, we had to buy a new pickup when the old one died. Mechanically, this would be a perfect time to make a long trip. If I waited, I'd just end up with another old truck and wouldn't feel safe making the journey alone. My husband couldn't take that much time off work to join me, and I didn't want to rush this journey. There would be too much to see along the way. Anyway, it was my dream, not his. He'd rather travel to warm climates and big cities, not long barren stretches. Truth is, I would prefer to travel alone.

Looking back over my shoulder down the aisle, the salesman stood behind a diminishing pile of *The Milepost* books. It's only ten dollars, I told myself. I went back to the book vendor, feeling detached from my hand as it passed a ten-dollar bill and took the offered book. I was already categorizing the next steps to planning the trip, my chest tight as I contemplated what I was about to do. Only four months to plan if I was to be on the road by the end of spring. With my mother's memory in my heart, I affirmed: "I WILL DO THIS."

Preparing the truck and camper was first. The new truck needed some modifications: a step and an openable rear window for camper access. Having it all to myself made packing in the limited space easy. Organizing work so I could do most of it online was a little more difficult. I work with my husband and both he and my employees were supportive (although his friends wondered why he was "letting" me go).

I went through the motions and made a to-do list with due-by dates alongside each task. I made lists of necessary provisions: cans of soup, tuna and corn, rice, crackers and peanut butter. I looked up the average high and low temperatures in Anchorage and Fairbanks. With expected lows in the thirties, I'd need clothes for cold nights as well as for warm weather while traveling through the south. I surveyed my closet for my most versatile items.

The planning seemed disconnected, as if I was organizing a summer camp trip for my son, but the stationery and stamps I added to my list were not for him to send letters home to Grandma and Grandpa. They were for me to mail communications or payments for office expenses while on the road. I still hadn't accepted the trip as one I was going on.

When I told friends I was driving to Alaska alone, I got strange reactions. One wondered if I was going to meet an old lover. "No one," she said, "goes on a long trip like this alone." Another offered to keep me company, at least to California where her son lives. It was hard to tell them I wanted to be alone. I like my own company.

I was tired of diluting myself; part of me caring for my elderly widowed father, part of me stressing about my twenty-plus son who still stayed out all night and slept all day, and the biggest part of me, living, breathing and working with my controlling husband.

• • •

I need air. I need to see if there's any me left in me. I look forward to the freedom of planning my own day, stop or go as I choose, eat or not as I want. To linger at a stream or zoom through a city at my leisure. To set my own pace.

Heading out of town, as the camper merges onto the highway, realization strikes me. I shout to the road in front of me. "Woohoo! I'm going to Alaska."

~Sheila Wasserman

An Object in Motion

*It is only in adventure that some people succeed in
knowing themselves — in finding themselves.*
~André Gide

I stared at the blinking cursor and took a slow, deep breath. "To Whom It May Concern," I typed. "I hereby tender my resignation." After finishing the letter, I returned to the date field and typed April 6, 2015 — exactly one year in the future. Then I printed the document, signed it, and placed it on the corner of my desk.

I'd waited ten years for a good reason to leave Indiana. I was done waiting.

Isaac Newton said, "An object at rest stays at rest and an object in motion stays in motion." If I wanted my life to change, I realized I had to put things in motion myself—no one was going to do it for me.

"There's more than corn in Indiana!" the billboards read once you get within thirty miles of Indiana Beach. The amusement park opened in 1926 and attracted visitors with its hand-dug beach (carved out of a cornfield) and its pair of thirty-foot-long toboggan runs. For the record, the billboards are true. There is more than corn in Indiana. We have soybeans, too.

After graduating from Indiana University, I had applied for jobs in and out of state. In the end, I accepted a position with a fast-growing tech start-up headquartered in downtown Indianapolis. It wasn't my intention to stay with the same company in the same city for a decade. It just happened.

I got promoted, developed a strong network of friends, and invested in grown-up purchases like a washer and dryer and bookcases that didn't have screw-on plywood backs. Before I knew it, ten years had passed.

To be fair, those years were not without joy, personal growth, and excitement. I took up kickboxing and yoga, got my master's degree, and wrote my first novel. I traveled abroad and across the United States. I went. I saw. I returned to Indiana.

I got comfortable — too comfortable. Each day became more or less the same — wake up, go to work, come home, watch TV, go to bed. Rinse and repeat. As I approached the ten-year mark, my company was acquired and my colleagues began to resign and move on to new adventures. Meanwhile, my circle of single friends dwindled. They married and had children, while I cooked dinner for one and took solo vacations. Indiana isn't an encouraging place to be single in your thirties.

"It's not like that in California," my older sister said whenever I called to grumble. "You've got to get out of the Midwest."

I also longed for the horseback riding days of my youth. The rich smell of freshly oiled leather, the gentle nickering of horses eager for breakfast, their velveteen muzzles — it was heaven on earth. But riding had faded away to make way for a career, grad school, and "more important things." Now, my only nearby options were head-to-tail trail rides.

The breaking point came one day during my morning commute when I had a startling realization. I'd stopped seeing anything. I'd stopped viewing my day-to-day life with any sense of wonder or curiosity. I'd seen this exact road — and these exact miles — more than five thousand times.

Indiana didn't need to change. I did.

If not here, then where? The answer came in the form of a memory — the first morning of my Cowgirl Yoga retreat outside Bozeman, Montana the year before. I had awoken to guttural, prehistoric squawks outside my window. I bolted upright and slid my sleeping mask to my forehead. Our yoga teacher had closed our practice the night before with a warning: overzealous songbirds often begin their chorus in the wee hours of the morning. But, it wasn't a songbird I'd heard. It was a dinosaur.

"Those are the sandhill cranes," our instructor said, when we unrolled our mats in the barn loft later that morning and settled into Sukhasana, or easy-seated pose. Part of the whooping crane family, the birds have exceptionally long windpipes that carry their primitive calls more than a mile.

It turned out the cranes were just the first of many surprises that awaited me in The Last Best Place. We moved onto our hands and knees and began a series of Cat-Cows to get the blood flowing. That was about the time hail began pelting the barn windows — in June.

After a blissful week of yoga and horseback riding, I drove to Yellowstone National Park to see geysers, American bison, and Old Faithful. Then, I traveled to Big Sky and over the lush green hills of eastern Idaho, and then down to Jackson, Wyoming, where I cheered for barrel racers and bronco riders at the rodeo, enjoyed a local yoga class, and visited Grand Teton National Park. I took my camera everywhere. There was so much to see.

As I stared at my resignation letter six months later, I couldn't get Montana off my mind. I'd already booked two more retreats for later that year. Maybe Bozeman was where I belonged? In the months leading up to my return, I researched. I planned. I watched the real estate market. I downloaded the Bozeman relocation guide and read it cover to cover. The more I put in motion, the more attainable my dream became.

When I returned to Montana for my second retreat, I met with real estate agents and visited dozens of local establishments — from the public library to doggie day cares, from martial arts gyms to the local co-op. I rented a little house downtown so I could get a better feel for Bozeman life.

I walked to the tea shop and uncorked tiny glass jars filled with dry leaf teas on the "sniff wall" before making my selections. I strolled aisle after aisle of fresh fruits and vegetables at the co-op. I visited downtown shops and cafés and drove through dozens of neighborhoods. One evening, a friend invited me to go horseback riding at her ranch. As we galloped through sun-kissed fields, her Border Collie hot on our heels, my vision clicked into place.

I would move to Montana, alone.

That night, I sent a text to a friend in San Francisco to share the good news.

"Guess what?" I said.

"You're finally moving to San Fran?"

"Close."

"You're moving to a town with a population of seven," he joked.

"Soon to be eight!"

"Three of which are horses...."

"Isn't it fabulous?"

My goal is to move next summer, and I set more of my plan in motion each day. I haven't resigned, and I may not need to if my company is flexible. It's not easy to make a huge life change when there's no one asking, telling, or making you. Seems like it'd be easier, but it's not. Because there's only you — alone in your apartment night after night — wondering if it'll all be worth it. You wonder if you can do this — if you can do this alone.

The thing is, you can.

Martin Luther King, Jr. once said: "You don't have to see the whole staircase. Just take the first step."

Put things in motion. Momentum will get you the rest of the way.

~Nicole K. Ross

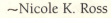

Just Me

*By all means use sometimes to be alone. Salute
thyself; see what thy soul doth wear.*
~George Herbert

I took myself out on a date last night. I was reluctant at first.
Though I travel extensively on my own, I had never taken
myself out to dinner. And when I say "out" I mean to an
actual sit-down, "Would you prefer a table or a booth?" restaurant. I always thought that having dinner alone would be a bit
uncomfortable. It would be awkward and completely out of my
comfort zone. But yesterday I was craving Mexican.

I walked into Casa Mexicana. "How many?" asked the handsome waiter.

"Just me," I responded, smiling. The smile was meant to hide
my mild embarrassment. Why was I doing this? I was seated in my
booth holding an oversized glossy menu. Just me.

I ordered water with lemon to start — my usual. As if I wasn't
already uncomfortable enough, I challenged myself to set my smartphone aside. Earlier in the day, I had read a book that discussed
the importance of cultivating solitude. Truthfully, it was what had
inspired this whole "date with myself" excursion. The book used Dr.
James Hollis's definition of solitude as "that psychic state wherein
one is wholly present to oneself." How often did I take the time to
simply be?

I had a difficult time remembering when I had last set aside my to-do list and simply sat in silence with my thoughts. With a combination of daily worries, fears of the future, and tendrils of self-doubt, the concept of sitting in the silence only to hear those thoughts grow louder wasn't too appealing. So instead, I sought distraction and packed my day planner—anything to stuff those unpleasant thoughts down a little deeper.

A few months prior, I had discovered the art of meditation—a wholly different approach to self-exploration that comes from being still. Through meditation, I could let go of the worry, fear, and doubt that plagued my mind. I awakened to the beauty that can be found through focused silence and deep thought. For years, I had been a regular yoga practitioner. But as a newbie meditator, I really had to practice being still and quieting my mind. Sometimes it worked. Most of the time, my busy brain continued to buzz. But, through consistent practice, I learned how to be more gentle and forgiving with myself, to always bring my attention back to my breath. And that helped. But then, life got in the way, and I forgot to take the time. The time to be me.

While it's challenging enough to observe your thoughts without judgment as they float by during meditation, I was attempting to do just that in a bustling restaurant with Pandora streaming fiesta songs. I supposed I could shut my eyes and pretend, if nothing else, to be meditating, even though my mind was still going a mile a minute.

Once my meal arrived, I ate from my sizzling-hot plate of vegetable fajitas. I wasn't altogether sure where to look while I chewed. So I admired the wall art.

I couldn't help it. I checked the time on my phone. Thirty-eight minutes had passed. I saw a missed text and resisted unlocking my phone to check the message. Thirty-nine minutes…

My mind drifted back to the book I had been reading earlier that day. A quote the book cited by Ralph Waldo Emerson came to mind. I pulled the book out of my bag to read it once more.

"It is easy in the world to live after the world's opinion; it is easy in solitude to live after our own; but the great man is he who in the midst of the crowd keeps with perfect sweetness the independence of solitude."

Amen, Ralph. Amen.

The truth is that it takes a lot of courage to be alone. How many times have we dived head first into a relationship with someone we knew was wrong for us because we were afraid to be alone? How long have we allowed fear to chain us in relationships long after they ran their course? It is only with compassion and love for ourselves that we gather the courage to simply be with what is, even if that means asking yourself out on a date to sit in the comfort (or discomfort) of your own company.

As the time ticked on, I relaxed more and truly enjoyed myself. I pushed away what would be tomorrow's leftovers and pulled out my journal. My journal—a precious collection of thoughts, prayers, rants, questions, answers, hopes and dreams. I've poured out my heart and soul on those pages, completely raw and vulnerable, to only myself and God. Why? Because I have learned how deeply I must trust—in myself and in my Creator. I must trust in the universal knowledge that I am exactly where I need to be, right here, right now, on this journey.

The waitress interrupted my writing reverie. "Will that be all?" she inquired politely. "Actually, no." I smiled. "I'll have the fried ice cream, please!" This was a special evening, after all. Finally, I was appreciating this evening out for what it really was—focused time to show myself love, fully and completely. And, whether a dinner out or a night in, I look forward to treating myself once in a while to the gift of reflection and solitude to just be, just me.

~Anna Lucas

Five Minutes a Day

You cannot always control what goes on outside.
But you can always control what goes on inside.
~Wayne W. Dyer

I could hear hesitation in my assistant Felecia's voice. "Do you mind if I ask you a personal question?"

"I don't have to answer it. But fire away." It was my standard reply but served to break the tension and make her smile.

"Do you have another job offer?"

"What? I wish! Why?"

Felecia looked me straight in the eyes. "Because you are so much nicer to be around this week. Not that you aren't always pleasant, but you know what I'm trying to say. You seem... happier, maybe? Something's changed. And I figured that you'd either gotten a new job or met a guy...."

I cut her off. "And I wouldn't have told you about him?"

"You don't have to tell me, but..."

I asked, "You'd like to know my secret?"

"Absolutely."

I motioned for her to close my office door. No need to share this with the world.

Observant, she had noticed the difference yoga had made in my life. When I had started, she mentioned that on yoga days I listened better and it took much more to fluster me.

"Like you noticed, days that I do yoga I find myself more centered, more grounded. So, last week in the class that I almost didn't take because of that huge deadline…"

Felecia nodded. Like a true New York native, she motioned for me to get to the point.

"Anita, my yogi, saw our stressed-out faces. She told us that one of the best things we could do would be to go into the office five minutes earlier than normal and use that time to do personal things, stuff just for us. Like, sip a green tea and meditate a bit. Or allow yourself to plan a getaway: write down somewhere you'd like to go to for half a day even. Perhaps a cute town on the Hudson or a museum you've been 'meaning to take your family to' or an art exhibit before it closes. And write down three things you're grateful for."

I could see from Felecia's expressive face that she was now clearly on the same skeptical page I had been.

I continued, "I know, right? That advice sounded easy, but everything seemed simple coming from Anita's lips. She's a yogi, for heaven's sake. Anita said deadlines work and suggested we do it before our next class. Get to the office five minutes earlier and before turning on your computer, checking e-mail or anything, give yourself those minutes. If you start your day this way, then the rest of the day your subconscious can be thinking about it and working for you." I shrugged. "Anita said it works."

A quick study, Felecia summed up, "That's all this big change is? Do something for yourself for five minutes before starting work?"

I nodded. "Well, in other parts of the country they might take fifteen, but here in New York City we pride ourselves on being more efficient. Seriously, anywhere in the world, if you give yourselves even that little bit of time, the results can be huge. I didn't even think it was working, but you caught it."

"Of course. I'm good." Felecia added a quick, "Thanks," and left.

I went over to my secret chocolate stash, pulled out M&Ms and walked to Felecia's cubicle. I knocked to get her attention.

"Hey! Here you go," and threw her the bag. "Chocolate is always another option."

Noticing her daughter's picture displayed in her office, I added, "Please don't take this the wrong way. Try the five minutes a day thing to be a good example for your daughter. It's like that stupid airline warning about putting your own oxygen mask on before helping others."

When I realized what I had said, I added, "Stupid, maybe, but it saves your life in an emergency. Let's not wait for that."

"See?" Felecia shook her head. "You're sounding all new-agey."

"Don't worry," I added, "it doesn't last forever. I'll be back to my old self in no time."

Knowing that Felecia had picked up on the change motivated me to keeping doing it. It took effort. I did it every day and I started to see differences: I stood up for myself more. I focused on changes I wanted to make, breaking them into smaller pieces. It worked, the days I did it. I gained momentum. Surprisingly, it's sometimes the smallest steps that lead to the biggest changes.

~JC Sullivan

Enough

Nourishing yourself in a way that helps you blossom
in the direction you want to go is attainable, and you
are worth the effort.
~Deborah Day

I was sitting at my dresser brushing my long red hair when suddenly Mom stormed through the door and started slapping me around, screaming and yelling. "I told you to stay away from those kids! They're nothing but trouble! Then you have the nerve to bring them to the house!"

I liked the brother and sister. I had spent all day with them wondering what was so bad about them. They didn't smoke. They didn't curse. They didn't shoplift when we went into stores; none of the things that I thought Mom considered bad. I even invited them to go to Bible study with me that night and they agreed.

So I brought them home with me.

Mom's face said it all. It was like standing in front of a judge, with my mother scowling down at the three of us standing before her.

"They're going with me to Bible study," I said hurriedly, hoping that would smooth her feathers and make her happy.

I thought a lot of things I did would make her happy. Going to church. Reading my Bible. Never hanging out with the wrong crowd. Obeying all her strict, religious rules. Living the squeaky-clean life of a Puritan. But in the end, I failed. She always raised the bar just a little higher, and like a fool, knowing I couldn't jump over it, I'd try. And fail. And try again.

Of course I understood. She had a terrible, abusive childhood. Her mother, an immigrant from Germany, couldn't raise her twelve children alone, so she surrendered the youngest two, my mother and her sister, to an orphanage.

As far back as I can remember, I lived and relived her childhood horrors. Not only in the stories she told, but also in the guilt and shame I felt for her sadness and pain. For her anger and rage. For not being enough to make her happy.

Trying to pay the debt I thought I owed cost me my life. I lost my identity, my thoughts, my hopes and dreams, my choices. When I looked in the mirror, I didn't see my youthful, freckled face; I saw her wrinkled, angry scowl.

By the time I married and had a child, I believed that everything that went wrong was my fault. A slap in the face till my ears rung was my fault. Slamming me against the wall and being chocked was my fault. Running out and leaving me all night was my fault. Ending the marriage in divorce was my fault.

When my son was five, I met and married a man who changed my life. He saw all the ugly inside me — all the hurt, anger and rage — and kept loving me. But it wasn't enough to save me from myself.

Just five minutes with my mother would set off a time bomb inside me. When I went home, I would blow up at my family. That's when I sought counseling. That's when all the bitterness and self-loathing, false guilt and shame began pouring out. That's when, with God's help, I began sorting through the rubble and found the little rag doll that was tossed and forgotten there. That's when I picked her up, tattered and worthless as she was, and embraced her in my arms. That's when my eyes began to see.

It was the hardest thing I had ever done, worse than going through my divorce. I walked out of my mother's life. I had enough of her power and control! Enough of her self-pity! Enough of her dumping the weight of the world on my shoulders! Enough! Enough!

After two years of counseling, my therapist suggested I try talking to my mother. Immediately, my heart pounded in my chest, fearing that one moment spent with her would destroy every bit of progress I had made. I told him I would consider it.

Several months later, I opened my eyes to a beautiful Saturday morning and knew this was the day. I jumped out of bed, and before I could change my mind, I asked my husband if he would take me to see my mother. I needed every drop of his love and support.

We pulled up to the curb as Mom and her new husband were walking to their apartment.

Rolling down the car window, I said, "Mom, can we talk?"

Like walking the Green Mile, I shuffled down the long, narrow corridor to her apartment. We sat down at the small kitchen table, and taking a deep breath, I poured out my battered heart.

And without a tear in her eye she said, "Sandi, if I have done anything wrong, I'm sorry. I just don't know why we can't let bygones be bygones and start over."

The same old story. Let's not get to the cause of our constant battles. No sense in delving into the truth. Let's just cover it up and pretend it never happened.

"Mom, why can't you see that you're not the only one hurting? You've been so consumed in your own pain that you can't see how you've hurt me. Right now, I don't know if I love you or hate you. That's why I have to stay away, to try and figure it out. I'm sorry, Mom. All I've ever wanted to do is make you happy. But I can't. Nobody can."

It would be six long years before I came close to trying again. Six long years of sorting through the guilt and shame of abandoning my mother. Six long years of facing it without the support and understanding of my siblings. Six long years of facing Mom's friends, seeing the shame-on-you glare in their eyes.

And during those six long years I learned that I am not responsible for my mother's abusive childhood and the physical and emotional pain she suffered. I learned that I'm not God and that He never expected me to take on the tremendous job of fixing my mother. He told me so. Loud and clear. And the heavy burden lifted.

Finally, feeling emotionally strong enough to allow her back into my life, we gradually built a relationship. Sometimes it was good, sometimes it wasn't. And although my mother never changed, I did. I grew stronger than I ever thought possible.

I still wish I had known a mother's unconditional love. I still wish I had seen just a glimmer of approval in her eyes before she died. But I've learned that I can live without it.

The relationship I had with my mother taught me that no matter how hard we try, we cannot fix people's broken lives. We cannot try saving them without losing ourselves in the process.

It was tough. It was painful. It was fearful and confusing. But I'm glad I did it. I have my life back. I've reintroduced myself to myself. Like a flower in the dessert, I've come back.

~Sandi Staton

Positivity
in the Wake
of Adversity

Happiness is an attitude.
We either make ourselves miserable, or happy and strong.
The amount of work is the same.
~Francesca Reigler

J oining the Navy was the most daunting and life-changing decision I have ever made. I still clearly remember the anxiety of being dropped off at the Naval Academy for my first day of "plebe summer," the boot camp–style session leading up to the first year of school at the Academy. Watching my parents wave goodbye with tears in their eyes, I was full of doubts, wondering if I would regret accepting my appointment as a midshipman. My fellow plebes and I were corralled from one group of red-faced, order-barking upperclassmen to the next as we recited mission statements, statistics, and songs from memory... and it was only day one! I was terrified—not of the calculated chaos enveloping me, but that I didn't belong.

Four years later, I proudly received my diploma from the Secretary of the Navy, graduating in the top one hundred of my class. I endured the trials of the Naval Academy for four years, and I have not regretted it for a moment since. The Naval Academy was a haven of success, an isolated, high-achieving society complete with a hierarchy of authority and an endless catalog of rules. It plucked young men and women from ordinary, unremarkable lives and sharpened them, transforming them into officer candidates with the tools and potential to become great military leaders. Upon graduating, I could see the ways I had changed since that first summer. But next came the true test — life in the fleet after four years of relative seclusion at the Naval Academy.

I reported to my first ship as the Repair Division Officer in 2011. I was immediately placed administratively and operationally in charge of seventy-eight sailors. Simultaneously, I was expected to learn all there was to know about the ship and its component departments. I qualified as Officer of the Deck, wielding responsibility for the safe navigation of a billion-dollar warship. I fought fires, flooding, and toxic gas leaks, and piloted the ship during a successful man-overboard rescue. Between visits to foreign ports, I spent hours in the balmy steam engine rooms learning the systems, and counseled and comforted my sailors when their fortunes took a turn for the worse. Over those first three years, I acquired a lot of knowledge and a little experience, and was once again transformed into a more mature and capable leader.

If joining the Navy was the most difficult decision I had ever made, embarking on a deployment to the Middle East onboard my third ship, an aircraft carrier, was the second most difficult. Not that I really had a choice in the matter. My ship was deploying, and everyone assigned to the ship, including me, had a compulsory invitation to ply the waters of the world with the ship.

I love the outdoors. Given the opportunity to choose, half a year cooped up on a gray-hulled ship was the antithesis of how I would spend my time. There would be times of suffering, no doubt. I would miss my husband, family, and friends with all my heart. I would miss the running, surfing, and hiking that was such a central part of my everyday life. I would miss sushi, driving my cute little hatchback car, and a good glass of red wine. I would miss being a girl — picking out clothes, jewelry, and shoes to wear.

In all honesty, I was terrified. I was afraid to "lose" so many months of my life—my life as I wanted to live it, anyway. This was to be my first full deployment. In the months leading up to our departure date, I found myself in denial, choosing not to think about what my future held. When the date drew near enough that it became imprudent to ignore my fate, it felt like a loss of control over my life. Accepting what I had to do changed me. It was a moment of great maturation and an opportunity to discover new ways to turn a less-than-ideal situation into an occasion for personal growth.

I deployed, and despite the many challenges of being stuck on a ship at sea, I seized the opportunity to prosper. I refused to view the deployment as a "prison sentence," as some of my more negative shipmates dubbed it. For me, it would not be wasted time. Instead, I viewed it as a chance to pull away from life and reflect on the person I was. If I didn't like the way I handled certain situations, why not use my months at sea to practice becoming the person I aspired to be? Indeed, this was a blessed opportunity to practice patience, kindness toward others, and discipline. It was also my chance to set and realize tangible goals, like finishing the first draft of my first novel.

An enthusiastic athlete, during deployment I participated in a variety of workout classes offered in the ship's hangar bay. I kept a workout log and made time for the gym on a daily basis. I chose to focus on the potential for personal growth rather than the negative aspects of my situation. I found that I was able to dictate my own attitude and outlook by actively pursuing personal and professional goals.

The days went by more quickly when I stayed busy, so I didn't allow myself to become idle. I emerged from deployment half a year older, but undoubtedly more mature. I was proud of the opportunity to serve my country, to truly give back in a manner that was wholly sacrificial. I believe that in overcoming daunting obstacles, we better ourselves because we gain fresh perspective on what we can truly achieve. Improving our lives, no matter what kind of complication we must surmount, is simply a matter of changing our own attitudes toward the cards we've been dealt.

~Katie Cash

Crazy Things

*Your own Self-Realization
is the greatest service you can render the world.*
~Sri Ramana Maharshi

It was 5 a.m. here in Alberta and the household was asleep. I, obviously, was not. I was visiting my sister and brother-in-law, and being with them was like being inside a wonderful, accepting, loving hug. I felt so at home with them. Could it only have been two weeks since my beloved passed away? It felt like forever yet also like a heartbeat; time seemed irrelevant now.

This was the strange place I found myself in. After thirty-one years of marriage, I was alone for the first time. I went from my parents' home to my first, brief, teenaged marriage. When that ended I still had my daughters to care for. Then I married my late husband. And now? It was just me. I had never been "just me." I had no idea who I was or what I wanted in life.

I felt like I was floating in an ocean on a little raft, and the waves were getting choppy. I had no idea what to do. I didn't know what I liked, I didn't know what I wanted, I didn't know even what I wanted to do for a living.

When my daughter flew in on the day my husband died, she brought me a lovely hand-bound journal. I wrote in it daily. As wacky as this may sound, I wrote to my deceased husband every day. It was my way of settling things in my mind, of gently letting him go, of assuring myself that he was okay, was happy and not hurting anymore.

The morning after my husband died, I got up and brought my beads out to the dining room table. After I had my shower, I found both daughters and my granddaughter at the table making necklaces. We proceeded to bead for the entire day and part of the next. We made lots of jewelry, and we reminisced about my precious husband, their dear dad and grandfather.

We talked candidly about what had healed inside us and what had been ripped open. We laughed about funny things from the past, and we ached knowing the pain that he endured during his long illness. We put words to feelings that had remained unspoken for so many years.

We did some big-time healing right there at the dining room table, with the power of women loving women, each passing her strength and her love, one to another. We shared our fears, our vulnerabilities, and our sick familial sense of humor (of which we are very proud — a gift of our dubious lineage). We were women doing what women know instinctively how to do — keep the home, heal the family, mend the wounds, be strong as only women can. And I was happily the crone, the elder, the earth mother, the matriarch.

In the face of my husband's death, it surprised me to learn how strong I was. I thought I would fall apart, perish even. I thought I would be inconsolable, incapable of reaching out to others. I thought I would be numb, frozen. I thought I would be broken. But I learned I just needed to be open to my spirit, open to the love of those I trust, and to the prayers and quiet power of love.

I needed to grieve, not with a petulant flavor that won't allow for healing, but with a fierceness that lets out the pain and lets in the light. I needed to allow the animal in me to writhe in anguish, let out her guttural cries, allow her time, feed her light. I needed to accept that grief does not come in a tidy little package that you open for X number of days or weeks and then wrap up again and put upon the shelf. It is an unpredictable, independent, wildebeest, and we ride it.

A twisted, delightful part of me revels in my newfound freedom to be whatever I want. I can be unpredictable. I can do crazy things. I can feel my way into discovering who I am.

So I go forward now, as I always have, putting one foot in front of the other, one step at a time. I do not look out over the entire mountain because it is too scary, too vast. I look down instead to where my feet are, and maybe a little bit ahead. I slowly take my steps. Maybe one day it will be different, but for today, this is enough.

~Ruth Knox

10

The Tango of Life

Life is a dance. Sometimes we lead, sometimes we follow. Don't worry about what we don't know, what's important is we learn new steps as we go.
~Author Unknown

"**S**tep... pivot, step... pivot," the handsome dark-haired instructor repeated the sequence as he moved succinctly to the staccato beat of the music. My gallant partner leaned closer and counted aloud as we practiced. "There is no need to talk," the instructor reminded us. "The dance is the conversation." So began my entry into the fascinating world of Argentine tango.

How did I end up learning to swivel and kick in a class full of strangers?

I'd always been drawn to the beauty and drama of tango. For years, I attended outdoor concerts and watched in awe as couples spontaneously expressed the alluring South American music with mesmerizing rhythmic movements. "Someday," I told myself, "I'll do that, too."

As I approached the mid-century mark and experienced the requisite soul-searching, my dream to learn to tango resurfaced. Eventually, I tracked down a local workshop. Finally, I decided to step out of my comfort zone and onto the dance floor.

"There are very few hard-and-fast rules in tango," the instructor said, smiling. "For that reason, 'sorry' is not part of the vocabulary."

He went on to explain further. "The idea is to dance fully in the moment; to simply surrender to and embrace whatever happens."

I had the feeling I was going to learn more than essential dance technique in this class. Perhaps an intriguing philosophy for life, too?

"Tango is defined by the leader-follower dynamics combined with the mood of the music at a given moment," he continued. "Every experience is special and unique."

I was both surprised and pleased to see the other tangueras and tangueros were close to my age and welcoming to newcomers. We agreed that this style of dance is a study in contrasts — while it appears easy, it's actually very difficult since it's based on subtle leads and weight changes. It's quiet yet dramatic. Most moves are small but precise. And it's one of the few dances that is done best by dancing more to the melancholic mood of the music than to every beat.

Before we knew it, we were rotating partners and dancing around the room. We applied important lessons on connection, trust and patience, which seemed relevant to everyday life as well as social dancing.

We quickly discovered that dancers need to stay connected, steady and balanced at all times. Through mutual upper body contact, my partner guided my movements and I practiced going with the flow. The key was to be solid in the basics, trying not to lose sight of the fundamentals while focusing on remaining consistently grounded.

My partner initiated the steps and I trusted him to safely propel me around the crowded dance floor. If we both vied for control, the essence of the dance was lost.

I patiently awaited his gentle lead before taking the next step, despite the temptation to anticipate his next move. If I made assumptions without waiting for him to guide me, I might actually interrupt his intention. It took time and effort to master moving together and gracefully expressing the passionate music. But the result was freeing.

As the weeks passed, I began to feel more comfortable in my tango shoes. I learned to lean in and embrace the beauty and mystery of the dance. I soon realized that tango dancing is a lifelong pursuit, not something that can be fully grasped in a six-week series. While

I couldn't expect to truly perfect it, I would be able to enjoy it one song at a time.

Even when I wasn't on the dance floor, my mind would replay the helpful advice of my instructor, reminding me of his wise words to dance and to live by:

Don't react if there is no action causing it.

Don't provide unnecessary resistance.

Develop tools, but don't expect to use them all of the time. Be mindful of the context without generalizing. What works in one instance may not work in another.

Don't try to oversimplify; welcome the complexity.

Take small steps. You don't need to take as big of a step as you think. It's an illusion. Practice, practice, practice — learn to enjoy the process.

Slow is the word. Be careful not to rush, thereby missing the subtle nuances. Take your time to savor each moment.

Be humble, accepting and gracious.

It takes two; stay in tune with each other and help each other.

Who would have thought that turning my *someday* dream into my *now-is-the-time* reality would dramatically change my life? Taking that one tiny step of faith not only introduced me to new friends, but also enriched my life with a challenging and fun-filled hobby that keeps me in shape and provides pearls of wisdom along the way.

The small door I entered when I nervously attended that first class opened into a big room filled with a world of opportunity. Offering more than just music and dance, it also provided a sense of accomplishment and camaraderie.

Did I mention that my instructor is planning an upcoming class trip to Buenos Aires? Now when I look at my well-worn tango shoes, I can't help but smile and be grateful that I took that first dance step.

~Kay L. Campbell

Along Came a Spider

It is in your moments of decision
that your destiny is shaped.
~Anthony Robbins

"Y ou're very brave," my colleague said, wiping her hands on a paper towel. Standing there in the ladies' washroom with her, I was feeling many things, but none that resembled courage. The woman complimenting me had, only the week before, edged me out of a promotion I needed.

"There's nothing brave about it," I said, perhaps more dismissive than I should have been. "The posting will only last six months."

"But you're leaving everything," she said. "Do you know anyone there?"

I've often thought of that small exchange. I believe in defining moments even when they stomp on my soul. Knowing they exist is much different from accepting where they take you.

And I wasn't in an accepting mood. She was right; I was leaving everything about my pathetic life behind. I was also faulting her for some of that, because she got the job I had studied for. We were tied in points, as far as the qualifying exam went. On our performance appraisals, however, I had a comment about not respecting authority. She did not.

I was rebelling against more than authority. My marriage was coming apart like a broken zipper. While constant re-zipping temporarily brought us together again, the fault was permanent. I got a divorce, we sold our home, and now I had a potential job 2,000 miles away. I actually believed it was no big deal. It was, after all, a temporary position, a minor reprieve from the rest of my life.

During the three months between accepting the temporary posting and the moment it would officially begin, I lived in a small apartment. My ex-husband and I worked through the tedious process of untangling what was his and what was mine. I repacked my life into boxes, stored some, gave some away, and put aside four that I would take with me.

Ironically, it was a small spider that gave everything clarity. As a child, daddy longlegs terrified me. As an adult, it's the quick little black ones that make my heart race. And it was a little black one that was mocking me as I zipped my suitcase closed.

He scurried across the wall. No longer able to call out "spider patrol" and have my husband come and remove it, I did what any responsible woman would do. I sat down and sobbed.

My life had been reduced to four boxes, two suitcases and no one to kill a spider for me. It was the most desperate moment of my life. The spider watched it all unfold from his place where the wall met the ceiling.

"You're very brave."

Wiping my tears with the back of my hand, I stood up. "I'm not," I said to the spider. "But I can be. And if I'm going to be alone for the rest of my life, it's up to me to find a way to be happy about it."

I reached into one of the boxes and took out a glass. I climbed the stepstool, and with a flick of the real estate flyer advertising my former house, I caught the spider. With a rapid fluttering in my heart, I opened the patio door and set the glass outside. He could find his own new life somewhere else. It's what I was going to do.

A defining moment — I was capable of facing the things that scared me.

Six weeks and several emotional breakdowns later, I understood why my colleague had said what she did. I enjoy people, but I don't make friends easily. I knew no one. I was surrounded by conversations in French that I did not understand, and a few in English that I avoided. I got lost nearly every day as I walked my new neighborhood and sorted through bus schedules. The job was frustrating because although the tasks were similar to my previous post, they were being approached in the most convoluted manner. The note about challenging authority still rankled. But that too was a defining moment—everyone, I realized, was afraid of change. Everyone was also capable of managing it.

On my fortieth birthday, I dined at a sushi restaurant alone. New options had opened for me, and they demanded thought. Would I move for a permanent job? Could I find happiness or security or belonging, or even worth, as a single middle-aged woman?

Defining moments. Reflecting on the previous eight months, I realized that yes, I would move. Financially speaking, I'd be better able to support myself. There were many reasons why my marriage fell apart—and I keenly felt my share of the blame for that—but the self-loathing that had become constant within that union was dissipating. If that could happen, then could happiness be far behind?

Ah, happiness. I realized no one else could be responsible for that, though others could augment it. It was up to me to make the most of the life I'd been given. It began with celebrating the fact I existed, and had for forty years.

I wanted more than a life sentence though. It wasn't enough to exist, so I began to make decisions that, while considering the needs of others, would best benefit me.

Why was that so difficult? I wondered. It was such a simple thing to consider my own needs, but it wasn't something I'd figured out before. So I chose me, and lived with my choices and learned how to be grateful for what I had. That gratitude opened room for joy.

Now, a dozen years later, I can see how each of those choices has given me the life I always wanted but never felt I deserved.

Defining moments. They've made all the difference.

Except for spiders. I haven't worked out what to do about those yet.

~Crystal Thieringer

Renewed Strength

The miracle isn't that I finished.
The miracle is that I had the courage to start.
~John Bingham

"Runners… on your mark. Get set. Go!"

Nike tights, shorts, and a jacket protect my muscles. A black headband covers my ears. Black gloves warm my fingers. Still, the chill of this 37-degree October morning pierces through the thin clothing.

Positioned two-thirds of the way back in the 1,133-person mob of half marathoners, I jog until I reach the starting line. Then the pack lurches forward. I advance with them, establishing my nine-minute-mile pace as the pre-race song lyric, "I would walk 500 miles," echoes in my mind.

Yes, I would walk 500 miles for you, I think. That's the only reason this forty-five-year-old mom is running 13.1. Even though you, Jenna, my teenage daughter and beloved firstborn, aren't here beside me.

Memories from the past ten months rush through my mind, while sidewalk well-wishers clap and cheer. I recall a single treasured, long-awaited run — looping twice around the neighborhood hills — with Jenna. I see her radiant dark eyes, her bountiful brown hair, her long slender legs that out-strode mine two steps to one. As we finished, she looked at me. Her eyes sparkled; her contagious smile emerged. She had been waiting to start pre-season track team conditioning. Wanting to run well, she had asked me to train with her.

I never imagined that first glorious run would also be my last with my daughter.

I never imagined that one week later death would unexpectedly steal her from this life.

Jenna's favorite verse was from Isaiah 40:31 — "those who hope in the Lord will renew their strength... they will run and not grow weary, they will walk and not be faint." I ran for her. And, I remembered.

The long-distance training runs were blanketed with memories. My steady strides carried me past the elementary school where Jenna laughed and learned, past the church where I worshipped beside her, past the cul-de-sac where she took her final breath.

It hurt. But one day at a time — one run at a time — I journeyed through the grief.

Confident I can finish this race now, I smile to myself. I have been waiting for this morning.

A quarter mile into the run, however, a sharp pain shoots down the inside of my right thigh. My first injury of the year from a moderate jog a few days earlier is worse than I was willing to admit.

The faithful fans continue to cheer. They display their signs, wave their arms, and ring their cowbells. The adrenaline should be spurring me on, but I am slowing down. I struggle to pick up my leg. It doesn't want to lift. I know I should stop before I damage my body more.

Running a different half marathon six months from now isn't what I want though. This one was my goal. This one is for Jenna.

I continue. But every time I plant my right foot on the pavement, I wince, unable to fathom twelve more miles of this.

Removing one glove, I touch the iPod armband and increase the volume. Worship songs stream through the earbuds. Tuning out the world around me, I focus. One step at a time, one tune at a time, I resolve to keep on running.

The route — through Greenville's historic neighborhoods, up and down Cleveland Park's winding wooded paths, across the tree-lined Swamp Rabbit Trail — is beautiful. I want to take it all in, but I can't. At mile six, pain shoots down the outside of my right thigh and across my hip. I am tearing multiple muscle fibers, one with names I can't even pronounce.

Rounding a corner, I see my dad. He can tell something is wrong.

"I'm hurting," I pause to tell him before passing by.

"Stop if you need to," he says. But knowing I won't, he strategically calculates three other places where he can encourage me along the way.

The ache, the throbbing, sears through me. I haven't felt such intense physical pain since childbirth. Somehow that seems appropriate, and I wonder whether a mother's pain and a mother's love aren't intertwined in an inseparable cord.

Though I see nearly nothing as I pound the path past ten tennis courts, a teenager's striking red hair captures my attention. She cradles a Starbucks coffee between her fingers, its steam rising to warm her. Then I recognize Abigail, one of Jenna's closest friends. She flashes a knowing smile. She cheers me on.

And so I continue, although the pulsing pain tries to stop me. In the middle of the course, the fans are few. But as I glance over at a neon-colored sign, I see Amy, my running partner before an injury removed her from the race. Then, at mile ten, Hope, who loves me as if I were her own mom. I wasn't expecting friends to come out to watch and root for me on this frigid morning. But I'd have stopped by now if they hadn't.

With three miles remaining, however, doubts assail me. Then I remember the words Jenna used to speak while wrapping her arms around my shoulders and resting her chin on the top of my head.

"Mom, it's gonna be okay." In that moment, I know that somehow it will be.

Sooner than I anticipate, I see my husband with my two younger children, Jenna's sister and brother. They applaud and stride beside me for several steps. Turning a corner, the tall walls of Fluor Field baseball stadium loom before me. Now I know the end is close. Finally, I round the outfield and enter the chute, two hours after taking that initial step.

I hobble, hardly able to walk, as a volunteer drapes a medal around my neck. That's when I remember the verse and realize that, for 13.1 miles, I hadn't really grown weary.

So, God was there, and His promise is true. I'm reminded that He never said the way would be absent of suffering, but in Him my strength will be renewed. He's probably smiling, I think, and Jenna most likely is too.

Amy is the first to reach me. As she receives my sweaty hug, she asks if I would do it again.

Without hesitating, I answer. "Absolutely."

Because now I know my heart can embrace the pain that comes with loving deeply... and still choose to run life's race well.

~Beth Saadati

Chapter 2

Time to Thrive

It's Time to Embrace Adventure

Taking Flight

*The first step towards getting somewhere is to decide
you're not going to stay where you are.*
~John Pierpont Morgan

Widowed fairly young, I was suddenly a free bird for the first time in my life. But where to fly? With two independent children and parents who still had each other, I wanted to start anew, to chance living differently. But how?

I decided to search for another place to live. My late husband's business had always mandated living in New York — I wanted to experience something other than "big city" life.

Interestingly, though my children approved of my decision, both of my extended families were aghast. I couldn't understand why they felt I had to remain in New York, where I'd even attended college while still living at home with my parents. It wasn't as if we all saw each other constantly. So why all the objections when no one ever questioned my children's decisions to attend out-of-state universities? Why shouldn't I leave New York when it was fine for my son to accept a position in Hong Kong and my daughter to work in Washington, D.C.? Was this a generational thing? Or was moving only sanctioned for work?

Over the next three years I visited eight different states. And nothing seemed to click. Lovely though they were, Vermont, New Hampshire, the Carolinas, Florida, New Mexico, Montana and Colorado didn't "speak" to me. All the while, my New York relatives and friends kept telling me it meant I wasn't supposed to move. And I could just hear their unspoken "I told you so's" loud and clear during each get-together.

But I was still hankering for a change....

So there I was checking out Denver and Fort Collins, the former too similar (albeit on a smaller scale) to New York, and the latter too similar to a New York suburb. Where next?

For the longest time a friend of mine who had purchased land in the Black Hills had been championing South Dakota. South Dakota? Well, I knew it was "out west somewhere, up there someplace." But really, South Dakota?

Still in Denver, and still perplexed, I made a snap decision—I was going to visit Spearfish, where my friend owned land. With no computer to search the Internet, no car, no maps, no GPS, no AAA TripTik, no concept of where Spearfish was in relation to Denver, and absolutely no idea of where I was going, I marched myself into a Greyhound bus station and hesitantly asked if they went to Spearfish, South Dakota.

"Of course," was the answer.

Surprised, I said, "Put me on the bus!"

And so the adventure began....

After an overnight journey driving north, a 3 a.m. vehicle change in the middle of nowhere, and long stretches of Colorado and Wyoming scenery, I was absolutely thrilled with my first views of Spearfish as we approached the small town. It was beautiful, it felt vibrant, and the air smelled fresh. And then there were those mysterious looking, dark, forested "black" hills ringing the area—truly, it was as if I were in a picture postcard.

The driver, upon hauling my valise out of the belly of the bus, looked around at the deserted early morning gas station "drop stop" and said, "No one's here. Who's picking you up?"

"Nobody," I responded. "I don't know anybody here."

As the driver looked at me incredulously, I explained I'd come to check out the area without knowing anyone in town.

"But don't worry about me," I was quick to reassure him. "I'll call a taxi."

"Lady, there are no taxis here."

"Okay, so I'll rent a car."

"Lady, there are no rental agencies here. Where're you from?"

As I answered "New York," he shook his head, laughing.

"Big city. Kinda thought so. Welcome to small town America."

And then, "C'mon, it's the end of my run, I'll take you to a car rental."

What I didn't realize was that this angel of a man at the end of his long drive had to take me to Rapid City's airport — an hour away — the only place where I could rent a car. And then he had to drive an hour back to Spearfish where he lived.

At the airport I offered him $50 for his time and courtesy. I was shocked when he refused the money — one of many acts of generosity and kindness I experienced during my subsequent stay. By week's end I had decided — I would move to Spearfish, South Dakota, a town of ten thousand, from New York, a city of ten million. It was beautiful, friendly, uncrowded, reasonably priced, with good water, fresh air, and high energy. It had a few amenities, and it was forty-five minutes from a small city.

All my friends and relatives thought I was crazy.

Before leaving South Dakota it was suggested I visit Bear Butte, a nearby sacred Native American site. The Butte, a dormant volcano, rises abruptly from surrounding plains. As one approaches, there is an overwhelming mystique and sense of power. Part of the Butte is inaccessible to non-Native Americans since the mountain is still used as a site for vision quests by local and visiting tribes. Standing in the visitors' section, I briefly meditated, asking for help regarding my imminent decision, and guidance with my upcoming move.

Suddenly, while meditating, a young Native American child appeared in a vision. About six years old, I couldn't tell whether the child was male or female. Bare-chested, sporting two long black braids, the figure wore nothing but a piece of tanned hide wrapped around its waist. Looking very serious, this child stared at me intently for what seemed like a very long time. And then it spoke, surprisingly in first person.

"I promised to return here one day," the apparition said, and then abruptly faded.

And that clinched the deal!

My mind raced on my trip back to New York. This had been my first visit to South Dakota. Had I lived in the area during another lifetime? Had I been Native American in another lifetime? Was there something unfinished that I needed to complete from time spent here previously? Why had I felt such an immediate connection to the area? Life suddenly seemed to have so many exciting new avenues to explore.

I didn't discover until this past year that all my naysayer relatives back east—after I moved to Spearfish—took bets on how fast I'd return to New York City. One month? Three months? Six? One even bet I'd give it a try for a year.

It's actually going on sixteen years now, and I've never been happier. I've never looked back, there's never been fear or loneliness, never been remorse, and interesting opportunities have been plentiful. My perseverance paid off, and I've never regretted my decision to take flight. From day one this has been home, almost as if it was, indeed, a return.

~Marsha Warren Mittman

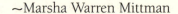

Caged

It is precisely the possibility of realizing a dream
that makes life interesting.
~Paulo Coelho, The Alchemist

Defining moments are not supposed to occur in the local fish market. Rather, they should be created on a wedding day, during the birth of a child, or at a long-awaited graduation. In addition, these life-altering experiences are supposed to be planned for, anticipated, or at least somewhat expected.

However, as I walked to our neighborhood fishery with my husband of twenty-five years, a sense of foreboding hung over me. I kept thinking, "Something is up, and I don't think I want to hear it." As seagulls squawked overhead and water lapped against the shore, my husband told me that he wanted to leave his job. Even though he was concerned about leaving the security of a pension, health benefits, a terrific staff, an expense account, and other perks, this was something he had to do.

My stomach churned. At fifty-something, I had assumed we were finally at the point where, financially at least, things had eased up. For two decades, I had paid my dues by clipping coupons, shopping sales, and taking public transportation. Over the years, I had also pre-paid our mortgage, kept a tight rein on our credit cards, and funded our IRAs. Finally, I could treat myself to a manicure without guilt, hire a cleaning service for the heavy household chores, and employ a local teen to maintain the lawn and shovel the snow.

Standing in that fish market, I could see my carefully constructed life begin to evaporate, just like the steam escaping from the enormous pots of chowder. Then, my eyes traveled to the lobster tanks against the wall. Like the unfortunate inhabitants, I realized I too would be imprisoned within my current career as the primary breadwinner. I would also be responsible for providing our health benefits. I resented my husband for putting me in this position.

The look on my face must have been telling because he suddenly looked like a remorseful five-year-old kid. "Oh, no, I'm sorry. Forget I even mentioned it," he said. "It was just a stupid dream I had. Just forget it." And he tried to force a smile.

But somehow I knew it wasn't just a stupid dream. It was real. And it was something he had been working up the courage to tell me for quite some time. I looked at him carefully. I knew the way I handled the next few minutes would have an impact on the rest of our life. I tried a weak smile.

"I've crunched some numbers," he said tentatively, "and while I know that initially, the financial burden will fall on you, I really believe that in one year, I'll recoup my current salary. Then, I'd like you to cut back. Maybe part-time?"

Part-time? That did sound nice. Before I could respond, the clerk behind the counter was asking for my order. "The usual right, Ms. B? Two pounds of flounder and a quart of chowder?"

"No, give us two of your best lobsters, and throw in a dozen shrimp." I smiled. "I have a feeling we're coming into a windfall."

And somehow I knew we would.

~Barbara A. Davey

Right Back Where I Started From

And I have loved thee, ocean!
~Lord Byron

When I turned five, I received a copy of *The Runaway Bunny*. The message it conveyed was that elsewhere was better than right here.

"I've got to run away today," I announced.

Mama nodded. "I understand, honey bunny," she said. So she wrapped a peanut butter sandwich in wax paper, tucked it in the pocket of my red boucle coat, and kissed me goodbye.

"Remember, you aren't allowed to cross the street," she cautioned.

I trudged to the corner, about three houses away. I peeked over my shoulder. Yep… Mama stood there watching me, so I dared not attempt to cross. I contemplated my options and decided to set up camp right on the corner and eat my lunch there.

As I nibbled, I raised my face to the noontime sun. I'd have loved to have flopped down and snoozed for a bit, but knew I was only supposed to take a nap in my bed. I took a final bite, stuffed the wrapping in my pocket and trudged home.

That night at supper when I recounted how I'd run away from home. Daddy and my first-grader sister didn't look impressed. "Looks like you ran right back," they observed.

They were right, of course, at least for the time being. For several decades, I pretty much stayed put. I married, worked, raised a son, and took care of a variety of houses that never quite felt like home. It all was just… California. I always imagined that home was out there somewhere beyond the horizon beckoning me. It was someplace else… across the street… around the corner… across the continent… on the other side of the globe.

So at age fifty I ran away a second time, this time joining the Peace Corps. At long last I'd have the opportunity to explore those faraway places I'd always dreamed of. Now I wouldn't have to stop at any corners. And maybe I'd find my home.

"You'll come back in two years, and won't ever want to venture far again," friends warned.

"I doubt it," I'd replied. In memory of my late mother, I packed a peanut butter sandwich to take on my first flight to Miami for a Peace Corps staging.

That Runaway Bunny would have envied my worldly adventures. I joined, joined again and rejoined. As a Peace Corps Volunteer, I hacked open coconuts with a machete outside my house in Belize City. I clung to my counterpart as we raced on her motorcycle to get across streams before they flooded in the province of San Juan de la Maguana, Dominican Republic. I helped paint murals on the Youth Center fence with teens on a rare dry afternoon when the monsoon winds had died down in Mont Fleuri, Seychelles. Vacationing in Singapore, I sipped Slings at Raffles and stuck a toe in the South China Sea.

Later, I continued to travel as a health programming specialist for Peace Corps. I heard gray wolves howl on the steppes outside Ulan Bator on the spring equinox in Mongolia. I thrilled to the spontaneous singing of Samoan chiefs and missionaries at a training session in Apia. I explored the corners of the earth in Guyana, Uzbekistan, Thailand, Saint Vincent, Bulgaria. I was still looking for home, though I'd been to more than fifty countries.

When I remarried during the millennial year, my new husband Ken began to talk about his vision of a dream house. "It's got to be somewhere with four seasons," he insisted. "I love sweater weather." So we settled in the far northeast corner of Washington State, and for a few years we shared what began to feel like home. And then Ken died.

I've continued to live in this huge old house, plodding through the seasons. I've hired handymen, gardeners, snowplowers to tend to the property, acres that I can't handle on my own. I've dragged my vacuum up and down the stairs. I've mopped, scrubbed and dusted until my aging muscles ache.

And I've shivered. Friends who've lived here all their lives perk up in the winter, wandering outside to cheer on mittened children who barrel down hills on cookie sheet sleds. Me? I huddle by the fireplace, sip hot chocolate and wish it were iced tea. I'd rather be basking somewhere on a beach.

But it's impossible, I decided, to attempt to move. I'm too old to be starting over somewhere else. Just thinking about the time and energy required to move again wore me out. Hopeless, I thought. I'm stuck here, and have to make the most of it.

Then I visited family in California last fall. I rambled across the beach to the edge of the Pacific. Suddenly, as the waves washed against my toes, I realized that this was home. Always had been. I'd grown up by the ocean. I'd gone fishing in it off a pier when I was a child. I'd sailed on it as a young adult. All my life I've loved the salty taste of my fingers after they've dipped in it, the delicious shock of the water's icy bite when I first would dive in to body surf, the distinctive scent of seaweed and sea spray.

"I never realized how much I miss being close to the Pacific," I told my son that night.

"Have you thought of moving back to California?" he asked.

"It would be overwhelming to even think about it," I said, shaking my head at the impossibility.

He raised an eyebrow. "I thought you were the lady who at age fifty set out on an odyssey that took her to the remote corners of the earth."

I stared at him, ideas clicking away in my mind. Yes, and I braved my way to the corner of my block when I was only five. I took a deep breath. Have I ever been too young or too old to refuse a challenge?

I'm ready to run away again. Challenging? Sure. But I've made a list and I'm checking it twice. I've already called the real estate agent. I've written to senior apartment complexes in my old hometown for rental estimates. I cashed in some frequent flyer miles for a ticket for a stepson to come and help clean out my garage and shed. I'm asking friends if they know of an art dealer who might be interested in the paintings and sculptures.

Each day I sort through a drawer, a closet, or a bookcase to determine what to donate, what to trash, and what to pack. I wake up each morning humming, "California, Here I Come."

I'm crossing the street. I'm going home.

~Terri Elders

Common Ground

Change the way you look at things and the things you look at change.
~Wayne W. Dyer

I maneuvered my rental car off the highway onto the main drag of the small town I had lived in nearly a lifetime ago, searching for the hotel I'd booked for my thirtieth high school reunion. I didn't recognize a thing. "This place has really changed," I thought. Then I realized I'd made a right rather than a left and was driving on a road that didn't exist twenty-six years ago.

I'd felt slightly disoriented by my reunion even before I got lost on that Louisiana road. What was I doing there? I hated high school.

It was because of Facebook. Back in the early eighties, I swore that once I graduated, I'd leave for good. It was an easy vow to keep—I'd mentally packed my boxes during eleventh grade. I fled the South for New York and didn't visit except to see my parents. Once they moved, there was no reason to return. But on our high school's Facebook page, a couple of women posted they were organizing our reunion. "Have fun," I mumbled to my screen. I never looked back at those days through the fuzzy nostalgia of middle age. If I thought about high school at all, it was with relief it had ended.

Then one of the organizers, a woman I hadn't known at all in high school, as she ran with the popular crowd and I hung out with the stoners, sent me a note saying she hoped I'd attend. We'd chatted by e-mail about our kids and our ex-husbands in an easy way I never would have years ago when I kept my vulnerabilities safely stashed away in an impenetrable lockbox.

On an impulse, I bought a ticket. I was curious. What were my classmates, these virtual strangers (and, thanks to social media, virtual "friends") like? How would it be to see each other without the screen as a buffer? On the notes line of my check, I scribbled "angst."

I wasn't sure what to expect. Indigestion. Panic attacks. Maybe a little part of me secretly hoped that those who'd been cruel were now old and fat. Maybe, actually, that part of me wasn't so little or so secret. (Of course, I was the same age as them and couldn't fit into my high school jean size either. But still.)

I headed off to Louisiana with one small tote packed with dresses and several huge bags of emotional baggage.

But something happened I didn't expect. We'd changed. There were the usual physical changes: gray hair, reading glasses, wrinkles. As a group pushing fifty, though, we looked pretty great. There were also more subtle differences. There was an openness I hadn't expected, one that only time and space allowed. Or perhaps it was me; maybe I was candid in a way I hadn't been all those years ago, when I wore my preconception of others like Kevlar—convinced that my classmates were robotic zombies marching lockstep in their Calvin Klein jeans and flipping feathered hair out of Maybelline-shaded eyelids in unison. I wanted to march lockstep too, but didn't know how. Each morning before school, as I unsuccessfully attempted to tame my hair into the Farrah Fawcett 'do all the other girls had, I felt like a fake. So I hid in plain sight, certain that by ignoring "them" before they ignored me, I'd win. Of course, it was hard to win when no one else was playing the same game.

At the reunion, a friend from my old social circle came up to me and we hugged. "Look, I'm shaking," she said, holding out a quivering hand, adding, "Lori and I talked about turning around and going home." I knew exactly how she felt. I told her that when I got to the reunion, I had to force myself to walk through the door. During the drive from the hotel, I'd morphed into a self-conscious adolescent. High school—even all these years later—provokes a visceral response. The grown-up part peels off, leaving only the burning emotional adolescent core. It's like being sixteen again, but with better shoes and no acne. High school, even thirty years later, still messes with the mind.

Clutching my seltzer, I mingled somewhat awkwardly, but less so than thirty years earlier. Conversations with my old friends, my fellow misfits, and others I thought I'd moved on from, or at least away from, quickly skipped over small talk and went deep. None of us were as forthcoming at sixteen when we tried to wear coolness like a cloak. In my case, it was a cloak that hung awkwardly off me, the wrong size and color. Now, we felt more comfortable, collectively, in our skins. I learned about siblings and close buddies who'd died, of suicide, alcohol, AIDS. A friend told me she grew up seeing her dad hit her mom. Another friend, who'd read something I'd written about mental illness, shared that two brothers had bipolar disorder.

I was humbled by the frankness of those I thought I'd left behind, who had stayed in the South. Mistakenly and obnoxiously, I'd assumed the town and its citizens would be exactly the same as thirty years ago. But everything and everyone had changed. I'd gone from resisting authority to being it, first as a teacher and then as a parent. My town had grown up, too. It now had a burgeoning arts district and a far more diverse population. What I'd mentally accused some who'd stayed of doing—not being open-minded—I was guilty of. Don't get me wrong; there were plenty of people at the reunion I avoided. But that's the great thing about being an adult: Thirty years ago, I cared about what people thought; now, I cared about what I thought.

The following day, I drove my rental car to the airport after what turned out to be a very fun high school reunion (five words I never thought I'd string together), its radio station a way-back machine playing groups I hadn't heard since then: Rush, REO Speedwagon, the Eagles. Instead of finding a station that was more to my taste, I left it on. Somewhere on the long bridge over Lake Pontchartrain, "Blinded by the Light" came on. I sang loudly and off-key and realized

I had no idea what the words were. I smiled as the high school angst I'd held on to for too many years dissolved somewhere over the lake.

~Sue Sanders

A Mid-Life Challenge

To think too long about doing a thing
often becomes its undoing.
~Eva Young

I stood in the middle of the vast administration hall, confused and bewildered. I didn't belong. My navy blue skirt and neat floral blouse told of a different generation. Standing hesitantly in middle-aged shoes, I surveyed the youngsters in jeans and T-shirts. They laughed and shouted greetings across the room. They belonged.

This was a stupid decision made in desperation. I turned to leave when through the cacophony I heard my name, "Ann, Ann." I searched through the myriad strangers to see a middle-aged woman waving and calling me. I looked enquiringly as she pushed her way through the crowds, dragging a friend along with her.

"Don't you remember me? We were at school together." Her eyes glowed with fun and recognition.

"That must have been nearly twenty-five years ago," I exclaimed. "How did you recognise me?" I waited wide-eyed and bewildered.

"You sang. Everyone knew you. Do you still sing?" She was right. I had sung my way through school — in concerts, the choir, shows and the cathedral. But in the last twenty years I'd settled into a housewifely routine and forgotten those uplifting schoolgirl events that had made my spirit soar.

"Anyway, I'm June and this is my friend Glen. Have you come to register?" She grabbed my arm. "Follow us. We can all register together. The three witches!" She laughed with the sheer enjoyment of the moment.

I was caught up in the excitement, and before I could turn and run I had signed and paid my registration fees. The three of us stood there giggling at our audacity. We had enrolled for studying towards a degree at university.

I hurried home, up the stairs and into my flat. I stood staring out the window across the bay. What a stupid thing to do, throwing away all that money. I had never shown signs of intellectual excellence at school and all I'd managed in the last twenty years or so was to cook and clean while I raised five children. But the mundane routine had dulled my zest for life. Surely there was more than endless cleaning up after others. This idea took root until I became ill with yearning for I knew not what.

I had left my husband, put my younger children in boarding school and rented out our family home. Why? For a small internal voice that nagged persistently, "There is more to life than domesticity. What's happened to the songs? There's a world to explore. Stop crying and feeling sorry for yourself. Do something." I felt I had reached the point of no return, but was university the answer?

I mulled over this conundrum for a few days, and then one evening the phone rang. "Ann, June here. I'll meet you tomorrow outside the main lecture hall just before 8 a.m. I need your support for our first lecture. Got to run. See you there." I barely had time to grunt a reply when she rang off. She sounded excited and I caught the feeling. A tingling sensation seeped through my body. I couldn't remember the last time I had felt such a nervous thrill. Maybe I'd give it a try. One English Literature lecture wouldn't be too embarrassing. I could at least read!

The following morning, I dressed in jeans and a T-shirt and set off to meet my friends who were watching out for me. We headed for the front row of the lecture hall. The hall soon filled with chattering students until the lecturer entered. Silence. The atmosphere hummed with anticipation.

Dr. Smails greeted us, picked up a book and read aloud the poem, "Stopping by Woods on a Snowy Evening" by Robert Frost. I was inspired as we debated the meaning of the poem. It could have been written for me. I sat entranced, all my senses on full alert. This was it. I had found something that inspired me. Something that required a new approach, a challenge for my rusty brain cells. Maybe I hadn't wasted my money.

I arranged with my generous and understanding boss to work shifts and flextime so that I could attend lectures. I sat with my friends in the front row listening to an analysis of either literary works or the human psyche (we had also registered for Psychology). My brain did gymnastics as it strained to understand and absorb concepts and revolutionary ideas.

The year passed and the magic happened as I perused reference books, read great literary works and studied the actions and reactions of the human psyche. At the end of the year we wrote exams, and all three of us passed with flying colours. I was the happiest I had been for a long time, but what to do with it?

I had no sooner asked the question when the headmaster of a school in the poorer part of town phoned. "I'm looking for someone to teach English. Our teacher is on maternity leave next year and we need someone to replace her urgently. Would you be prepared to fill in?"

"But I only have English I, and I have never taught," I protested in fear of taking on such a task.

"Well," he responded, "you'll be one year ahead of the scholars. Please, help me out?"

I accepted the challenge, plunged into the deep end and loved it. The children were keen learners and I was used to being surrounded by teenagers. My salary increased and I had time to study.

Slowly, step by step, I passed more university subjects until I was eventually capped with an English Honours degree. That Honours degree led to me procuring a lecturing post at the local university.

With this new confidence, I had started singing again; I joined a choir and sang in shows. Life was a great adventure again.

~Ann Hoffman

18

Mountain Dreams

Get excited and enthusiastic about your own dream.
This excitement is like a forest fire—you can smell it,
taste it, and see it from a mile away.
~Denis Waitley

Our family had enjoyed a happy home in the small community where we lived. Yet, as life often does, our situation changed. The town had grown, but we had not. We decided to move and start fresh.

That night, unable to sleep, my husband and I discussed our plans, or lack of them. We had no idea where we were headed or what we should do with our lives. The more we talked, the more I thought about one of our family's favorite Disney movies: *So Dear to My Heart*. This wonderful movie portrayed the lifestyle my husband and I longed for. We had always dreamed of owning a tiny chinked-log cabin like the one in the movie, but we'd live in the mountains. I'd spin wool by the wood stove, milk goats, make cheese, can food and work a garden. My husband would harvest wood, hike, fish, snowshoe and make maple syrup. We imagined our children thriving and pursuing their interests in the great outdoors. The longer we chatted, the more I felt our answer had been in front of us all along.

"Do you still want to live in the mountains someday?" I asked.

"Of course," he answered, "but we can't do it now."

When I asked him why not, he presented me with our usual collection of problems: east versus west, how we would finance our land,

and how we would make a living once we were there. "The bottom line is that we can't afford it right now," he said.

"That's how you felt when we wanted a baby," I reminded him. "If we'd waited until we could afford one, we'd still be childless today." He nodded. "Why not live our dream?" I continued. That did it.

We were excited and terrified at the same time. Naturally there were obstacles, but fighting for our dream made it worthwhile. The eastern mountains won. We financed and found land. We put our home up for sale while we built our cabin from thousands of miles away. Questions and concerns from well-meaning friends and family were addressed.

"Why such a hard, meager life?" my in-laws asked. "Why not move closer to a city? Why not move closer to us?"

"Because we've always dreamed of living in the mountains away from it all," we answered.

Eventually we packed up our three kids, six cats, seven parakeets, and one dog and we made the cross-country trip eastward. Living in the mountains had been our big dream, but there were plenty of mini dreams that we fulfilled along the way. Each dream required a separate leap. We homeschooled our children. I milked goats, made cheese, spun wool, grew my garden, ground wheat, and baked bread. We heated with wood stoves. We made maple syrup, picked berries, and canned our food. We hiked and enjoyed nature and our peaceful surroundings. But most of all our children thrived and so did we.

This year we celebrated the twenty-year anniversary of living our dream. I can't believe how quickly the years flew by or how many changes have taken place. We're older now. Our children are grown. We've got grandkids. Time moved on and now there are new dreams on the horizon. We are grateful that we took this risk. Not only did we survive—we thrived!

~Jill Burns

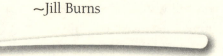

19

Taking a Leap

You don't always need a plan. Sometimes you just need
to breathe, trust, let go and see what happens.
~Mandy Hale

There was no question I had a good job—a six-figure salary, stock options, and potential for advancement. Best of all, I enjoyed my work researching herbs for the treatment of common ailments. My formulas offered a safe alternative to traditional over-the-counter drugs, and that gave me satisfaction. I worked with folks who were for the most part congenial, and my office in downtown Chattanooga was only a short commute from my home. I had nothing specific to complain about and yet I was not content.

I felt like a very large person stuffed inside a very small box. I wanted room to swing my arms, stretch my legs, and reach my full stature. Perhaps a career change was in order. But to what? I had no idea, and altering course in mid-life wouldn't be easy. Still, a wee voice prodded me to take a risk—to leap even without knowing where I would land. I toyed with the idea, but I was too afraid to make a move.

And then I remembered that time in Maui.

I had lived close enough to the beach to hear the surf pound the shore, but I was in love with the region the locals called upcountry. It was dotted with eucalyptus and jacaranda trees and offered spectacular views of the island. I longed to spend time there, but I was terrified of driving the narrow road that wound its way up the volcano. Though

I told myself that one day I would do it, that day never seemed to come. Then a wise friend asked me, "If not now, then when?" I had no answer for him, and that simple truth coursed through me like a bolt of electricity. Life was unpredictable and short. Why not now? With my stomach churning, I got in the car, snaked up the Haleakala Highway, and looked down at the sea.

The drive had been liberating. I had pushed past my boundaries, mastering those hairpin turns despite my fear. I knew I could do it again. I could take a leap. I considered a sabbatical, a complete break from the 9 to 5 that would give me the time to explore my possibilities. It was a radical notion, but I had savings. I could make it work. I tried to picture myself lingering over my morning coffee as my husband Andy grabbed a bagel and rushed off to his office. But I couldn't quite see it.

And then a new idea came to me. It was one that would require Andy to take a leap as well. Before we married, Andy had told me that he dreamed of living in Israel. He had spent six months on a kibbutz after high school, and in college he spent his junior year in Jerusalem. He loved the people and the land, and he wanted to go back. I had no particular draw to Israel, and the wars and terror attacks hardly made it a vacation paradise. I made it clear to him then that I wasn't interested in emigrating. Still, I had left the door open for an extended visit someday.

Maybe, I thought, this was the time for that visit.

That night, as I placed the last of the dishes into the drying rack, I turned to Andy. "You know how I've been saying that I want to make a change? What if we both did? What if we went to live in Israel?"

"Really? You mean leave our jobs, and just go?" he said.

"Yes. For a year. That's all."

It didn't take any convincing to get Andy on board. He began planning out loud. Other engineers had taken a leave of absence from his workplace. He would ask for one too. I told him that I would resign, that I wanted to do something different when we returned. We were both quiet after that. I could hardly believe that I had voiced such unlikely ideas. I began to quiver and to backpedal.

"Well, what I meant to say was that maybe I could see myself in Israel if we were participating in an organized program."

Andy was an adventurer. He was fine with taking off for parts unknown and figuring it all out as he went along. But not me. I explained to him that I was not prepared to just hang out in a country where I didn't speak the language. That would be too hard. I wanted us to go on a program for English speakers that provided room and board, classes in Hebrew and Israeli studies, and the opportunity to travel.

Being the resident Israel expert, he took on the assignment of finding a program that would meet my specifications. Day by day, my list of requirements grew along with my anxiety. I was like a baby bird stretching and flapping her wings but not quite ready to leap from the nest. The day Andy announced that he'd found the perfect program for us my knees buckled. I took a few deep breaths and to shore up my courage whispered the words that had become my mantra: "If not now, when?"

We filled out an application, plastered the envelope with airmail stamps, and dropped it in the mailbox. The wheels were set in motion. Not a week later, Andy got word from his boss. There would be no leave of absence. If he left, we would return from Israel without a roof or a job between us. Andy was still game. It was up to me.

One by one, my second thoughts melted away under the bright light of opportunity.

"Okay," I said. "Let's go for it."

Days rolled into weeks as we put all our stateside affairs in order. We both gave notice at work, made care arrangements for our mutt Tova, and began paring down the contents of our three-bedroom house, tossing or giving away whatever wouldn't fit in a ten by fifteen storage unit. Then at 5 p.m., on the very cusp of the new millennium, I hugged my co-workers goodbye and left my office for the last time. I had a copy of *Herbs of Commerce*, a framed photo of Andy, an African violet in a clay pot—and my own heart bursting with possibility.

~Lorri Danzig

A Not So Trivial Twosome

Regardless of differences,
we strive shoulder to shoulder...
[T]eamwork can be summed up in five short words:
"We believe in each other."
~Jerry Smith

The announcement in the newspaper enticed me: "*Trivial Pursuit* Competition… $500 First Prize."

The competition, for teams of two, was to be held at a nearby mall. My wife Carol and I loved playing the game with friends, but this competition would be in full view of the general public. I waved the paper at Carol. "Did you see this?"

"Yes, and the answer is no! Ask Clive!"

Trivial Pursuit, a board game that tests your general and pop culture knowledge, was the latest fad and had become an "intellectual hula hoop" for adults. To be crowned the local champion would bring us glory and gold.

But there are in life some things that loving couples should avoid doing. Partnering to play a game based on knowledge and memory, in a public forum, is on that list of relationship testers. Thus Carol's firm answer to my query.

My friend Clive made a good fit. We were prepared and eager, but just hours before the Wednesday night qualifying round, Clive took ill. Now on the cusp of the competition I needed a replacement. This called for desperate measures… "Carol!"

We arrived and found Table 8 set to accommodate eight couples. Although Carol was clearly uncomfortable, we took our places, nodding greetings to those present. A group of spectators had gathered and that made her all the more nervous. An announcement was made and play began.

The first couple started strongly, answering correctly and acquiring a few "pie wedges" in their scoring token before missing a question. The following two teams had very brief runs before losing their turns. Next up, we did well, garnering two wedges, but an Art & Literature question confounded us and we became spectators again, hoping for another chance. As the games continued, we could hear cries of joy and groans of despair from the other tables. Our table played on and elimination loomed; however none of our opponents filled their game pieces and we got a second chance. We did not waste it. Thanks to some favourable rolls, Carol's knowledge of birthstones and anniversaries, and a run of correct answers, we won our table and earned a spot in the finals. All the talk afterward was about the couple at Table 3 who had run the board on their first turn, answering over 100 consecutive questions correctly to sweep into the championship. We would face them on Saturday at "high noon."

Saturday's table was centred in the mall's rotunda. We were seated side by side in the eighth spot and selected a green (for Forrest, our last name) playing piece. The team that had been perfect on Wednesday sat almost across from us. This was a promotional event for the mall, and spectators surrounded us, standing three deep. The media was well represented and the local cable TV channel was taping the event. The judge called us to order and the questioner began.

Team 1 got off to a shaky start. They only answered four questions before missing one. Team 2 did better and half filled their game piece with wedges before faltering. Team 3 took the die and lived up to expectations. A mixed female/male team, she took the lead in answering and they seldom conferred, rolling strategically and answering about seventy consecutive questions. Without missing an answer, they ran the board. Technically they had won the game, unless another team could match their performance and force a playoff. The next four teams were clearly intimidated and unable to mount a serious run. During play, I watched the couple as their confident smiles became almost smug.

We were up last and started quickly, rolling on to the required squares and acquiring about half the wedges needed. Even though one of us thought we knew the answer, we always conferred before replying. Then, we ran in to a stretch of rolls that forced us to answer many questions without acquiring wedges. Every question threatened sudden death; but eventually we made it to the centre and then nailed the final question. We had done it — run the board to force a playoff.

Team 3 was up first, knowing as well as us that a single miss could mean defeat, yet they seemed quite calm. The audience had increased and even they too were tense, often being warned to silence by the questioner. Picking up where they had left off, our opponents breezed along, acquiring wedges quickly. Then an Entertainment question drew blank looks from both. They conferred and argued and then answered… incorrectly. The audience groaned. Our hearts, already in our throats, began to pound. We were up.

Frankly, I doubted we could run the board again, but it was do or die. Initially it seemed the game gods had deserted us. Our dice rolls were not placing us on the required spots to acquire wedges. That meant answering many more questions, with a single miss meaning failure. But with hands held and knees knocking, we pressed on and our luck turned. By the judge's count, on the one hundred and third question, we gained the centre of the hub. The scene became deathly quiet. The pressure was almost unbearable as Team 3 considered the deciding category and chose, Art & Literature. The tension increased and we held hands tighter. The audience buzzed, then hushed as the question was posed.

"In *Alice in Wonderland*… What did the Knave of Hearts steal from the Queen of Hearts?"

Carol shoulders slumped and she sighed. We conferred. She knew the answer. I agreed. We delivered it together… "Tarts!"

"Correct!" The audience exploded in cheers. We hugged in relief, first like shipwreck survivors and then in joy at achieving both fame and fortune. Our opponents congratulated us, the cheque was presented and the media interviews followed.

At home I poured a celebratory drink and toasted Carol. "Here's to you; thanks for stepping up, honey! You were a rock and saved us many times."

"At least it was worth it!" Carol replied.

Years later when telling the story to friends or family, they always ask the ultimate trivia question, "What did you get?"

Carol had that answer too. "John got the glory and I got a granite countertop!"

~John Forrest

Getting Our Groove Back

You can't always wait for the perfect time;
sometimes you must dare to jump.
~Author Unknown

In retrospect, our "big decision" probably took about three years to make. It was a crazy three years in which we gave birth to our second child, Hannah, and two years later our baby boy, Charlie. As much joy and happiness as this brought to our lives, we also faced some of our most devastating times—two of our parents passed away.

I was a mother of three, working part-time from home. I owned my own executive coaching business and was finishing my certification course, often at night. With my coaching business being international, I was often on calls in the evening or early morning—which suited me as it did not take time from my children.

My husband enjoyed his work, though he was getting a bit tired of his role and feeling restless, looking for more. To make up for the lack of stimulation at work, he studied for his MBA. He also travelled internationally for his job, anywhere from Chile to South Africa, Tucson to Perth, which took him away approximately 120 days a year.

During the night, we had young babies still waking. And during the day, we did fun child-oriented activities like swimming lessons and dance classes. We visited shopping centers, had health checkups—all the things you do with three little ones, five and under. Weekends often included travelling to visit family and friends, or they visited us. We spent time watching our eldest, Jackson, in his junior lifesaving club, Nippers, or in his local soccer competition. You could say we were happily living in the chaotic rat race.

When I was up with the children at night I would often wonder, "With so much business, noise and life swirling around, how will we focus on what is important?" It was time to hop off the hamster wheel. We needed to take action towards our own long-term happiness. Because as good as this was, it wasn't great.

The first step was to stop thinking about what we did not want and start thinking about what we did want. We wanted more family time, more work-life balance, and to live an inspired life. We wanted to have many fun, loving and positively memorable adventures with family and friends. We wanted the kids to have experiences that would make them say, "We had an awesome upbringing."

We wanted to truly love what we did for work. I wanted time to focus on my relationship with my husband; I wanted to be a role model for my kids. Less time in the shopping center and more time making memories. I did not want to sit on the sidelines and watch; I wanted to join in. I wanted to give back to society. I wanted to be able to relax and have fun and laugh, every day. I wanted to explore the balance of living life to the fullest and still have time to stop and smell the roses.

That's when it happened. My husband started applying for jobs overseas. We had lived overseas before and knew we loved the adventure, but we were torn because we'd have to leave our families, friends and stability. That would be a lot for a young family.

Part of our decision was karma or fate, call it what you will. My husband saw the perfect job online. While speaking to the hiring manager in Canada, he was told, "We are located in a small mountain town. You would never have heard of it." Except that my husband ski-bummed in that town for two years before we met—only leaving because of the lack of work in his field. He had always dreamed of going back there!

We believe in living our lives on purpose, and it was time to move forward into a new chapter. It was about creating less craziness, more work-life balance, less stress and more adventure and happy memories. It was time to pursue our passions and dreams. We had always believed in loving what you do and doing what you love. It might sound obvious, but for us it was a massive and courageous decision.

I asked my eighty-two-year-old mother for advice. Even though she is elderly and would not see us as often, she replied with such clarity and wisdom. "You do not want to get to my stage of life and look back and wish you had done it."

We now live in that little ski resort town in Canada. My business is flourishing; my husband loves his job, and travels less. We have been back to Australia to visit our family and friends three times in three years. My mother came and stayed with us for two months; I speak to her regularly on the phone.

We've undergone a transformation. We move our bodies, our stress is low, and we've got our freedom and our balance. Now we have time to stop, breathe and feel grateful. In the summer, we travel and explore as much as possible. Every weekend during the winter our family skis together. We aren't getting benched from our own lives. Now, we live.

~Kate Wan

My Theory of Relativity

In the middle of difficulty lies opportunity.
~Albert Einstein

I n October of 1992, at the age of fifty-eight, the aerospace company I was working for offered me and 1,200 other senior employees early retirement, also known as the "golden handshake." Up to that point in my career, I had not planned to retire until I was sixty-two. By then I would have had an additional four years, which would have given me a greater pension and allowed me to obtain early Social Security. Had it not been for my wife working at the time, I would not have been able to support the two of us plus a son who had just started law school.

A few months prior, my middle son quit the law firm where he worked and opened his own law practice. Recognizing that I was in dire straits, he offered me a part-time job creating forms from special software for attorneys. At the same time, I had already sent out résumés to obtain another job in the aerospace industry. As good as I was at what I did, no one was hiring fifty-eight-year-olds.

After a few months working in my son's office, another attorney who rented office space in my son's suite of offices approached me and asked, "Has anyone ever told you that you look like Albert Einstein?" With a puzzled look on my face, I simply said, "No." He basically ignored my answer and told me to buy a mustache, take some black and white pictures of myself, and turn them over to him so he could send them to a lookalike agency. I had no idea what he was talking about. But, like he had said, what did I have to lose?

I did exactly what he said. I happened to have a good camera with a portrait lens and a tripod. I bought a roll of black and white film, set up the tripod and took some pictures of myself. I wore an old black sweatshirt like the one I saw in an old picture of Einstein. I should note that although my hair was white, it was cut fairly short and neatly combed. I never had long straggly hair. But for the picture, I messed it up a bit, glued on the mustache and removed my glasses.

A few days later, after the film was developed, I handed all the pictures over to the other attorney. He looked them over, chose a few and handed the rest back. He said he was going to send them to a lookalike agency.

Two weeks later, I received a telephone call from an agent. He told me his name was Brian Mulligan. Out of nowhere he asked me if I was available for a gig on a certain date. He explained that the gig was for a one-day film shoot for a Japanese production company. I thought someone was playing games with me and I hung up. A few minutes later he called again and convinced me that this was for real. He wanted to know if I had a headshot and résumé to give to the film producers. When I said I had neither, he told me to get an eight-by-ten glossy print made from one of the negatives.

He then told me he would help me create a résumé. "Are you kidding?" I said. "I haven't done anything as an Einstein lookalike to put on a résumé."

"Don't worry," he told me, "we'll figure something out." At that point, I told him to forget it and hung up again.

But he persisted. Since he lived close by, he asked me to deliver the headshot to him and that we would work on a résumé. How the hell was he going to do that? Worse yet, what was I going to do once I got on the set? I couldn't have felt uneasier about going through with it. To this day, I don't know how I allowed myself to get involved in something I had absolutely no training in or knowledge of. And what kind of agent throws an unknown out there, not knowing what he is capable of doing?

What I didn't realize at the time was that it was all about "the look." The next thing I knew I was in a Beverly Hills office auditioning for the part of Albert Einstein in front of Japanese producers and the director of the film. In the end, it didn't matter that I didn't understand Japanese. I could tell by the look on their faces how happy they were with my look. The following day my agent called to let me know that I got the gig.

That was the beginning of a twenty-two-year second career, which continues to this day. My résumé now includes commercials made all over the world, film and TV, trade shows and print ads. I even did a Pepsi commercial, for which I had to become a member of the Screen Actors Guild. I also became a member of AFTRA in order to be on TV shows like *The Tonight Show with Jay Leno*, among others. I was in a movie, *Breaking Up*, with Russell Crowe and Selma Hayek. Then there was the Disney World production, *Ellen's Energy Adventure*, with Ellen DeGeneres, Bill Nye, Jamie Lee Curtis and Alex Trebek.

I had no idea how much money I was going to make just because I happened to look like Albert Einstein. The Pepsi commercial alone made me $70,000 for the year it was on TV. Commercials made in Japan, Korea, Barcelona, Greece, and Panama City allowed me to earn $10,000 for one-day commercial shoots plus all expenses paid.

Although some years were more lucrative than others, I have been able to average $15,000 a year. After twenty-two years, that comes to $330,000. Not bad for just looking like the smartest guy in the world.

~Benny Wasserman

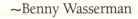

23

Chicken Soup for the Soul

Sweat, Blood and Solitude

Only those who will risk going too far can possibly find
out how far one can go.
~T. S. Eliot

"Y ou know, there are better ways to go about this," the hotel receptionist said as she cast a doubtful glance over my fully loaded bike. I had just told her of my plans to ride across the country by myself.

"Why don't you take a car?" she asked, helpfully.

"I can't. I sold mine yesterday," I answered. I felt the panic swirl in my gut as I thought back to handing over the keys at the dealership. I had no choice but to go forward with this crazy plan now.

She trailed behind me as I pushed the heavy bike outside. As Yorktown, Virginia is one of the official trailheads for the TransAmerica Bicycle Trail, I hadn't expected to draw any attention. But I was surprised when no fewer than three people remarked on how unusual it was for a woman to attempt this alone, something I heard often throughout my trip.

A few people strolling by paused to watch as I finished my preparations. I smiled and waved at them, pushed down on my pedal… and didn't move an inch. This was my first time riding with the extra weight of my panniers, the bags slung over my wheel. I gritted my teeth and tried again, breathing a sigh of relief when I inched forward.

I moved slowly down the road, houses and buildings gradually transitioning into woods, though the trees lining the road offered little relief against the sweltering heat. The unaccustomed weight of the panniers on the front wheels created a pronounced wobble when I went uphill, throwing me off balance. I didn't even complete two miles before I tipped over, falling like a little kid riding a bike for the first time.

That first day, I fell three times, lost a bag in the middle of a busy intersection, and made it a whole fifteen miles into the 4,241.5-mile journey. When I sat down in my hotel room that night, all I wanted to do was call my parents and beg them to come get me.

Pushing my doubts aside, I continued the next day, and every day after that, progressing at a snail's pace. Once or twice a day, I crossed paths with other cyclists and exchanged a few friendly words, but otherwise I was left to my own thoughts. With little else to do, I reflected on how I ended up here in the first place.

If I had to pinpoint where this idea first took root, I would say it was in Afghanistan. During my first deployment, I discovered a blog written by a man who rode his bike from Japan to London. I was fascinated by the stories he told of the people he met and the obstacles he overcame. His adventures reminded me of the vast world that existed beyond the narrow confines of the camp we lived in.

When I left the military, I found myself with a few months before school started. I was unhappy with the marked changes I had undergone in the past few years. I had become more cautious, and looked to others for confirmation before stating my opinions. Frustrated with a system that rewarded personal relationships over merit, I began doing only the bare minimum required of me. I wanted to shed this negativity, to relearn how to think for myself, and to once more rely on myself to solve my problems. And above all, I craved solitude. This seemed like the perfect solution.

This trip, however, was definitely not what I had expected. I became hopelessly lost early on, making it unlikely that I would finish in the few short months I had. To make up for lost time, I switched to a more direct route. The catch, of course, was that I had to go through West Virginia. I could have kicked myself for not paying more attention in geography class when I belatedly discovered that West Virginia is the only state located entirely in a mountain range. Coming from South Florida, where the only elevation you can train on is the speed bumps in the parking lot, mountains really suck.

As I approached that first mountain, I pulled over and looked up. I took a deep breath and began pedaling furiously up the steep incline. I made it around the first bend before I lost all momentum and came to an abrupt halt, forcing me to get off and push the bike. I trudged up the mountain, the pebbles flung by the passing vehicles stinging the raw and blistered skin on my legs. The 100-degree heat sapped my strength, and the sweat running into my eyes made it difficult to see. The duct tape I had wrapped around my feet quickly slid off, unable to stick to my damp skin, and the straps of my sandals sliced into my bloody skin.

Working from dawn to dusk, I made it up and over nine mountains in two days. Though I spent more time walking than riding, by focusing on a spot just ahead of me I could ignore my exhaustion and force my feet to keep moving. And with each new mountain, I could ride a little further before I had to get off and push. More importantly, something clicked in my head, and I was able to look at the bigger picture of my journey rather than getting swept up in the minute-to-minute misery of it.

One of the most meaningful encounters I had occurred after I had emerged from the mountains. The flat, paved roads of Ohio were a welcome relief after the pounding I took in West Virginia. The cyclists on their road bikes still zoomed past me, but I had stopped caring. One of the cyclists pulled over briefly to say, "You know, I've completed three Ironmans, but I could never do what you're doing." I looked over at him, startled, then smiled.

I don't mean to make this sound like a fairy tale where everything worked out in the end. My journey abruptly ended in South Dakota when I quite literally got stuck in the flooded dirt roads. It was lonely, it was exhausting, and in terms of finishing what I set out to do, I failed miserably.

Despite this, I felt like I finally regained that sense of self that I had lost in the military. I found a balance between relying on myself and knowing when to ask others for help. And most importantly, I learned that no matter how tired you are, you can always ride fast up a steep hill when a dog is chasing you.

~Krystal Klumpp

24

Taught by Teens

*You gain strength, courage, and confidence by
every experience in which you really stop to
look fear in the face.... You must do the thing
which you think you cannot do.*
~Eleanor Roosevelt

The group of teenagers led the way through the heavy iron gates onto the campus surrounded by cement walls. We were in Kingston, Jamaica, a city fraught with danger, but the teens laughed and joked, secure and unafraid. I was worried. It wasn't the setting, however, but the new experiences I would face inside the safety of the campus walls that caused my anxiety.

As a child, I had lived in a prison of fear. Like a host of my friends, I was afraid of bugs and spiders, but I was also afraid of places too dark and too high, spaces too close, and spaces too open. Mostly, I was afraid of people. What did they think of me? Would they laugh if they knew what I thought? Would they like me?

With adulthood came maturity. I realized I was bigger than insects. I rode the fastest, highest roller coaster at Cedar Point to prove my fear of heights had vanished. Just once, mind you, but I did it. I joined Toastmasters International to conquer my fear of public speaking. Self-help books and friendly counsel helped me put aside other fears, but still, I spent too much time in hiding.

Then I volunteered to chaperone teenagers on a work team to

Jamaica. For one week, we would work on this campus for deaf children. Most of the deaf students had left for summer break, but five teen boys remained.

As the gates locked behind us, the teens ran to meet the deaf students. They quickly discovered that basketball was a universal language. By evening curfew, impromptu lessons in sign language had planted the seeds of friendship. I watched the play from the safety of an open-sided, tin-roofed pavilion, wanting to join the fun, but too afraid of failure to try conversing with the deaf students—especially in front of an audience.

We spent our days painting, welding, installing a water storage unit, and pouring a cement roof. We worked hard, but our youth group wasn't afraid to try new skills or laugh at their mistakes. Following their initiative, I took a deep breath and climbed the scaffolding to join the bucket brigade manually passing cement to pour the new roof.

Each evening, sweat ran down our dusty, paint-splotched bodies, making everybody race to the showers. Once again I retreated. The other women and girls didn't mind the open locker room. They giggled and shared stories, but I dressed behind the shower curtain, longing for their freedom yet unwilling to be seen.

One afternoon, we visited a home for severely handicapped children. As our teens engaged wholeheartedly in this new adventure, I watched from the shadows. One of them, a macho, brawny football star, squatted in the dust and blew bubbles with a little girl, unashamed of the teardrop sliding down his face. His actions gave me courage. I cast my fears aside, picked up a crippled child, and danced a Ring Around the Rosie jig.

By week's end, I leaned new skills, tried new foods, and learned simple phrases in sign language. I let the girls braid my hair and laughed with them at the results.

On our last evening, we gathered in the pavilion to share what the week had meant to us and the lessons we had learned. I knew my turn was coming. Rubbing my cold, clammy hands against my skirt, I thought, "Maybe if I go to the restroom and then sit with those who have already spoken, no one will notice."

All week long, the teens showed me how to put aside my fears and live. They inspired me to laugh at mistakes and learn. I realized that if I didn't speak they would never know how much they had taught me. The person beside me sat down. I stood up and faced the group.

"I came to chaperone you. Instead, you have taught me…."

Today, I have overcome almost all my fears and I gain more independence every year. Freedom is a wonderful thing, but I am not finished learning; there is always room for personal growth. Maybe I should chaperone another work team of teenagers.

~Rhonda K. Maller

25

When in Rome

*Being naked approaches being revolutionary; going
barefoot is mere populism.*
~John Updike

"W hen in Rome…" I thought as I flattened my back against the rough cedar siding of the sauna. The glance in the window had revealed more than I had wanted. My month in Sweden had been a great adventure, faced head on, but this seemed more daunting, intimidating. I slowly shook my head, scolding myself. "You can take trains across Scandinavia, ride the buses of Stockholm alone, yet you can't take your bathing suit off with your family?" I stole another peek in the window. There they were, perched on benches, all of their blond loveliness, stark naked. I felt like an uptight, stupid American.

As I stood there, I realized that I would be more obvious in my bathing suit than nude. Could you truly be less conspicuous naked? I slowly peeled down the black straps over my frigid shoulders, giving a shudder in the cool air. I finished the job with a determined yank, steeling myself for the next step.

The handle of the cedar door was smooth as I grasped it in my moist palm. I inhaled sharply and straightened my spine. I sucked in my stomach. I tried to walk nonchalantly into the sauna. No one had done more than glance my way and the conversations continued, enveloping me in the rhythm of the Swedish language. I suddenly felt very silly.

Fifteen minutes, maybe twenty passed as the easy conversation continued. I listened to the talking, joined in for a few words and tried to become immersed in the moment. The rhythm of the language started to lull me into a more relaxed place. I wanted to be adult enough, sophisticated enough, to think that public nudity, well at least among distant family members, really wasn't a big deal. I wanted to act like I was every bit a casual European, comfortable in her own skin. I had done this thing and now should relax in the moment.

My cousin Kia's voice startled me back into the sauna. "Are you ready?" she questioned. My mind flew back into high gear. "Ready for what?" What else could there be?

"A sauna isn't complete without the cool down. Now is the time we end the sauna."

My heart started to thump. How could we cool down? There wasn't any snow outside in July. Was there a shower? I knew in my heart it wasn't going to be a shower.

Kia looked amused. Her blue eyes twinkled.

I didn't want to ask the question because then I would have to choose my next step. It's funny how sitting naked on a hard wooden bench in a roomful of relative strangers had now become the comfortable choice. I did have to laugh at the absurdity.

It was as if Kia was reading my mind. She didn't wait for the question but answered it as if it had been spoken. "We run into the Baltic."

"What?" I had heard the words and it wasn't that I didn't understand them, but my brain refused to comprehend how they could have anything to do with me. The loop replayed over and over; "we run into the Baltic, we run into the Baltic." The sauna stood at least 100 yards from the shore. Across the yard, in view of all of the other summer homes, the other vacation residents, the entire population of Sweden, and all the satellites hovering overhead.

My throat went dry. There would be bouncing and jiggling in places that had never shook in Sweden before.

I stood, my knees feeling a little weak as Kia firmly clasped hands with mine, fingers locked together. "*Vi ska ga nu!*" she crowed and we were off.

~Karen Coffee Nicholson

Chapter 3

Time to Thrive

Thrive on Your Own Path

The Wine Epiphany

Choose a job you love, and you will never have to
work a day in your life.
~Confucius

H ave you ever heard anyone say "I have the BEST job on the planet?" Anyone? Well if you haven't, then I will be the very first to tell you. I have the BEST Job on the planet! Seriously, it's not a joke. I really mean it. I wake up feeling happy, jazzed every morning, and looking forward to what my workday will bring. Are you thinking, "That's too good to be true?" Well, believe it. I'm a Master of Wine (MW), which means I taste wine for a living. I literally get paid to travel the world and taste wine! Most would agree that is definitely a dream job.

It wasn't always like this though. In fact, there was a time when I was miserable in my career and in my life. I felt lost, alone, and depressed while walking the tightrope of a breakdown.

Most people, I'm sure, can relate to this at some point or another in their life. I worked so hard for years to get a high-end position in London with an international financial firm, thinking that would bring me happiness and success. I never thought I would end up hating my prestigious international job that made me six figures.

I would work non-stop all hours for months straight, including weekends. I had no life, just 100-hour workweeks. "Churn 'em and burn 'em," "sink or swim" and "only the strong survive" were common mantras. Being one of the very few women not an administrative assistant, I felt even more pressure to succeed.

After one particularly long night, at 3 a.m., I begged my boss to let me go home for just a few hours sleep (and a shower because, frankly, I stank). The financial world is NOT known for compassion. The cold response I got was, "No, you are going to complete this client presentation." I couldn't even see straight. How anyone could expect attention to detail at 3 a.m.? This meant a higher risk of mistakes, which only led to one place, me getting screamed at by various people until I cried.

Shortly afterward someone came up to me and said, "Don't worry! After ten years of this, you'll have 'paid your dues' and you get to be the boss." I felt trapped and couldn't breathe because for the first time I realized that I didn't want my boss's job or my boss's boss's job.

I was bound by the infamous "Invisible Golden Handcuffs." What to do?

Then, one business lunch changed my life forever.

On this particular day, I was honored to have been invited to a business lunch and participate in a client presentation that I had created. Our firm's executive dining facilities overlooked London's Thames River right near Tower Bridge and the Tower of London. While most days are gray and overcast in London, on this day the sun peeked out.

The servers came out from the kitchen with an herb-crusted salmon. Excitedly, I saw servers pouring white wine they called Sancerre. In the UK and continental Europe it is not taboo to drink a glass of wine with lunch.

When I tasted the salmon with the wine... WOW! I was absolutely blown away by my first food and wine pairing experience. The fresh grassy notes in the wine created a bridge to the herbs crusted on the salmon. And the lemony acidity of the wine cut through the fattiness of the fish. This made the dish seem lighter, the flavor of the fish pop and it created a cleansing sensation, preparing me for my next delicious bite!

Then came another epiphany. It occurred to me that the chef in the back intended for this reaction! He didn't just say to the servers,

"Hey, give 'em whatever we've got." There was a conscious decision to put these two things together to create precisely this experience. This was a revelation and it opened my eyes to an entirely different world I never knew existed. At that moment, I vowed to learn more about it.

In between the evening work hours, I took a wine class, still returning to work afterward to finish my day in the wee hours of the night. To say my first wine class was casual is an understatement. Our "teacher" would go out and buy six bottles, pour us tiny amounts and we'd chat. At this point, wine was a newfound hobby, so I didn't complain that the information wasn't very good. Trying the wine and being out of the office for an hour was satisfying enough.

Some months afterward, all of us expatriates were sent back to our respective countries because our firm merged with another. So I went back home to New York. It was there I took my first "real" wine class and I fell in love… with wine.

Insatiable for any information I could find, I bought books, read wine magazines and spoke to people in the industry. I spent hours in wine stores looking at labels and writing down what I saw and looking them up on maps when I got home.

The concept of TQM (Total Quality Management), states "if you pay the highest attention to the quality of your product, the money will come." So I concluded that if I invested in the quality of the product (ME of course and my knowledge of wine), the money would come in.

I began to realize that wine was not a mere passing fancy. I was now studying into the wee hours and loving every second. I loved the viticulture, the science of winemaking, the business and finding out exactly why each wine tasted so different. This was my passion and I was delightfully obsessed.

I made the decision to leave my firm and my six-figure salary to go work for a wine store in Greenwich Village at practically minimum wage. I did not blame my family for thinking I had lost my mind. People tried talking me out of it, because, quite frankly no one makes money in wine (or at least so they thought).

My passion for wine and knowledge, however, would not be swayed! Before taking the job at the wine store and then a wine distributor, I insisted that I would have to leave early to take wine classes and I took any wine classes I could get my hands on.

Then someone mentioned the Master of Wine title. This is the highest certified title in the wine world. It requires passing a four-day exam, including identifying thirty-six wines blind, days of essays on viticulture, winemaking, global wine business, contemporary issues and QAQC (quality assessment and quality control). The exam is given only once a year and the limit is only three chances to pass half of it. The exam has a ten percent pass rate and after passing, one had six months to complete the third part, write a dissertation.

Challenge accepted and won! It was strenuous, exhausting and arduous work but this time, I loved it. I became the fourth woman in the U.S. to obtain the title of Master of Wine (MW). It was something I could really be proud of.

The road was not easy, money was tight, and it took the better part of a decade. I worked full-time while pursuing all of this, and—yes—I made a ton of mistakes. But investing in oneself is NEVER a mistake. It may take a while, but if you keep moving forward (even at a snail's pace) you will get there! I now make more money doing what I love than I did in international finance and I don't regret a second of it. I was worth the investment.

~Jennifer Simonetti-Bryan, MW

A Man of Letters

Risk more than others think is safe. Care more than
others think is wise. Dream more than others think is
practical. Expect more than others think is possible.
~Claude Thomas Bissell

O f all places, it began in the physics laboratory. I had been scattering photons—those immeasurably small packets of energy, those tiny sparks whizzing around—the source of all light. They were amazing particles—I knew they were—but at the time I could only think of the annoying burning sensation that they were leaving in my retinas.

It was late. My stomach hurt from crunching too many salt and vinegar chips, and my head hurt from crunching too many numbers. I wanted to go home, but as I rose to leave, my professor called me back.

"Come have a look at this, Kluftinger."

Through the buzzing, whirring dim of the lab, I could see a scroll of paper in his fist. It was the court order for my continued imprisonment, written in my very own hand.

Last week's lab report.

"You have some corrections to make before you go. The data is good, but the write-up is too long. Too fluffy. Give me facts, not fancy writing."

It hit me, right then and there, as fast as one of those photons—a tiny packet of light.

I wanted to be a writer.

That was the spark. It was a flash of illumination, just long enough for me to see a better, thriving version of myself. I didn't have to live my life imprisoned by data cells. I could have a clean sheet. Even better, I could have a pen to fill it. But the spark didn't last.

I have to admit it. Buried in that basement, deep in the dungeon of the laser laboratory, I killed a part of myself. Taking back my lab report, I axed my own creation. I slashed descriptive words, superfluous sentences and unneeded elaborations. I replaced metaphors with metadata. And what did I have to show for it? A perfectly clean science paper. A skeleton—functional but lifeless.

That was the death. The rebirth came later. Near the end of semester—I don't know how many lab reports later—I climbed the stairs from the physics building for the very last time. With each step I felt my body growing lighter. With each breath, that tiny spark flared into flame. I continued on, faster, until I looked up to see nothing but the clear, cold night sky. It was all wonder and sparkling light. I didn't see binary systems or stellar dust, held together by electron degeneracy pressure. I didn't see fourteen billion light years of expansion. Instead, I saw mystery and beauty, held together by the outstretched arms of God. To me, at that moment, the stars were something to be felt—not counted or measured.

I wrote a poem that night, and I think it had more truth in it than any astrophysics paper I'd ever written.

One year later, I graduated. I knew that it was time for me to pursue my writing. But how much time could I give? More degrees were beckoning, and the bills were piling up.

"The great thing about being a physics professor," they said, "is that you can always do some writing on the side."

On the side. Is that what we're supposed to make of our passions? A sideshow?

"Become a man of letters," they said, "it will give you security."

PhD, MSc., MBA. It's true, these letters do bring security. These readymade letters—little packets of prestige and success—they are good. But they are not good for me.

My letters are the ones that come together organically. My letters are driven by emotion and the un-assured, unpredictable chaos of creativity. My letters are the ones that make words, paragraphs and books. They make people remember and forget, laugh and cry. They make imaginary worlds in my mind, and real truths in my heart.

So I said no. I said no to "safe" jobs.

Thriving is not about finding time for your passion—finding secondhand seconds, hidden away between the giants of your life. Thriving is about giving time. It's about giving the time that you could use elsewhere, the time that costs you something, and the time that might not give anything back.

If this seems too risky, then look down. Right here. This word, this page—these are my dreams. This is me, thriving, every time my letters are read and felt.

~Ryan Kluftinger

An Activist Is Born

I wondered why somebody didn't do something.
Then I realized, I am somebody.
~Lily Tomlin

As far as I was concerned, I had no future when I lost my husband in April of 2013. His death was not a total surprise but he'd survived a nasty brain infection and was living well, I thought, although with less-than-par lungs.

I was very depressed. My husband had just turned sixty-one. I was a relatively young widow with a couple of lonely decades stretching before me.

It was the day after Billy's death that I received a notice from the county that my fence was on my neighbor's land. I had new neighbors who must have complained. I was told to remove the fence by a date certain or "the county will take action."

I was so wrapped in grief and preparing for my husband's funeral that I thought there had to be some mistake. I'd been living in that house for more than ten years; I'd obtained all legal and required documents. The offending fence was there when I bought the house and I had a legal county-recorded survey showing my fence to be very legally on my land.

I got through the funeral and dealt with the post-service reception, which was at the house that Billy and I so loved. It was on that awful day, when my friends and family had gathered to comfort me, that surveyors from yet another neighbor behind me were measuring my fence. I asked them to leave and after a few words, they did.

I vowed that I would get to the bottom of this—just give me time, I prayed, to get over the death of my husband.

Over the following few weeks I was bombarded with letters from builders behind me, from new neighbors I'd never even met, and I heard from old neighbors to my right and left who were receiving recriminating notices from the county, too.

It was the last thing in the world I wanted to do, but I methodically got out all my house settlement papers and considered the situation. All of sudden some new people behind me got new surveys, and mine was no good? Something was wrong with this scenario.

My husband was a kind and gentle soul. He would have been overwhelmed by this, but at least I would have had company. Tears poured down my face as I pondered fighting this battle alone. Nevertheless, I was determined.

First, I compiled and copied all my documentation, including my own legal survey, and sent packages to everyone involved with this mess, including the builders and my county councilwoman. I was lucky to get a quick response. My survey was perfectly legal, and perhaps the surveyors made a mistake, and perhaps the really nice people behind me who hadn't bothered to introduce themselves or even move in yet were right, but it belonged in a civil court, not with the county.

My pressure on the county council people, my letters to builders and the county property boundary czar, and my straightforward letters to my new neighbors worked. I managed to stop any action against me by the county.

That bit of pressure over, I began investigating. I checked out the date and times my county council met, and I decided to take action. I went to the next county council meeting and discovered that I could sign in to comment before the council. So I did.

As I sat and listened to the meeting, I was mesmerized. I learned how building height limits were calculated, how county employee benefits were computed. I listened to the testimony of other citizens like myself, talking about their wells or septic situations or generic county laws. When my name was called, I said my piece and did it very well. The county council, under the directive of my own council-woman, agreed to look into how property dispute procedures were handled by the county.

Over the next few weeks I began attending my county council weekly meetings, and really liked it. I am a blogger and I began writing a weekly column for a local political site about all the things I'd learned from the meetings.

One day I got a phone call from a local newspaper informing me that the county council had rewritten all procedures for handling property boundary disputes. The reporter wanted to come to my home and interview me.

Thus I ended up in a half-page spread in a local paper: "Sussex County woman behind county council revamp of property dispute laws." They took my picture in full color, in front of my fence. Everywhere I went, people greeted me as a local hero of sorts, a citizen ombudsman if you will.

Then I read that the county was considering a new law for excessive dog barking. I pondered this notion. The county already had a noise ordinance and I often had to deal with a particularly fractious neighbor who complained about my dog barking when every other dog in the neighborhood was barking at your evening passers-by, bicyclists, strollers and the like.

I signed in to the county council and when my time came I stood tall and told my story. "This is a beautiful place to live," I pleaded with my lawmakers. "Please don't encumber us with excessive laws."

After I left the county chambers, I was besieged by TV and radio reporters. Goodness, I didn't have any idea. I did give an interview with a local radio guy, and a local TV station asked to go back to my house and film my dog. A week later, the county tabled the proposed law—not necessarily because of me, but hey, it happened.

Soon, I couldn't go anywhere without somebody recognizing me either from the newspaper report or the television story.

I continued to write my local political column and began to get interest from many of the local politicos. I was writing about them, and they were interested in what I was saying.

It wasn't a planned thing, this change that moved me from quiet citizen to vocal activist. In fact, had my husband lived, I doubt I'd have become involved in such things. He was quiet and I spent much of my time attending to him medically. I never denied him a second of my time, but after his death I found my new passion and I had the time to pursue it.

As of this writing, I don't know where I'm going with this. I do know my political column is doing very well and I have a large following.

Next week I am going to Dover to check out what the state politicos are up to.

I always said I wanted to change things, but I never expected this.

And I'm not done yet.

~Pat Fish

29

A Magical Life of Possibilities

Never mind searching for who you are.
Search for the person you aspire to be.
~Robert Brault, rbrault.blogspot.com

When we first landed at JFK airport I was eight years old. I instantly realized that this 747 Air India jet plane had taken me from Kolkata's oppressive schools and transported me to a candy store called the United States of America. I found school easy, so I had time to explore other interests, such as art. That enthusiasm would not be easily dampened until one fateful day when I was twelve and my father had his first heart attack. In one day, my world changed from childhood freedom to heavy responsibility. My mother in turn suffered from hypertension and pondered the possibility of becoming a widow. How would she manage two kids and a house mortgage that she was still calculating in rupees instead of dollars? My own question became how I could make their struggles worthwhile, and make my life count somehow.

Though my father miraculously survived his first massive heart attack, it changed everything. Every expectation for my brother and me intensified: straight A's; all household chores done with a smile; and plans to attend Ivy League colleges to ensure a livelihood of a certain social esteem. On the surface, I acted like an angel and made good grades, but with equal zest I participated in hidden acts of rebellion.

I often skipped school, choosing instead to hop on a bus from Livingston, New Jersey to New York City. I would usually find my way to the Museum of Modern Art to study paintings. All my transgressions were well hidden because my grades were good enough to get me into the Engineering School at Cornell. I was the daughter of an engineer who had left his homeland as part of the seventies "Brain Drain"—when the USA was granting work visas for doctors and engineers from Asia.

While my mother had jumped at the opportunity, my father came reluctantly to the new land—giving up his own dreams to be a writer, actor and musician in order to raise his young family. With that kind of family history, I was not allowed to take advantage of the art scholarships I had received. It was much more practical for me to get a degree in Electrical Engineering. My parents' gloating rights amongst their social circles would only grow as, over time, I got my Doctorate in Biochemistry from Stanford Medical School, and my brother got his PhD in mathematics. The unspoken part of our story was that my brother and I had fled from our parents to the West Coast for continuing our education, in an attempt to create distance from the pressures of keeping up appearances amongst our East Coast Bengali community.

Having graduated from Stanford I had moved to Seattle for postdoctoral research, still searching, still wanting, still waiting for my real life to show up. By all measures, I was a good scientist who had received many awards and grants, and I had impressive publications of my work. Yet there was a seemingly intangible element that was still missing from my life. Meanwhile my father informed me that I was being talked about as a loose woman in his Bengali social circles, still unmarried at the advanced age of twenty-nine. I stopped speaking to my beloved father for a month after that comment. But then I caved and said yes to what happened to be my seventh marriage proposal. My first husband was unaware that he was asking for my hand at a time when I was most lost and confused.

He may not have been the man of my dreams, but one fortuitous day, he brought home a brochure on a health product that gave me goose bumps the first time I read it. I was not a pill taker in general as they usually made me nauseous. But this product was made with a technology that struck my scientist brain as ingenious. Add to that, it made a huge difference in my health when I started to take it. I immediately started sharing this revolutionary product with everyone who crossed my path. I also started researching the benefits of nutrition. And this led me to a big moral dilemma. The National Institutes of Health and the American Cancer Society were funding my research to find a "cure" for cancer and Alzheimer's. Yet, this product represented a larger possibility that chronic illness could be prevented in the first place through lifestyle and proper nutrition.

At that time, I saw myself as a scientist and a scholar. Furthermore, my Bengali upbringing had led me to believe that making money was not important. Yet, I was enamored with this product and wanted to get the word out. Another big catalyst for things to come was the fact that I had shared the product with a friend, Doug Barlow, who was an engineer looking for a career change. When presented with this new concept in nutritional supplementation, he figured there was money to be made here. And so I had the added impetus to help him find a new career. Thus began my new business venture.

What happened in the next few years is certainly a good story line for a novel. There were many trials and tribulations, as I turned the delicate vessel that was my life upside down, and shook out all the contents of my personal and professional existence. As a result, my existing social and professional circle raised their eyebrows in many shades of disbelief, contempt or genuine concern. However, I met some amazing new people that introduced me to the concept of owning my life — every bit of it. I opened my heart to a different kind of education, reading books and taking courses I had never considered before. But I still had nightmares for six months that I was throwing away my career and reputation. And there was the inevitable divorce, after which my parents avoided interacting with me for years.

Awkward and bewildering as those few years were, I slowly got used to the concept that I alone was responsible for my happiness. I began to see my parents in a new light and have compassion for their own struggles. I appreciated them for what they were able to give me, and I began to remember moments where they too had sought out moments of pure joy and self-expression.

I ended up marrying my friend Doug, as we grew very close working night and day for several years to build a marketing team that would span the globe and provide us with a very comfortable residual income. He also had the same zest for life as I did, and together we had two beautiful girls. The greatest recognition I have ever received for having chosen the road less traveled has come from them, now teenagers. They have often expressed their gratitude for having such cool parents, and a magical life of possibilities abound. I am truly blessed.

~Mitra Ray

30

Keeping Less, Living More

The more you have, the more you are occupied.
The less you have, the more free you are.
~Mother Teresa

"Y ou have breast cancer." It was the fourth time in seventeen years I'd heard those words.

The doctors gave me surgery and radiation. Then they wanted to put me on a drug for five years. I knew it would suck the joy out of my life. Widowed the year before, I understood that nobody has five years to spare.

I prayed for guidance. Hoping I heard the answer right, I told the doctors, "No thanks."

Usually I don't pay much attention to my bookshelves, but it was about this time that I happened to notice how crowded they looked. Most of the books had been worth reading once — but not more than once. Why were they still hanging around?

I fetched a dust rag and some old grocery bags from the kitchen. I pulled books off the shelf, dusted them, and put them in bags. I kept only the Bible and a few old favorites.

With each book I bagged I seemed to feel a tiny burden come off my shoulders. I hadn't thought my old books were any burden at all, but the idea of not making room for them any longer lifted my spirits.

I stowed the books in the trunk of my car and donated them to the Friends of the Library the next time I drove by there.

My kitchen cabinets were stuffed with paraphernalia I'm embarrassed to admit I never used, like six muffin tins, an embellished earthenware wine chiller, and dozens of quart canning jars. I gave my kitchen extras to the Salvation Army and in return received a cheerful word of blessing.

Life felt a lot easier with a little less stuff, although I couldn't see why. Owning fewer books saved me maybe ten seconds a month on dusting, and with less junk in kitchen drawers and cupboards I found what I wanted faster. But why should losing a little clutter feel like a big relief?

Leaving that question for philosophers and psychiatrists to debate, I began to scan the house for things to get rid of.

The Salvation Army got the jeans I'd outgrown, the high heels I teetered in, and the what-was I-thinking sweaters. I dumped broken flowerpots, dried-up paint, and margarine tubs that lacked lids. I shredded or recycled obsolete paperwork. I gave shabby towels to the animal shelter. I cleared space like a pioneer clearing land.

Sorting out needless possessions taught me what was my job and what wasn't.

Using shabby towels—not my job.

Serving wine stylishly—not my job.

Re-reading mediocre books—not my job.

No longer did I have to squeeze my life into the space my possessions allowed. I found time to join a Bible class at church. There I finally got to know some of the good people I'd been sitting by every Sunday—plus, of course, I got deeper into Scripture.

I bought several different translations so I could gain the different insights they provided. After all, I had plenty of space on my bookshelves. Spending more time with God's word gave me more confidence in Him.

Then my life changed again. "Will you marry me?" Richard's smile glowed.

I knew God had brought Richard and me together. "Yes!"

Richard pulled me close in a long, strong kiss.

Our late-life marriage is teaching us to drop nonessentials. We have what we need, and we value what we have: this place, this time, this companion.

Five years have passed. Cancer has not shown up again.

Whatever comes my way tomorrow, I have lived today.

~Alison P. Martinez

31

They Took My Picture

Know me for my abilities, not my disability.
~Robert M. Hensel

At six years old, I saw myself as pretty typical. However, much of the world saw me as Tiny Tim. I was a scrawny kid with skinny arms and legs, pigtails in my hair and a smile that was waiting for the tooth fairy. Because of the cerebral palsy that had affected me since birth, I walked with crutches and wore leg braces, which weighed me down more than just physically. They were a tangible reminder that I was different than my peers. Wearing them made me feel as awkward as my unsteady gait.

I thought it was special when I was selected to be poster child for the county where I lived in New Jersey. At a time when I was often excluded from games of tag and climbing trees with friends, I saw this opportunity as a benefit of my disability. I was singled out, but for once in a way that I thought was positive. To my six-year-old mind, this was important stuff.

The day came for the first photo shoot. My new dress, freshly shampooed hair and big brown eyes all reflected the excitement bubbling inside. Standing on the designated mark, leaning on my canes, I smiled big into the camera as the photographer set up the shot in such a way that nobody could miss my braces.

They took my picture.

The meaning was lost on me at the time, but that image was put on donation cans all over town that year, in grocery stores, banks, and restaurants. The idea was that people should donate their spare change to raise money for cerebral palsy, and, to some extent, people should also feel sorry for me. Even at my young age, I took note of the stares, and the vibe some people had that my circumstances somehow made my life unbearable.

I am not sure I can adequately describe what it is like to be the object of someone's pity. The look in their eyes is a mixture of sorrow and "I am glad I'm not you." I've lived with it all of my life, and see it often in my day-to-day activities. When I can't reach something on a shelf or struggle to open a heavy door, most people rush to help as they give me that look. Some are compassionate, some are insensitive, some simply don't have a clue. But that look always leaves me feeling like I have inadvertently swallowed lemon juice.

As I got older, I met other people in high school and college who also had physical disabilities. Through conversations and shared experiences, I learned I could do many things because of my disability, not in spite of it. That realization resuscitated my soul.

Over time I fell in love with advocacy. Learning my rights and to use my voice made my confidence swell with each success. When I was able to speak to government officials about programs that would increase the quality of life for those affected by disability, I felt the satisfaction of Superman after he rescued Lois Lane.

One day, in 2007, I got an application inviting me to participate in the Ms. Wheelchair Kansas pageant. At first, I scoffed. I would describe myself in many ways, but beauty queen is not one of them. But as I read more about the program, I learned that the Ms. Wheelchair Kansas pageant is not a beauty contest. Instead it is a competition based on advocacy, achievement, communication and presentation to select the most accomplished and articulate spokeswoman for persons with disabilities.

Ever since I was young I have wanted to be a public speaker. Talking to various audiences about issues that challenge people with disabilities, as well as ways to empower and respect us, would enable me to do my small part to change negative perceptions. Because contestants in the Ms. Wheelchair Kansas pageant had to have a platform, write a speech, and communicate about disability awareness, I thought participating would be good practice for my future career. To my shock and amazement, I won.

One of the highlights of the year was traveling to Bethesda, Maryland for the Ms. Wheelchair America pageant. I think anyone who is affected by significant disability sometimes dreams of a world where there is no discrimination and everyone is given the respect they deserve. That was my overwhelmingly empowering experience at the Ms. Wheelchair America pageant.

Though I had decided previously I didn't want the national crown because I didn't think I could handle all the travel required, I wanted to get to know the twenty-six other state title holders, and to do my best to impress the judges. The women were incredible. All were wheelchair mobile and all had impressive stories to tell. Ms. Wheelchair Texas went to college on a wheelchair tennis scholarship. Ms. Wheelchair Virginia taught special education when she was diagnosed with multiple sclerosis. Ms. Wheelchair Illinois was part of a dance company, and Ms. Wheelchair Massachusetts was a quadriplegic who had lost nearly fifty pounds by working out regularly at her local YMCA. As bonds were formed, we communicated about our common struggles, and on comedy night we continued to laugh about our disabilities. The power that I drew from that group will keep a light burning inside me for decades.

At last it was the night of the crowning ceremony. In a formal gown with my hair and make-up professionally styled, I felt like Cinderella, except my life had already changed. When the announcement was made that I was not one of the top five finalists, I thought I was done. Then the head judge said he had a special announcement. There was another award that year.

"They say wild flowers thrive in the Midwest," he began. "One of them holds the title of Ms. Wheelchair Kansas." I was so stunned that I could barely process what he said next. The judges were giving me the Bouquet Award, because they said I had "the uncanny ability to leave the judges with a little more joy than they had before I entered the room." No award of its kind had ever been given before in the pageant's thirty-five-year history.

When I regained my composure, the head judge asked me to join him on stage. When I did so he knelt down by my wheelchair and gave me a hug that encompassed all the joy and pride I was feeling. In that moment, I understood that no matter how other people looked at my life in the future, I would never feel pitiful again. I looked up and smiled big.

They took my picture.

~Lorraine Cannistra

32

Chicken Soup
for the
Soul

Today Is Your Day

The people who get on in this world are the people who
get up and look for the circumstances they want, and,
if they can't find them, make them.
~George Bernard Shaw

I was a triple major in Economics, Policy and Management at Rice University so when I got a summer internship at Goldman Sachs, I was supposed to be thrilled. Driving to work in the dark at 4:30 a.m. and leaving in the dark around 8 p.m., I slaved away at a cubicle as an Excel monkey, chipping away at my soul and heart every hour. I was focused on making the rich richer, and lost my path to what I truly wanted.

Here I was, on top of the world, focusing on data analysis at the top bank in the world. It didn't feel like success, yet everyone around me praised me for getting this internship. Luckily, I had a mentor at Goldman who gave me good advice. He said I would succeed in anything I tried, and that I should try doing something creative if that was what I really wanted. My banking job would still be there for me if I wanted to come back to it.

I then landed an internship at Coach in New York City. Leaving Texas for the first time, I signed a lease through the Internet, hopped on a plane, and headed off for the Big Apple. I had a closet-sized apartment, but I had walked into the world of *The Devil Wears Prada*, except everyone was dripping head to toe in Coach. As a fashion assistant and color expert, I got to pick colors for wallets and small handbags that were going to be produced in the thousands around the world.

After three months, I was one of forty interns who were hired full-time. Although the work hours were much more controlled than at Goldman Sachs, there was still something nagging at me. I couldn't understand why I still felt unhappy.

It was then that I sat down with a mentor, a vice president at Coach, who said to me, "Neha, the world is your oyster." It was that day that I quit. I quit working on the corporate track where I felt like a cog in the system. I gave myself time to breathe, time to find out what it was that my heart was aching for.

Over the next few years, I realized that my passion lay with something I had stumbled across at sixteen. I had been hired by three second-graders to choreograph and tutor them for their dance talent show. Greer, Ana, and Sarah—bubbly little second graders—loved coming to my house to learn dance as we danced the evenings away to Beyoncé. I was making good money at sixteen, and I loved every single minute.

So, after quitting two of the most prestigious companies in their industries, where hundreds of people vied for the positions I had, I turned to tutoring. I launched my tutoring company, Elite Private Tutors, where I was able to start focusing on the value of contribution, instead of significance. Before, I was focused on a title, on an end goal, and on having a level of certainty in my life. As an entrepreneur, I am able to focus on growth and contribution. My mission statement changed: the more I grow, the more I contribute.

I built my company into a six-figure company in a matter of months, finding new and unique ways to reach my audience of moms. I was able to connect with moms from the heart and started to truly make a difference for their children. In the last year, I was inspired to write a book that could help students across the nation, instead of just making a difference with the clients in my area.

I know that many people look at a twenty-something as noncommittal, flighty, and not dependable. But, I have to say that with our focus on thriving, growing, and finding our passion, this trait is beneficial.

We make extremely happy employees or entrepreneurs because we know that our goal in life is to thrive at a deeper level—to find real meaning and fulfillment in our daily lives.

~Neha Gupta

The Dream
We Didn't Know
We Had

*When I go out into the countryside and see the sun and
the green and everything flowering, I say to myself
"Yes indeed, all that belongs to me!"*
~Henri Rousseau

If someone had told me five years ago that I would be living happily ever after on a small farm in western Oklahoma, I would have adamantly denied the possibility. Back then, I was a confirmed city girl. I enjoyed the amenities of city life. Then my husband and I decided to move from our longtime home in the city. We looked at houses in several surrounding communities, but nothing suited our needs or our budget.

One day, while we were checking my mother's farm for her, I looked around, liked what I saw and asked my husband, "Why don't we build a house here on the farm?"

To my surprise, he said, "Yes!"

And so began a new and very different chapter in our life story.

From its earliest days, the farm has always been called the Home Place. My great-grandparents, grandparents, mother and uncle all called it home. I spent many happy childhood summers there doing farm chores that were more fun than work for a city girl. No matter my age or the stage of my life, I often returned to the Home Place for peace, quiet and sanity. When my sons were growing up, I would treat them to a day at the farm so they could experience a bit of country life. It was a nice place to visit, but I had no intention of living there.

When we started our new life on the farm, it was far from a magical retreat. It was rugged and unkempt. Cattle had roamed it for over forty years with evidence they had toured the outbuildings.

My husband and I set out to tame the land. We took down dead trees, bulldozed dilapidated outbuildings and planted vegetable and flower gardens and an orchard. We learned new skills as we worked and provided the locals with humorous moments as they answered our naïve questions. We built a home to welcome family and friends, to share the beauty and bounty of the land.

We soon realized the land had played a marvelous joke on us: it had changed and transformed us in our efforts to tame it. We lost weight and gained muscles.

We've learned to recognize and honor nature's cycles and timing instead of clocks, calendars, schedules and to-do lists. With only two clocks in the house, we enjoy the flow of days into nights. Our time-less life allows us to appreciate sunrises and sunsets—each a unique, spectacular event that canvas, camera and words only partially capture.

Living a simple life in the country has led us back to common sense and personal empowerment. We've learned to be creative and resourceful in solving problems. I often consider how my grandparents would handle a situation with fewer resources and conveniences than I have. The nearest large town is thirty minutes away, so we have to think and plan ahead instead of hopping in the car and "running" around the corner for something we forgot. We keep a pantry of staples, preserve much of our garden's abundance and share with family and friends.

In the quietness of the land, we hear and appreciate nature's music—birds, crickets, cicadas, frogs, coyotes, cattle and the ever-present Oklahoma wind. We also listen to the silence. In this silence, we allow the land to guide us to do what needs to be done—where to plant a flower or tree and how to share the blessings of the land with others.

Nature entertains us with the antics of rabbits and raccoons, and a parade of possums, armadillos and an occasional snake. Coyotes saunter and deer leap across the fields. Migrating pelicans and geese serenade us along their seasonal journeys. Hawks soar in the big sky. Our TV is seldom on as we enjoy nature's big screen, with surround sound, instead.

Walking through the grasses, gazing at the century-old trees and wondering about all the changes and history they have witnessed are relaxing pastimes. My bare feet feel the pulse of the earth and connect me to God and the eternal. I walk down the same country road, noticing the same red anthills in the same places as in my childhood. Some things do not change.

While this picture is idyllic, I have to be truthful: caring for the land is a full-time job—but it's a joyful job. My ancestors left me a rich heritage—not the kind of wealth you can spend, invest or save, but a wealth of spirit, perseverance and love of the land. They taught me to "take care of the land, and the land will take care of you." That's our intention.

As we open our doors to family and friends, we want them to feel that they are at home in the piece of quiet that is the Home Place. Friends who questioned our sanity after our many years as city dwellers feel the magic of the peace and quiet and are reluctant to leave.

Life has brought me full circle to happy, busy retirement days on the land where I spent many happy summer days as a child. We're living the dream we didn't know we had.

~Linda E. Allen

34

Not Giving In

*Continue to work hard at what you love no matter
what the odds are. Eventually, someone will
praise and appreciate what you do.*
~Author Unknown

I am living proof that how we choose to react to things in life can dictate our outcomes. We can either navigate to peace and happiness or we can be our own adversaries.

My childhood was messy, to say the least. My parents had money, and then they lost it all. Our family went from comfy suburban rancher to the roughest project in town. Also, I was biracial and learned quickly that I didn't quite fit in. The black girls didn't like me. They said I was trying to sound white. They said I thought I was better than them because I was mixed, and then they threatened to kick my butt. The white girls ignored me when I tried to be friends with them because of where I lived. Maybe I was dangerous in some way? At the very least I had nothing in common with them, and just plain didn't meet their standards.

My dad had to work two jobs, so he was gone most of the time. He still tried hard to instill in us a deep underpinning of family and faith. My mom started to show signs of paranoia. She would accuse my father of being with another woman instead of at work. She began to have paranoid delusions of people following us and told us that someone was breaking into our house at night, although nothing was missing! Then one day, exasperated and panting, she told me that she just finished wrestling with Satan in our kitchen. That's when I knew my mom was mentally ill.

Soon after, she started hanging with a new group of friends. Her children were once her priority, but now we were just in the way. So I guess it was no surprise that my mom's next move was to leave my father. Even though she didn't want us, she didn't want my dad to have us either. She manipulated my sister's thinking against our dad as best she could. She even dreamed up false accusations of child abuse to stop him from getting custody of us and forever tarnished his reputation.

As years went by life only got worse. All around me I saw other kids with normal lives—they wore nice clothes to school; they took ballet and tap; they had nice things; their moms were in the PTA. I was dressed in rags, never had anything to eat at home, my mom didn't care where I was or what I did, and my stepdad smoked crack, beat me senseless, and molested my brother. Life was a mess. I was failing in school. I was terribly lonely and I felt unwanted. I had no idea what kind of future I would have.

Despite the situation, I had big dreams. I wanted more than anything to become an oncologist. I loved gymnastics and horses. While my mom would never sign me up or commit to any of these interests, I studied the things I loved. I worked out daily and taught myself gymnastics from books and on playground equipment. I dreamed that one day my life would be good. I never stopped dreaming.

When I was thirteen, in a crack-fueled fury my stepdad beat me on the kitchen floor until I was coughing up blood and begging him to stop. I called for my mother to help me but she stayed in the bedroom; I knew she could hear me. When he finally was too tired to kick me in my chest anymore, he snatched up a plastic grocery bag and threw it at my face. He told me to get out and not to come back. I didn't want to leave, but since my mother wasn't intervening, I realized that she wanted me to go, too. I saw no other option. As I turned and headed out the door, I thought, "Big deal, you're making me leave somewhere that offers zero comfort. What's to miss?" That night I cried myself to sleep on the roof of the school.

From there I bounced around and stayed at friends' houses. By fifteen I had a fake ID and was dancing in a gentleman's club on the west side. It was the only job I could get, but it was also a trap. I noticed that the girls who worked there were all on drugs and had legal problems. The men were mostly rude and talked down to me. When I told them I wanted to go to college, they laughed. I started to grow angry. Angry at them, and angry at life. I had big dreams and felt like I was born without a chance. Still I was determined to make it. There was a fierce fighter deep inside me. I managed to avoid the lure of drugs and other major issues, but I wanted more. I remembered to have faith in God, although I wasn't proud of the way I was living.

I signed up for GED classes when I was sixteen. The more that people told me I couldn't do something, the more I wanted to prove them wrong. I used that negativity as the driving force to have some say in how my life would be. I still had financial hardships and other typical obstacles, but I said over and over, "I don't accept this for my life."

I've come a long way. Today I have four years of college. I was licensed in real estate and am a licensed home inspector as well as a writer, wife and mother of four. I am blessed with a great family. If you're feeling discouraged and unsure about life, sometimes you have to adjust the way you see things and have a little faith. I could have felt sorry for myself and given up. I could have gotten pregnant as a teen and entered the cycle of welfare and government housing. I could have chosen drugs to numb the pain of a lonely and desperate childhood. I chose to find an inner strength I think we all have, I chose to not give in, and you can too.

~Lauren Ball

Chapter
4

Time to Thrive

Make Time for Your Most Important Customer

35

My Mondays

The best days are unplanned, random and spontaneous.
~Author Unknown

Six days a week, I devote my days to others. One day a week, I assert my independence by making sure I am responsible only to myself. I believe that time is the most valuable currency we have, which is why I am committed to giving myself time each week that's all my own.

Tuesday through Saturday, I work. I have two part-time jobs and they are both social and customer service-oriented. One job is as a circuit trainer at Curves where my priority is making sure our members get a fantastic workout while having fun. This often means entertaining them while coaching, compelling (and sometimes outright cajoling) them into "working harder and really feeling the burn!" My other job is as an innkeeper at Channel Road Inn. There, in addition to baking homemade goodies, I greet the hotel guests and help them make plans for their time in Los Angeles.

That is time-intensive because it requires taking their individual desires and interests into account. Guests rarely tell me up front what they're interested in. I don't think they're being evasive—I just think we all run at such frenetic speed in today's modern world that we lose touch with who we are and what we like to do. Even when I ask what their interests are they often say, "I don't know; we just want to do 'California things' and have fun." But I know each person is an individual and there are hundreds of "California things" to do.

Through the course of conversation I hear patterns emerge. It becomes clear that some guests are the outdoorsy types, so I steer them toward surf lessons, horseback riding and hiking through the Santa Monica Mountains. Some guests need to be pampered and have calming experiences, so I steer them toward botanical gardens, day spas, yoga classes and meditation centers. Some people love amusement parks, so Universal Studios and Disneyland are the obvious recommendations. Others are intrigued by art and find fulfillment by going from museum to museum. To create a meaningful experience, it's important to help the guests slow down and think about who they are and what activities they would really enjoy doing. I always remind them, "You can't do everything, so it's important to find the activities that would make you happiest."

My Sundays are devoted to spending time with my husband. We are both homebodies so we love to pad around the apartment in our pajamas and do NOTHING for the entire day. We call Sundays "Pajama Days" because more often than not, we never even get out of our pajamas. Sometimes he wanders in and out of his music studio if he gets a song idea. Sometimes I sit at my computer if I get a writing idea. But for the most part we lie in bed, watch movies, read books, and order food to be delivered. Sundays provide a sanctuary of time for us to reconnect as a couple after a busy workweek.

And then there's Monday! Monday is my day. For this one day, I am neither a circuit trainer nor an innkeeper. I am, of course, still a wife but, barring an emergency, I only consider my wants and desires on this one day. I assert my independence by doing whatever I want, whenever I want, from the time I wake up to the time I go to sleep.

Most Mondays I'll spend writing, but sometimes I just wander aimlessly through department stores, browsing and looking at all the beautiful dresses, shoes, jewelry and furniture the world has to offer. Such reverie! I love the way the various patterns and textures look and feel. Whether they're in my size or not, I delight in running my hands through racks of dresses just to see all the beautiful colors whoosh by. I love to touch the zippers and buttons on the shoes and purses. I like to peruse jewelry, especially pearl jewelry. I can get lost for hours looking at furniture and imagining which pieces I'd buy if I ever won the lottery and could build my dream home.

Sometimes I'll go out to eat by myself and sometimes I'll meet a friend for lunch. Either way, it has to be a restaurant that offers vegetarian options because this is my day and I don't want to have to struggle with the menu.

Sometimes I'll stay home and play with my cat, Anaïs—or if she's not in the mood, then sometimes I'll go by an animal shelter and play with their cats. I have my favorites!

If I've gotten a coupon or a Groupon-type deal, I'll go get a mani/pedi. I love getting manicures and pedicures. The massage aspect is fantastic, and the end result looks great, but my favorite part is choosing which polish I want. Even though I almost always pick a neutral color for my toes and clear on my fingernails, some days I'm feeling sassy and have my toenails painted red!

Sometimes I'll have a second "Pajama Day," but this one all by myself. When I have a "Pajama Day" by myself, I sleep in the middle of the bed, use all the pillows and set the air conditioner to exactly the temperature I like.

Mondays (or My-days as I like to think of them) are important to me. I anticipate and plan them throughout the week and bring particular focus to them as I go to bed on Sunday. Just like with the hotel guests at Channel Road Inn, I know that to create a meaningful experience, it's important for me to slow down, clear my mind, reorient my thinking to putting my needs and desires first, and to think about who I am and what activities I'd really enjoy doing the next day. I try to get re-centered, so come Monday morning I will be able to honor myself as an independent person with individual tastes and desires.

Not everyone likes to window shop or play with cats all day, but these activities relax me. Some people might not like to spend their day in front of the computer trying to write a story, but that's often what I'm drawn to. Some people don't like to eat alone at a restaurant, but I do—so I do. As I plan my Mondays, I always remind myself what I tell the hotel guests, "You can't do everything, so it's important to find the activities that would make you happiest."

I know we can't all have an entire day to ourselves each week. My friends who are parents tell me that it is an incredible luxury. Even so, I hope we can all find at least a few hours each week to assert our independence and do whatever we feel like doing. It is unbelievably freeing and empowering to re-remember that. Even if you are a mother, a grandmother, a daughter, or a spouse—you are also an independent, free-spirited, unique individual with idiosyncratic wants and desires that deserve to be listened to and honored.

~Rebecca Hill

36

Guest Treatment

You're worthy of it all. You just have to believe you are!
~Tony Gaskins

My mom had guest soaps in the bathroom. In a home with very few luxuries, those tiny roses of avocado green and lemon yellow represented something special to her; they were something she wanted to keep nice for our guests. So she kept them in a covered glass container, where they would be safe from the many sets of little fingers in our household that needed washing. Only the guests never used them. We never used them. Those soap rosettes decorated the shelf in the bathroom for as long as I can remember. There they stayed, displayed until dust caked in the crevices of the soap petals, and the roses lost their luster. But they were never used. They were saved for guests.

Fast forward to my adult married life. We were visiting my in-laws when the marriage was still shiny and new. New traditions, new family members, and new relationships were just beginning to be forged when I received the gift. It was casually given. No big deal; everyone got one. It was just a bar of soap, a chunk of green marbled glycerin, lightly scented and wrapped in cellophane with a lovely label proclaiming that this soap had been handcrafted by an artisan who just happened to be my new brother-in-law. That soap was only a few ounces, but I carried the weight of it for years. It was guest soap.

It was too pretty to use. It was proudly set out to be looked at—but not used—for about a week. My practical husband did not see the point of it cluttering up the countertop. So it found a new home, wrapped and cushioned, set aside in my scarf drawer. There, its gentle scent would drift between the layers of nylon and silk, and waft up to greet me when I opened the drawer. With its cellophane wrapper and label intact, that bar of soap was a hidden gem that gently reminded me of nice people and nice things whenever I saw it. My life went on. My children grew. An empty childhood bedroom became a craft room, and in this newly created space there was a glassed-in display shelf—a place for the soap. It found a new home.

I loved my craft room. Bright and sunny, soft and cozy, it was filled with quaint furnishings and things I cherished. When I got sick, the craft room became my recovery room. I could rest there surrounded by happy memories. As I got better, I took inventory of my life, and of my surroundings. And, I saw the soap.

I saw something that was meant to be used, not admired. Long ago it was given to me, a simple gift of special soap. Except that I had decided I wasn't special enough to use it. Cancer changed that. I took that carefully wrapped soap off the shelf and opened it with a sense of childish delight. The scent was as lovely as I remembered it to be. However, without its wrappings, the glycerin was rather dull, and as I stood there with that hazy chunk of soap in my hands, I wondered what all the fuss had been about. Then I ran it under water.

It was transformed, and so was I. The running water turned the soap into a shining jewel in my hands. The surface became slick and the colors gleamed. The irregular angles gave texture to the glycerin rotating between my palms as the suds slipped through my fingers. A regular bar of soap does not feel like this. No, this was something different, something special. So I took my time, savoring each sensation, totally immersing myself in the moment. As I concentrated on the bubbles building between my hands, reveling in the feel of the flowing water over my skin, the ritual of washing my hands transformed into a meditative experience. I let it all go. I felt my troubles washing away with those tiny bits of foam. It became a small moment of pure joy. My heart was at peace; I felt pampered and loved. After all those years, why had I been waiting to use it? I was waiting for me.

Cancer was an unwelcome visitor in my life, but it taught me to live. So, from now on, I will use the guest soap. And while I'm at it, I might as well use the good towels, too.

~Paula Klendworth Skory

37

Making My Health a Priority

The greatest wealth is health.
~Author Unknown

As the daughter of a doctor and part of a loving family, I was always taken care of. I wasn't responsible for my health and nutrition for the first eighteen years of my life. Besides, back then, there really was not too much knowledge about nutrition.

In 1984, due to the national war, dictatorship, and communism in my native country, Nicaragua, I moved to Costa Rica to pursue my university studies. I was on my own and had to figure out a way to take care of myself. I was busy studying; therefore my meals consisted of whatever fast food was available between the university campus and the National Library.

After graduating, I got married, but we couldn't go back to Nicaragua in the midst of war, and we couldn't stay in Costa Rica as our student permits expired after graduation. We had nowhere to go. Then we learned about a beautiful land that was opening opportunities for immigrants… Canada. After some research, I was convinced of the fact that Canada was the best place to live in the world. There was true democracy, freedom, no violence, no judgment, and countless opportunities for our new family. Even though it sounded too good to be true, we immigrated to Canada in March 1988.

My husband and I came to Toronto with one small suitcase and a box of books, with no clear awareness of what Canada was about, just hoping that the war and dictatorships we experienced our entire life would be over for good. As an immigrant, there were many challenges to overcome, and no time to think about my health; it was not even an issue, so why should I care? We had so many other things to worry about, such as finding a job, working on our language skills, adapting to the new culture, and learning to live without the extended family connections. I missed my mom, dad and siblings very much during an age when there was no Internet, Skype or cheap phone calls.

Our finances were very tight, but I was so happy to think I could live in a democracy; I didn't pay attention to small details such as the weather. We didn't realize that moving in the middle of winter might not have been the best idea. We encountered our first challenge, moving from +30 degrees Celsius to -30 degrees Celsius, a 60-degree difference overnight! We handled the challenges one by one and appreciated them as big opportunities in our newly found dreamland.

A couple of years down the road we obtained permanent residence in Canada, which was a major gift from God. We finally had a place we could call home. Our first kid, Sergio, was on his way, and I was so happy to finally look forward to a future. I forgot about myself again, and for the next twenty years I dedicated one hundred percent of my efforts and my time to my family and to my newly founded business, a translation agency. I thought success was having a happy family, perfect kids and a growing business, and I was so focused on all that, that I just forgot about my body. I gave birth to Adriana and when I had my third child, Juan, I was already carrying thirty-five extra pounds. Even though I would prepare what I considered back then "healthy meals" for the kids, I was not doing the same for myself. There was no time allocated to taking care of myself, and since I had no medical issues, I had no worries. I thought I was made of steel.

In 2008 I attended an Anthony Robbins event that motivated me to work on several areas of my life. The big breakthrough that impacted me the most was working on my health. I realized that, unless I did something right then and there, I would not last for too long. I had three amazing kids, teenagers at the time, who still needed me.

Being in my early forties, I only had mild health issues; it was easy for me to "catch" a cold or flu, I had headaches, allergies and some temporary conditions. During the seminar, I understood what could happen to my future if I didn't take immediate action, so I did. I decided to eliminate from my diet all red meat and coffee, and I decided, for the first time ever, to be in charge of my health and prioritize it in my life. From then on, I started to add small changes, one at a time. If I could stop drinking coffee, I could do anything! I knew I had too many things to learn and correct to do it all at once.

After eliminating red meat and coffee, my next step was to introduce water with lemon to my diet. I also started to do yoga regularly, I switched my office chair for a stability ball, I drastically reduced my intake of acidic foods, such as meats, dairy (switching regular milk to almond milk was huge for me), commercially prepared products, canned foods, sugar, bad oils, and much more.

I finally understood what juicing could do for the body, and this was a major change for me as it required some of my "precious time." I strongly believe that my daily green smoothie has a lot to do with the fact that I have not had a cold, flu or allergy symptom in over six years! After twenty years of carrying thirty-five extra pounds, I released them and kept them off, and my pants size went from a size 10 to a size 4. I feel fantastic!

I understood the impact of stress and excess cortisol in my health. I regularly do guided meditations, I learned to breathe properly (which most people do not know how to do, by the way), and I do it daily as part of my routine. I have gone through forgiveness exercises that allowed me to be at peace with myself and others. Stress and negative emotions create more acidity in our bodies than the worst foods we could ever eat. I am still in the process of learning to slow down while cultivating positive emotions on a daily basis.

I am happy that I have been influencing my family, friends and colleagues to also take care of themselves and have become, as I define myself, an ambassador of health and happiness. I have more energy than ever before and I am still on the journey of taking care of the only body I have. I finally made the time to take care of myself and thrive!

~Lola Bendana

Recharge Rental

The sea, once it casts its spell, holds one in its net of wonder forever.
~Jacques Cousteau

I hit a wall. I am the girl who rarely says "no," the one my friends say is the busiest person they know. A sometimes demanding career, chairing a local professional group, helping to found an international professional group, becoming a condominium association board member, participating in writing and Bible classes, caring for a parent's affairs, providing stateside assistance to a deployed Army brother, and caring for two dogs had burned me out. I needed a vacation.

I scheduled a week off from work and searched for beach rentals. At first, the search was futile. Most properties were too expensive, some would not allow dogs, and some were too far away from the beach. At the last minute, I found a property for the right price, with a dog-friendly fenced yard, across the street from the beach. Was this property too good to be true?

I took off for the rental with my dogs in tow. Finding the condo was easy. Inspecting the premises, the first thing I noticed was the same throw rug in their kitchen as in my own. It felt like a good sign. I let the dogs loose to run and roll in the yard and continued my inspection. The condo was very clean, the bed and sofas were all comfortable, and there were plenty of pots, pans and dishes for a week of meals. Settling into this strange place felt like taking a deep breath.

We went on unleashed walks and runs on the beach. Schools of playful dolphins offshore kept pace with my walks. Sitting under the pier in the shade, I traded technical manuals for fiction for the first time in years. Fresh air and sunshine, surfers, cooperative birds and interesting flowers growing in the sand inspired creativity with my digital camera.

I now refer to this place as my recharge rental, and it has become the one calendar entry each year written in stone. Each trip yields a new adventure. One year, I took a boat tour around Cumberland Island, where John F. Kennedy, Jr. was married, and saw wild horses. That trip was especially eventful because such a bad storm hit us on the way back that you could see nothing but torrential rain and wind from the boat windows. Comforting the terrified woman sitting next to me, I learned she too was visiting from Atlanta. When the storm finally subsided, we saw the actual lifeboat from which Navy SEALs rescued Captain Phillips, bullet holes and all.

Every visit, I meet nice people. A man on the beach told me how to recognize shark teeth in the sand. I never found any teeth, but I collected lots of beach glass and unusual shells. Another year, during a beach walk, a woman stopped me because she thought she knew me. It turned out we have a friend in common in Atlanta. One year, I met a local author. Last year, I met the owners of the condo upstairs, joining them for wine and pizza. That's how I found out about and witnessed a turtle hatching where they count the hatched eggs of endangered sea turtles.

Enjoying an annual visit to the beach has allowed me to step out of life's hamster wheel and replenish my energy. An added benefit is that it is the perfect halfway point for my mother's trip home. When my mom visits Atlanta from South Florida, I meet her halfway and drive her in, or travel with her halfway back. This year was the first time she joined me at the condo on her way home. The night before she left, we ate dinner at a wonderful beachside restaurant with live music. The evening was one of the best that either of us could remember. It was the perfect end for her visit to Atlanta, and the perfect beginning of my annual retreat.

~Bonnie L. Beuth

39

Race Against Time

Who forces time is pushed back by time;
who yields to time finds time on his side.
~The Talmud

Three numbers in Sharpie down my left calf and three more down my right upper arm brought home the reality that I was about to participate in my very last triathlon. After two years of competing, I found myself no longer physically able to participate in the swimming, biking and running event. My body, unfortunately, was giving way before my spirit was ready.

Please do not be mistaken; erase the image of me you've just created in your mind. Now, re-adjust to a slightly overweight, middle-aged brunette mom of three. There you are; that's me. I am the one who didn't rush to the results board with the others to search for my name and results upon crossing the finish line, because it was always there patiently waiting for me at the bottom of the list. With each event I completed, a part of me would berate myself for not being fast enough or good enough. I saw myself as the "feel good story" of the event, the person you patted on the back and congratulated for managing to finish the race.

At one point, I couldn't take it anymore and I pushed incredibly hard and watched my time like a hawk. While I achieved what I set out to that day, and it felt fantastic, that was not my "time to thrive."

No, that lesson came for me on the day of this very last event, one early summer morning in 2013.

I had signed up for this particular triathlon once before but then I hadn't shown up. This time, I signed up and embraced the race as my farewell to the triathlon piece of my life journey. My goal that day would once again include time, but in a much different and unexpected way. I was going to ignore time, unheard of amongst a sea of competitors donning timing chips on their left ankles. The goal was to not allow time to be the measure of success or failure at my last event.

As my turn came to enter the pool, my thoughts went back to when I first began swimming as an adult. Finding a nice evenly paced stroke, I ignored the clock and focused instead on the way I felt in the water. I embraced the peace swimming always brought me, and the lightness of not only body, but of spirit. As I completed my laps, I emerged from the pool with a feeling of serenity. Averting my eyes from the large clock on the wall, I made my way over to my bike, ready to take on the next challenge.

With the cheers of the people around me, I hopped onto my bike and turned off the timing device on the handlebars. I settled myself into a rhythmic dance with my bike, tuned into the feel of the summer breeze on my skin and the energy of the ride. As I rode into my last lap, my smile grew.

In the past, this is where my negative mind would take over the race. As I switched out my riding shoes for my runners, my legs were always heavy and my spirit growing more so—and the real battle against the clock usually began. The running part of the race was where you make or break your time. Could I fully surrender time?

As I began to run, I once again turned my mind away from the pressure of time. I took my thoughts off my tired feet and reflected on the things that make me, well, me. I love to laugh. I love to smile and I absolutely love to encourage others to do the same. And so my run that day became less about the countdown with the clock and more about all that I could and did bring to this triathlon to make it mine.

A favorite moment was when I made my way to the water station at the halfway mark of the run, out of breath but full of joy (joy! can you imagine?). Usually grabbing a cup and pushing on was my way so as not to lose a moment on that clock. This time, I stopped. I rested. I chatted with the volunteers and joked about who was going to give me a ride back. After a while they reminded me. "Hey! You should get moving. This is a race against time, you know!" Thanking them for the water, I moved my feet once again and made my way up the hill to the turnaround point and smiled. Today was not about racing time for me, it was about learning to let it go.

Across the finish line, I lingered before making my way over to the results board. I had to take a peek, right? I knew where to look, but my name was mysteriously absent from the bottom of the list. I searched a few lines up but didn't go too far, because I knew it wasn't there. I headed over to the timing table and inquired about the discrepancy. Upon giving my timing chip number, the man grew extremely apologetic and let me know that there was a malfunction with my timer. From his body language I could tell he expected me to be upset. As I said, time is of the upmost importance at these events. Slapping my hands on the table, I threw my head back and laughed. Taken aback, he asked if I was okay. Smiling brightly, I replied with a victorious smile, "There could not have been a better person to have a malfunctioning chip today than me. Thank you."

And so it was in an event designed to conquer time that I would do exactly that by simply ignoring it. I thrived on a new personal level that day, releasing the power that the clock had over me. Letting go of the harsh and negative way I would judge myself after crossing the finish line.

My last steps in the triathlon world became my first steps into the journey of transforming who I am, how I speak to myself, measure my worth, and so much more.

~Angela Wolthuis

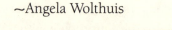

40

Chicken Soup for the Soul

Walking to a New Me

An early-morning walk is a blessing for the whole day.
~Henry David Thoreau

"The finish line is just ahead! You've got this, girl! Don't slack off now!" I panted to myself. My heart beat rapidly and beads of sweat covered every inch of my body—still, my self-cheerleading did not stop.

Although I had been fitness walking (about four miles) for six months, this was my very first 5K race. The feeling of competition was exhilarating, and the thrill of it pulsated through my entire being. I was not going to let myself down! I would NOT give up!

After moving into my mother's home to care for her following a stroke, I found myself neglecting my own health. Although my new duties kept me somewhat physically fit, my emotional life had become rather stagnant. It was obvious that I needed to find something that would inspire me to get out of the house more often.

I found my answer while standing in line at the grocery store checkout one sunny spring day. Bold red lettering on the cover of a magazine caught my eye—"Walk Off Weight!" I picked up the magazine and tossed it on the counter with my groceries. Who couldn't stand to lose a few pounds?

That special edition changed my life! After reading about the multitude of benefits derived from walking, I knew I had found the perfect activity that would not only get me out of the house more often, but would also improve my overall wellbeing.

I read that walking was a great way to get rid of the blues, tone the body, lose weight and cut the risk of heart disease. It could even ward off cancer. The publication also professed that, although any walking was good, a faster pace was better. The possibilities intrigued me, and I couldn't wait to start.

I didn't start walking four miles right away; I began slowly, taking my camera on long leisurely strolls. The walking and fresh air were invigorating, revitalizing me. Within a couple of weeks, I challenged myself with a more intense exercise regimen.

Calculating distances and speed, then writing them down on a calendar, inspired me to increase my workout a little more each day. After a few weeks, I progressed from walking two consecutive miles to between four and six several times a week. My speed increased from about three miles per hour to over four.

My walking routine was intoxicating, and it wasn't long before I began to notice the many positive changes in both my physical and emotional health.

I lost weight! As the excess fat I'd been carrying around my waist melted away, my self-image improved. I felt less sluggish, and the added bonus of lowering my risk of having a heart attack elated me. Even my chronic lower back pain had completely disappeared!

I made a conscious effort to maintain good posture while I walked, and that carried over into my everyday life. My legs strengthened and my calves became more attractive and shapely. I was ecstatic when people noticed the changes in me, remarking on my healthy glowing appearance and the new bounce in my step.

Prior to my new routine, I had been diagnosed with osteoporosis. My doctor was thrilled to hear that I had taken up walking because it's one of the best exercises to help strengthen bones and maintain bone mass.

The benefits to my emotional wellbeing were equally impressive. My spirits lifted with each passing day. I could hardly wait to get up each morning. I finally had a goal! With my newly gained self-confidence, I also found myself to be more sociable and outgoing.

Caring for my mother became less of a chore—feeling completely refreshed, I was able to tend to her with renewed enthusiasm. I encouraged her to strive to become as healthy and as happy as I felt.

For the first time in ages, I felt great! Wanting to challenge myself even more, I started looking into organized walks with my daughter-in-law, Jo.

Our first walk was the Tofurky Trot in Portland on Thanksgiving Day 2014. What a thrill it was to cross the finish line in record time!

On New Year's Eve Jo and I walked in First Run 2015, which began at the stroke of midnight. It went along the waterfront and across two bridges in downtown Portland. We couldn't have chosen a more wonderful way to enter the New Year, and at seventy-two years of age, I looked forward to a healthy and happy year ahead of me.

~Connie Kaseweter Pullen

41

Time Out
for Better Time In

I like the physical part, but I'm also drawn to the
spiritual. For me, yoga is not just a workout—
it's about working on yourself.
~Mary Glover

"I do not like you," my three-year-old daughter Fiona hissed one difficult afternoon. I didn't really like her in that moment either. Everything from putting on her favorite pink socks to taking a much-needed nap was a battle of wills. I was exhausted and depleted, but I kneeled down and listened to her.

"Why don't you like me?" I asked, searching her hazel eyes and willing myself to have role-model-worthy patience and kindness.

"You're not being nice." Her lips scowled, yet her eyes were pleading.

This was deeper than a child not getting her way. I stopped to consider what she was saying. The weight of my total responsibilities was crushing me. I worried about the work I needed to finish after our two children went to bed, the chores that I was neglecting while teaching them to read and write, the supplies that had to be ordered while making wholesome meals. There was never enough time.

I had let taking care of myself sink to the bottom of the list. The responsibilities of family life displaced sleep, travel, exercise, and most other things that replenished and inspired me. I was emotionally exhausted, creatively depleted and physically drained, which did not make me the most positive and enthusiastic nurturer.

"You're right," I said, drawing Fiona in for a hug. "I'm sorry, sweetie. I will be nicer."

Later that afternoon my phone buzzed with a text message from my friend Vicki: "Want to go to yoga tonight?"

It was her fourth request. I had previously turned her down, not because I didn't enjoy her company or the rejuvenating stretches, but because the deadlines and responsibilities in my life made relaxing exercises seem frivolous. Lying on the floor half-asleep in Shavasana? That peaceful posture seemed reserved for a woman with much more free time, not an anxious, overwhelmed mother of two with too much on her plate.

But before I could type, "I can't," I stopped myself. I knew I needed to make time for friends and rejuvenate myself. My lack of exercise was taking a toll on me inside and out.

"Yes," I told Vicki. I would meet her at yoga that evening.

Rushing into the studio after dark, I unrolled my yoga mat and quickly said hello to my friend. Since silence is the studio policy, I was able to soak in the serenity of quiet for the first time that day. While I love the loud, loving togetherness of family, pausing to hear my own thoughts was deeply replenishing.

As the class started, my anxious mind analyzed everything from the instructor's brisk tone to the woodsy smell in the air. But as the gentle stretches and strong stances took over my mental state, I started to calm and focus on the present. I noticed my body and heart opening up, my spirit awakening. By Namaste, I felt more alive and centered.

Instead of collapsing exhausted into bed that evening, I cheerfully tackled tasks that had been looming over me. Sleep was peaceful and satisfying, and I awoke the next morning refreshed. Ideas and energy flowed freely, as if from a newly discovered stream; but most importantly, kindness and enthusiasm made me buoyant. I felt better equipped to fill my children's cups.

"Come see the surprise party I planned for you," my daughter cooed, ushering me to her play set.

"For me?" I chirped.

"My best friend," she said beaming, wrapping her arms around me.

Like me, she seemed like a happier version of herself. Perhaps my moments in child's pose had been just as beneficial for my offspring as they had been for me.

Taking "time out" for yoga didn't detract from my busy life. It made my "time in" more productive and purposeful.

~Cortney Fries

42

Just Say No — and Sometimes Yes

Learn to say "no" to the good so you can say "yes" to the best.
~John C. Maxwell

The phone rang. It was the president of the library board of trustees. Three months previously I'd resigned from that board; it wasn't a good fit for me. I did remain on a non-board committee, as I believed in the mission, but the process had frustrated me and eaten up more time than I anticipated when I joined.

"Good morning. How are you?" His cheeriness put me on guard. Something was up. "Janet is stepping down as chair of the public relations committee and I hoped you would be willing to take over. It requires, you know, writing letters and refining talking points for speaking to groups and since you've done a lot of public speaking and you write…"

"No. No, I'm sorry I can't do it."

Wow! I'd said that?

After a few pleasantries and best wishes for him to find a new committee chair, we said goodbye.

I poured a cup of coffee and sat at the kitchen table to watch the blue jays bully the other birds for space at the feeders.

I felt light, free, amazed at myself. I'd just said "No" with no explanation. I gave him no opening for discussion. No exaggerated excuses about other responsibilities, problems, too many commitments, not being up to the challenge. Not even, "I'll think about it," while gathering the courage to call back and say no. Just "No." And surprisingly, I didn't feel guilty about it. I could have done the job. My calendar had lots of space. I had the credentials and experience in both writing and public speaking.

But I was done with all that. After more than twenty years on the local animal shelter board, twenty-eight years as a 4-H leader, an officer in the Cancer Society and garden club and other organizations, I needed my life back. Now retired, I dreamed of uninterrupted time to tackle writing a novel, to try pastel painting, and to experience other new things. It was time to stop saying "as soon as…."

One by one I had resigned from each responsibility as my term finished, or when someone else could step up in my place. The next years would be mine. I wanted to write, to learn to paint, to take classes instead of teaching them, to try yoga, to spend some days doing nothing.

I wrote it on the refrigerator memo board. "Choose wisely. 'As soon as' is here."

I don't plan on being a hermit. And I will take on short-term volunteer tasks, such as manning a yard sale booth for three hours, or giving one lecture on canine behavior, or spending one morning weeding the county courthouse flowerbeds. Saying no to the big obligations and recurring commitments will let me look forward to the things I choose to do, instead of resenting the time it takes to dress, drive, and attend yet another meeting of an organization.

I realize that sometimes I did choose to do the things that were on my calendar, to rise through the ranks, to take responsibilities that ate up more time than I believed they would. The trouble is, many times when you assume the mantle people expect you will continue to wear it year after year.

From now on I will be chary of chairmanships. Bored with boards. I don't want to be in charge of, president of, chair of, leader of… anything. Been there, done that, successfully, if I do say so myself. I will now be a happy occasional soldier instead of a general.

I will be gleeful when I awake to nothing more pressing than brushing the dog or hanging laundry out in the sun, and reminding myself that "as soon as" is right now.

When the phone rings, as it will, asking if I can edit one letter or arrange one luncheon for a visiting author, I will probably say, "Yes, I'll do it. Just this once."

~Ann Vitale

43

Solo Gig

Alone time is when I distance myself from the voices of
the world so I can hear my own.
~Oprah Winfrey

A flier was stapled to the telephone pole by the Q76 bus stop. It featured a grainy photo of a rock band, a hand-drawn logo, and some information about an upcoming gig. The group was probably a bunch of high school students who played cover songs, but I was thrilled to see their flier. To me, and to my enthusiastic twelve-year-old mind, it represented possibilities.

I'd grown up with my mother's albums—a colorful cornucopia of '60s and '70s rock and folk—but I had my own musical style. I'd started to refine it when I was in elementary school. When I'd stayed up late one night, I'd spotted a new band, Guns N' Roses, on MTV. They weren't yet superstars, but they were already in the press, and I'd followed their activities with an almost religious fervor. Guns N' Roses had opened the door to an entirely new and novel world for me, and they had helped me expand my horizons. I'd started reading *Rolling Stone* magazine when Axl Rose appeared on the cover, for instance, but I'd kept reading it whenever I could because it was fascinating.

There was one impediment to my budding career as a rock aficio-nada: I never got to see any of my favorite bands perform in concert. The arena shows were just too expensive, and the club gigs were off limits due to my age. My mother once took me to CBGB during the day so I could see what it looked like, but there was no way she was going to let me set foot inside that club, or any other, at night. In hindsight, I suppose I can grudgingly admit that she was being a responsible parent, and that as a twelve-year-old I would have been out of place at the Limelight, but it stung at the time.

This band flier, though, seemed like a breakthrough. The venue was the fellowship hall of a local church. The tickets were cheap. It was in the neighborhood. Best of all, there wasn't any age limit.

My mother agreed that I could attend the concert... on the condition that I went with a friend. The trouble was—and maybe she knew this, and was being sneaky—that nobody I knew was able to accompany me. I asked friends and classmates at school and at dance class; I broached the idea with my neighborhood pals and my best friend. In desperation, I even asked the acquaintances who waited for the bus with me. Most of them wrinkled their noses at the very idea. They were into New Kids on the Block and the like; they detested my music and I loathed theirs. The few friends who were receptive were unable to get their parents to agree to it.

That meant that I couldn't go either, because Mum wouldn't budge. No friend... no show. On the night of the gig, I slumped morosely on my bed at home. I opened my journal and wrote a screed about the unfairness of it all. I drew a picture of myself crying. It didn't even dawn on me that I might not have cared for the music; I was bereft about missing a real concert.

I also made a promise to myself: when I had things my way, I would not allow other people to dictate what I was able to do. If my friends didn't want to go to a concert, a museum, a play or any other event, I would go alone. The idea of flying solo did not faze me, and I didn't see why I should let other people's reluctance to participate hold me back.

As I grew up, I had many opportunities to follow through on this resolution. Throughout high school and college I attended plenty of concerts with friends, of course. We went to talk shows and Broadway musicals and took advantage of all New York had to offer. However, I also struck out on my own on a regular basis. I decided, on the spur of the moment, to check out off-Broadway plays and performance pieces. When Zucchero, a famous Italian rock star, played at the Beacon, I didn't even ask anyone to go with me; I simply booked myself a fabulous ticket and went alone. I had a wonderful time. By the time I was twenty-one, I was entirely comfortable doing everything and anything by myself. I traveled around the world, ate in restaurants, and went to amusement parks alone. I was amazed by how much my perspective changed—for the better—when I could focus on the sights and sounds around me, and not have to worry about anyone else.

In 2006, my love of music returned in force, and I started going to concerts again. Ninety-nine percent of them were solo ventures. I discovered that even when I was alone at the gigs, I could have as much—or as little—interaction with others as I wanted. At some shows, I chatted with my neighbors. At others, I didn't talk to anyone. Whatever I decided to do, I minded my safety and had a wonderful time. When you're on your own at a concert, you have a chance to really explore the environment and learn from it. In a lot of ways, it's better than going with friends.

When I was alone, for some reason, I had a knack for falling into interesting situations. Often, I inadvertently got up close and personal with the bands. When the B-52s played a small club in New York, for instance, I accidentally ended up in the VIP area and watched the concert with the Bs' friends and spouses. At a Cure show, I somehow managed to get backstage when I was only trying to get from one level of the venue to another, and spent a panicked five minutes trying to find my way out again. After a performance by The Cult in Boston, I decided to wait around to meet the band. When Ian Astbury finally emerged from the theater, I was too tongue-tied to say anything. One of the friendly strangers nearby grabbed my camera, explained that I was shy, and asked Ian to pose in a photo with me. And he did.

I am still out there, and I'm still going to shows as often as my budget allows. I still fly solo most of the time. It gives me the opportunity to truly lose myself in the music, to drink in every bit of the ambiance, and to quietly process everything I see and hear.

Every now and then someone will be disturbed by this, and will offer sympathy: "You're here all alone? That's too bad." I always smile and nod at them. Being alone at a concert doesn't mean I'm antisocial or friendless. It simply means that I'm enjoying a night to myself. My friends will hear all the details about the show the next morning. They always ask, and they're always entertained. And secretly, they're probably also grateful that I'm not trying to drag them off to see bands they don't like.

~Denise Reich

44

Getting Real

Sometimes you just need a little bit of time for yourself
to clear up your mind and see things
from a new perspective.
~Author Unknown

Clutching my steering wheel, I stared at the cracks in the pavement in the parking lot at the Presqu'ile Beach Motel in Brighton, Ontario. Up until that moment, the destination had been just another familiar sign on a well-traveled road, one that would normally have signaled the half-way point of my regular two-hour commute to the city.

But on this occasion, it was proving to be an historic landmark—a tipping point—the scene of the unexpected mutiny from my life.

The cheerful hanging baskets and colourful plastic chairs belied the dark mood that had brought me there. While my car idled, an internal debate about whether or not to check in—and check out for a few days—raged within me.

I wasn't a camper, sojourner or wayfarer. I had none of the seasonal trappings of the other guests—there was no canoe strapped to my roof or flip-flops on my feet. There was no good reason for me to be in that place at that time, except that I was a tired working woman who was dangerously close to crossing the centre line of sanity for no apparent reason. I guess that made it as good a place as any to stop and try to catch my breath.

What would people say? This was the main point on which I was stuck.

A friend of mine had done the very thing I was contemplating and not only did she live to tell the tale, but her reputation as a dedicated wife, mother and working professional remained intact in spite of it. She told me her story over a glass of wine one night, in matter-of-fact tones, as if she were weighing the merits of shaving versus waxing. Exhaustion is a very common condition amongst working women, and I bore the signs of one who was similarly afflicted, so she had every reason to trust that I would lend a listening ear without judgment.

You see, the real trouble with "leaning in" and trying to excel at both career and family—with a bow to Sheryl Sandberg—is that unless you have paid staff keeping the home fires burning, the chances of catching a steep angle and finding yourself prostrate on the floor are pretty good.

I was impressed by the methodical nature of my friend's revolt. Even in her darkest hour she was the consummate planner. She brought enough food to sustain her for forty-eight hours so she wouldn't need to leave her hotel room.

While she was there she had a good cry, a long bath, and watched a couple of movies. But mostly she just slept off the dark cloud until some glimmer of a silver lining helped her find her way back home.

"I just need a break," I said to myself as I turned the engine off and reached for my purse.

I knew I couldn't make the trip to work, but could I really make the decision not to go home? Taking a sick day is one thing, abandoning your family, even briefly, is quite another.

The fear that had been manageable while the car was idling now began to make me tremble. I needed more time to weigh the pros and cons, to make a list of some kind that would prove that this was a totally ridiculous idea. I quickly turned the engine back on.

My friend had checked into a hotel, not a motel—there's a huge difference. Motels never have bathrobes, fluffy towels or plump mattresses. And worst of all they are a haven for those hideously patterned, quilted polyester bedspreads—the ones contoured to fit old beds with rusty springs, like some sad, stain-screening shrink-wrap. How could I get the rest I so desperately needed in such a low thread-count environment?

I shuddered to think of it and then I remembered my bedroom at home, a linen aficionado's paradise with cozy cotton quilts, a feather bed and, yes, my very own terrycloth bathrobe. My rational voice said, "Just go home, woman, and call it a day!" If fretting about the sheets was my biggest concern, maybe I hadn't hit rock bottom yet.

Home is comfort, that's true. But home is a lot of other things, too, like expectation, routine and the unending call of duty. To the occasional visitor home is a showcase of all that you've done, but for the permanent occupant it is more often a screaming chorus of what you've left undone. It's no small wonder that home, for many people, is the least restful place on earth.

I was about to turn the engine off once again when I thought about the call I would need to make to my husband. I couldn't do this without at least telling him where I'd gone, that I was okay, and that I did intend to come back home, after about forty-eight hours of self-imposed isolation.

"Blindsided!" was the word I imagined him using when he, inevitably, called his mother or my mother or one of his friends to tell them what I'd done. I could see him with his face in his hands sitting at our craggy old kitchen table repeating the word "Blindsided!" and alternating between rage and disbelief.

Realizing the extent to which Mark would be completely shocked by my taking such a desperate measure to deal with my exhaustion—a situation about which I hadn't given an adequate voice—was, even more than the abhorrent flame-retardant textiles, what made me realize I had to go home. It was time for me to grow up and finally learn how to speak the truth, to make up for all the times I'd lied to my husband, saying "I'm fine" even though I wasn't. Like many women, I had made the classic mistake of secretly (and stupidly) wishing he could read my mind.

And so with at least one curious onlooker, I slowly backed out of the driveway, turned my car around and pointed it in the direction of home. I would take some unused vacation days and I would tell my husband what, exactly, I needed by way of a couple of days off the grid.

More than anything I would ask him not to judge me. Maybe other women were coping with all of the demands better than me, but "compare-and-contrast", while great for book reports, is a horrible way to live your life.

As for the title of my book, instead of *Lean In: Women, Work, and the Will to Lead*, I'm thinking about *Get Real: Women, Work and the Will to Survive*.

~Michelle Hauser

45

Learning to Fly

*The truth is, unless you let go, unless you forgive
yourself, unless you forgive the situation, unless you
realize that the situation is over, you cannot move
forward.*
~Steve Maraboli

I t has been said that you are never more vulnerable than when you become a mother. It's easy to interpret those words to refer to the way we, as mothers, feel about our children. It's easy to identify the panic we feel when bad things happen to our kids. It's easy to acknowledge that we would do anything, really anything, to keep our kids safe. What's not so easy is to recognize the other ways in which we become vulnerable as mothers.

I had my first two children at ages thirty and thirty-one. A divorce and nine years later, I had three more children in less than thirteen months time. Not only did I become even more vulnerable through my incredible emotional attachment to my children, but I became vulnerable to the loss of myself.

When the twins were babies, the physical toll was tremendous. Trying to combat postpartum depression and a wicked case of sleep deprivation, I fought to keep myself upright and my family moving forward. I struggled to keep my wits about me at the job, and to stay focused on what mattered. Family, friends, and other mothers of multiples supported me and shared resources, but every day was a battle.

Even as the children grew and matured, I realized that the feeling of vulnerability and fragility still remained. I recognized that our marriage was suffering, and that I no longer felt the joy that I had earlier on. I came up with solutions for making life easier, for attending to the obligations and the opportunities, but below the surface, my fears were mounting, threatening the very core of who I was. While on the surface I appeared to be fearful of nothing—supermom to my kids, superhero to my patients, family and friends—the charade was killing me.

During the summer, while my husband and children were away, I tended to my long to-do list, once again failing to refuel myself, and instead putting the needs of others before my own. I had all but eliminated days off and nights out and I refused the dinner invitation that came that week from a friend. Following nearly an hour of badgering, I relented and agreed to meet her downtown. She was accompanied by her boyfriend and one of his colleagues, in from out of town. Despite my protestations that I couldn't possibly take the time away from my projects, I found myself relaxing as dinner progressed. I enjoyed the smiles we shared, the laughter, and the unbearable lightness of being that emanated from the experience. I noticed a feeling I hadn't had in such a long time: I felt grounded, yet alive. My friend snapped a few photos to memorialize the unthinkable: me, out at a restaurant, on a weeknight. After a few hours, I wished them well for their return flight and headed back home.

The following evening, my family returned and I listened intently to tales of their week away. In turn, I shocked the lot with the news that I'd actually gone OUT to dinner with friends. Later that evening, I shared the photos with my husband and tried to articulate the feeling that I'd noticed while at dinner. I failed miserably in my attempt to communicate and eventually ended the conversation with the feeling that something was somehow changing below the surface.

For the next few days, we talked, but each time, I felt as if I was floating further and further away from him. I pulled out the photos from time to time and kept noticing a look in my eyes that hadn't been there in very long time. I realized that there was a light behind them, a twinkle that had been buried deep below the fears I had been accumulating. During the course of the marriage, I'd overcome my lifelong fear of heights as well as a terrifying claustrophobia. I'd even relinquished my fear of death, but what I'd desperately held on to were my fears associated with losing control.

Only weeks later that thirteen-year marriage ended. Life fell into millions of tiny fragments around me, and when my children left for a two-week vacation, I came undone. I did what I'd NEVER done for myself: I took two weeks off from work and sat with my feelings. With the support of some dear friends, I let the waves wash over me, at times feeling as if I would disappear beneath the surface. Memories of traumas and tragedies rose to the surface, demanding that I deal with them, and in my weakened, fragile state, I allowed myself to be vulnerable.

I didn't die under the weight of it all as I expected. Quite the contrary: I rose to the occasion, unlike the woman I had been in the decade before. Gone was the superficial superwoman, and to the forefront came a force to be reckoned with. Armed with embers aglow in my core, I drove my daughter to college and then continued north alone to my favorite retreat spot. There, I wrestled with the grief that had remained capped about the loss *in utero* of three babies, whom I had named Emily, Melanie and Hope.

While I had allowed myself time to grieve Hope's loss during my twin pregnancy at forty, caring for the remaining twin consumed me. But never before had I allowed myself to grieve the loss of Melanie and Emily. At age twenty-five, after two years of fertility procedures and protocols, the news that Melanie was on her way was sublime. But, unbeknownst to me, my husband had already chosen to leave the marriage. In the wake of his departure, I lost my long-awaited pregnancy and Melanie was gone before she'd had a chance to arrive.

As I grieved for Melanie in my room by the sea, I realized that I had never really grieved the loss of the marriage because it had been so unhealthy. I let go of the judgment I'd weighed on myself and let the tears come—for her, and for it. As I found resolution with that loss, I realized that I had to reach farther back and to finally allow myself the courage to grieve for Emily.

As strong as I had learned to be, and with all that I had survived, I had never felt capable of acknowledging the depth of that loss. Seventeen, battered, and pregnant, I had given up. I overdosed with a bottle of Valium, and while lucky to have survived, lost Emily in the process. Because of how she came to me, I'd never let myself be present with how deeply attached I was to her. Secretly, I'd believed that I didn't have a right to mourn her loss, but as I finally allowed the waves of desperate sadness to move through me, I found peace. Each day I realized I was growing stronger, while each night the sadness steamrolled my heart. By the time I returned home, I could feel the spirit of my girls with me, uninhibited by my fear of the grief surrounding their deaths.

During the months that followed, I learned to open my heart more with every passing day, and even found myself learning to share with the mate I'd had for those thirteen years. There were good days and bad, but our love for one another and our children enabled us to morph into friends and co-parents. The memories didn't stop coming after our divorce, and more than a time or two he listened as I grieved for the traumas I had endured and never shared with anyone. Each experience of disclosure and each layer flayed from my fear base left me more and more willing to venture forth.

Just two weeks after our divorce, we attended an Accelerated Free Fall (AFF1) class and with the support of an instructor went skydiving for the first time. A week later, we dove into the waters of the Pacific and completed a mile ocean swim. We repeated the experience just days later, in even rougher waters. I attended an entertainment industry event and embraced my role as a future producer of one of the actresses being honored. I committed to writing and publishing a series of books and I finally relinquished the desire to remain stuck and small. I recognized that it was time to fly.

Six months later, I am no longer bound by the fears that threatened my very core. I am willing to be all that I am meant to be, and to give to myself all that I deserve. I have accepted invitations to do activities that I never believed I could engage in, and have committed to performing functions that I'd always believed were meant for others to do. I am embodying the sage that I am and the wisdom that comes through me and I am finally ready to thrive.

~Sage de Beixedon Breslin, PhD

Chapter
5

Time
to
Thrive

Say Yes to Thriving

46

The Summer of Yes

We must walk consciously only part way toward our
goal and then leap in the dark to our success.
~Henry David Thoreau

In April of 2012, my writers' group struggled to find speakers. I loved my group enough to drive two hours on a Saturday morning once a month to be there. But I felt the meeting quality had started to slide. Several meetings that year had no speakers at all, just members reading their work out loud to the group. I offered to help out the speaker committee and shared a list of ideas for future topics with them.

Two weeks before the meeting, I hadn't heard from anyone on the committee. So I followed up. No one had even contacted a speaker, let alone booked one. A fellow member told me, "I can't find a speaker. I don't even know where to look!"

I'll admit I got annoyed. A lot of members stopped showing up when we didn't have outside speakers. So I told her I'd take care of it. I had no idea what to do either, but this dithering wasn't getting anything done.

Ten minutes later I had an idea.

Five minutes after that, Google provided a telephone number to call.

Twenty minutes after the "I don't know where to look" conversation, a librarian from the local university thanked ME for the chance to share his knowledge on short notice with a bunch of strangers.

For free. I didn't know if he was a great speaker, or if anyone would be interested in his talk on Internet research techniques, but I let the committee know the name of our speaker and arranged for him to have a projector and screen for his presentation.

Afterward, I sat in my chair thinking, "Wow. That was so easy. Why couldn't anyone else do that?" Then enlightenment smacked me in the back of the head. It wasn't that no one else could do it; it was that no one else DID. Which made me wonder: How many opportunities had I lost because I didn't make an effort?

I decided one word would rule my life and that word was "yes." Yes, I would make the effort. Yes, I would participate. Yes, I would walk that 5K race for charity. Yes, I would attend that concert in the park. Yes, I would go to that science fiction convention. Yes, I would sit in the driver's seat instead of on my love seat. I declared that summer the Summer of Yes.

The next morning, the mayor hosted a 5K walk along the River Trail. So I got off my couch at 9:00 a.m., put on the jogging shoes I never jogged in, and went down to the park. I doubted my sanity in walking a 5K with no preparation, but when the shotgun went off I started moving my legs. My couch potato behind walked all three miles that day. I hovered near the end of the pack, outpaced by women with strollers, but I finished. I applied a little effort and accomplished something that just the day before I wouldn't have even tried.

After that, "yes" became my mantra. I'd get invitations and reply, "Of course, it's the Summer of Yes!" I looked for things I wouldn't normally do. I entered costume contests. I rode my bicycle to work instead of driving. I tried recipes from magazines and shopped at the farmer's market. Most of the time, "yes" was easy. Once I put myself in motion, momentum kept me moving forward. I finally felt my real life had begun.

Soon the Summer of Yes spread to my friends. I'd ask them to come along on my adventures, and they would say, "Well, it is the Summer of Yes!" They invited me along on theirs, reciting the mantra when I was reluctant. The Summer of Yes infected them, then mutated, infecting me with the new strain. Because while the Summer of Yes started with 5K races and concerts, it quickly reached beyond such trivialities.

Yes, I will be president of my writers' club. Yes, I will finish my degree in Database Administration. Yes, I will submit my short stories for publication. Yes, I do hate my toxic workplace, and yes, I will apply for other opportunities. The Summer of Yes focused me on the things I really wanted from life; it showed me I didn't have the things that were truly important to me.

By the end of the Summer of Yes, I had a new job. I got published that fall. By Christmas, I earned my associate's degree. And my writers' group meetings had speakers scheduled at least a month in advance. "Yes" literally changed my life.

My friends still talk about the Summer of Yes. They think it's over. For me, the Summer of Yes didn't end. It became the Year of Yes, then the Life of Yes. I'm still saying "yes" even though the tasks have gotten harder, accomplishing them more complex. "Yes" got me a stellar performance review and a promotion. "Yes" is taking me to Europe for the first time.

The Summer of Yes started with a moment of frustration. I hope it never ends. And in case you are wondering, the librarian who spoke at our meeting was fantastic.

~Ericka Kahler

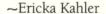

47

It's MY Life!

There came a time when the risk to remain tight in the
bud was more painful than the risk it took to blossom.
~Anaïs Nin

I'd heard the expression "jaw-dropping" before, but had never experienced it until that day. I could almost feel my chin slam into my chest with shock.

"You're kidding, right?" I asked my father. "You're not serious!"

He took another swig of his ever-present weekend beer before replying. His eyes were bleary, his words slurred, but there was no mistaking the stern gravity of his words.

"Do I look like I'm kidding, girl? You can attend school for one more year to get it out of your system, but then you're taking a secretarial course."

"But why?" I protested.

I had already been accepted into my second year of CEGEP, our version of pre-university in Quebec, Canada. I hadn't decided on a major yet, but I was fully counting on many more years of higher education. My father's pronouncement stunned me.

"You're going to be married, so you'll need a job when your husband comes here," my father announced.

"Comes here?" I asked. "From where?"

He emptied his bottle, slammed it on the kitchen table and jerked his head toward the refrigerator, indicating I was to get him another. Too stunned to move, I could only stare wordlessly.

"Get me a drink," he hollered, spurring me into action. I scurried to do his bidding, opened a fresh bottle and handed it to him. I watched him take a long swallow. When he was done, he continued to speak.

"It's almost arranged. I haven't decided which man yet, but I have four possibilities."

A sense of dread washed over me as I recalled the many bulging envelopes that had recently been coming in the mail from Poland, Papa's homeland. Pictures of men about my father's age whom I didn't know, but presumed were his cousins or brothers, littered my parents' nightstand. Now I realized they were prospective husbands. My father was arranging a marriage for me!

It wasn't a common practice in our small immigrant community, but it did happen. Two daughters of family friends married brothers their parents selected for them. And though they didn't seem miserable or mistreated, there was a dull hopelessness in their eyes when they became pregnant almost immediately. They lost their zest for life and were no longer the carefree, optimistic girls with whom I'd shared whispered dreams and giggled about teenage crushes at sleepovers. Papa had never indicated he had the same plans for me. I was terrified.

Ours was not a happy home. Laughter seldom rang through it. Though my three older brothers and I were rowdy and boisterous with each other, we were all taught to be compliant and meek around our parents. If we misbehaved, the discipline was swift and painful.

I had always been a "good girl." I never argued with Mama or Papa or crossed them in any way. I brought home the expected exemplary report cards. I was neither allowed to date nor attend extracurricular school functions, but unbeknownst to my parents, I did have a boyfriend. We had met several weeks earlier and I was already deeply in love with him. The thought of marrying an older stranger repulsed and frightened me, igniting a flame of rebellion inside me.

I realized that my father had stopped talking and was staring at me. "Go to bed now," he commanded.

I glanced at the clock and saw it was only nine o'clock, but I obeyed. I needed to escape—to hide in my room and absorb every-thing—and to plan.

I waited until everyone was asleep. When I was sure it was safe, I tiptoed into the kitchen and retrieved several large empty bags from the pantry.

I didn't have many personal possessions. I crammed all my cloth-ing into an overnight bag I always kept under my bed. The rest of my belongings fit in the three other sacks. When I was done, I pushed everything back under my bed and lay down, fully dressed.

As soon as the sun started to rise, I opened my door and stepped into the hallway with my arms full. I came face to face with my oldest brother, who I knew had overheard the conversation the night before. Our eyes met and he stared at me for a long time, noting the possessions spilling from my arms. Without a word, he tucked a twenty-dollar bill into my pocket.

Just then my father emerged from his room. He immediately grasped the situation and strode toward us. To my utter shock, my brother barred his way, his stance rigidly confrontational, and his expression mutinous.

"Go! Get out," he told me. "Now!" he added hoarsely, still standing defensively between my father and me.

I looked at Papa one last time before I ran. "It's MY life," I shouted at him defiantly for the first time ever as I left.

He couldn't stop me. I had just turned eighteen two weeks earlier so I was legally considered an adult under Canadian law.

I didn't go far. I walked two streets over to my best friend's house and begged her mother to take me in. She agreed, but warned me I couldn't stay long and that I would have to pay rent. I immediately handed her my brother's money, leaving myself with only seven dollars to get a job and start my new life.

The next day, I used some of it to take a bus and get my tuition money back from school. Two days later, I had a job waitressing, and shortly after that, my own apartment.

Eventually, I married my boyfriend, and through hard work and determination, we built a good life together—one based on mutual love and respect.

I didn't see my father again for almost seven years. One December, he sent a message through my brother that he wanted our entire family together again for Christmas. His stern attitude had mellowed over time, and he greeted me with open arms.

Surprisingly, he and my husband became good friends. Papa died twelve years later, but by then we had completely reconciled. He doted on his only grandson and admitted that he was proud of me, voicing his regret for not allowing me to follow my dreams to continue my education. I assured him that, after becoming a parent myself, my priorities had changed. Simply being allowed to make my own choices and mistakes was enough to ensure my happiness. I thrived on the life I was living and felt as successful as if I'd graduated college with a degree.

It took all the courage I had to stand up for my freedom and leave home that day, but by doing so I discovered an inner strength and independence I never knew I possessed. The man who tried to stifle those very characteristics in me inadvertently made them rise to the surface, freeing me to live my life exactly the way I wanted to with no regrets.

~Marya Morin

48

Perspective

*Live the way you want and believe in what you want
and never let anyone make you think any different.
The one in control of your life is you.*
~Nishan Panwar

As my two-year-old twins chased each other up and down the hallway before their bath, I stared into the water rising in the tub. It was then, inside a beautiful house on a lake, living a lifestyle that looked ideal to the outside world, that I accepted the ugly truth: my ten-year marriage was going to end. It had to.

Our parents lived on opposite coasts. Little by little, my husband had driven most of my friends away. Isolated on a rural property away from everything but him and the kids, I found myself alone, exhausted and increasingly worried for my own health and sanity. Now, instead of one demanding husband, I also had two demanding children and my energies were being spread dangerously thin. And, as was typical, his demands only increased as my energy levels decreased.

Prior to children, of course, my focus had always been on him. Now with kids, he had competition. From his perspective, I thought about them too much. I coddled them too much. I paid them too much attention. What this all really meant was simple: I paid too little attention to him.

From my perspective, there were two helpless infants and one grown-up man all endlessly vying for my attention. There was a fourth person, of course, who also needed attention, but that person was the easiest to shut up: me.

Anyone who has taken care of even one baby knows that infant care can be exhausting, thankless and mind-numbing even under the most loving circumstances. I had two babies and no outside support. We did not belong to any outside organization, church or group to at least allow me something different to look at other than the walls of our home. I would suggest such a thing and be told, "What, your family isn't good enough for you?" I asked to take part in a women's golf group or to ride a bike in the mornings before the kids got up. I was told that I was selfish, and anyway, if I went biking, he might have to change his schedule.

I tried for space on the weekends for a while as well. A few hours. Even an hour. Just to get away and breathe and not have someone needing me. My body simply ached with exhaustion. My mind was dull and sad. I desperately needed to rejuvenate somehow, but without support to do so, there wasn't any escape. And the guilt trips he would lay on me when I asked to even walk to the mailbox on my own made fighting for my sanity hardly worth the effort.

According to him, I didn't love my family. I didn't love him. I was a bad mother. I was selfish. I was self-involved. His mother never needed space, so why should I? Selfish. Selfish. Selfish.

That is one thing they will tell you about controlling, manipulative men. They are acutely aware of your weak spots. My weak spot was being called "selfish." People who haven't experienced an emotionally abusive relationship might ask, "Why would you put up with that?" It's a question that makes sense only when you aren't involved in the terrorism that is a controlling spouse.

And the answer is pretty simple actually: because to fight back is to expend the little energy you do have left, only to dig yourself a deeper hole. A hundred pounds of flesh extracted for disagreement is worse than the ten pounds of flesh normally taken. It becomes about pure mathematics.

So, on that day sitting at the edge of the bath, two years into being a mom to beautiful kids, but ten years into being a wife to a controlling manipulator, I shook the basket of their little foam letters into the water and wondered how I would escape. Many times, he had threatened to kill me if I ever left him. He worked at home and was nearly always there. I was truly a prisoner in my own house.

Moreover, he controlled all of the finances and I knew that if I left he would make every attempt to destroy me and leave me penniless. He couldn't even lose at a board game without becoming furious. Leaving a man like him was opening Pandora's box. I would be willingly placing an enormous target on my forehead. What would he do to us if we left?

But more to the point: What would he do to us if we stayed?

My soul, year after year, had shriveled by degrees into almost nothing. His existence had nearly snuffed out mine. And now I looked at my little children and envisioned what a household with the four of us in it would look like during their upbringing. No empathy. Constant, unreasonable demands. Disrespect for their thoughts and their feelings. The role model of me as his emotional punching bag.

The kids were wondering if the bath was ready. They ran to me, throwing themselves at me full force for a big, raucous hug; their little chubby arms holding me tight, their sweet-smelling heads nestled in close. I hugged back, feeling the tears well in my eyes at their pure, unadulterated love. This is how it should be, I thought.

Reaching over to turn off the faucet, my glance down at the water was My Moment. There, floating among the boats and the squirt toys, were three little foam letters that had gathered together by the drain: J-O-Y.

Joy.

It was ours for the taking.

~Heidi FitzGerald

Sparked

Happiness is not something ready-made. It comes from your own actions.
~Dalai Lama

My journey toward creating a life that has meaning started about nine years ago. I was married, mother of a beautiful four-year-old daughter, and owner of a successful clothing store. Though I looked great on the outside, inside I was running ragged.

From a distance, I looked like I had it all together: nice clothes, darling child, athletic body, good-looking husband, nice home, regular travel to exotic places. Still, as I looked at my life more closely, I wondered, "Why don't I feel happy and joyful? Why do I feel I'm just surviving every day?" However, in the same breath I was asking myself, "Isn't this the kind of life that I always wanted, strived for and desired? Shouldn't I be grateful for what I have?"

Like many people, I could not remember what excited me anymore or what my "purpose" was. I felt exceptionally sad and empty inside and didn't know how to change. I knew I wasn't living in harmony with my values. I was drinking too much, bingeing late at night, eating way too much sugar, hanging out with very toxic people, not exercising, and consuming anything that might help me not feel what I was feeling. I was not being true to myself. I asked myself, "Is this how you want to live? Is this how you want to feel?" Without a doubt I knew I wanted to feel a sense of worth and value and living this way wasn't getting me there.

That year I attended a seven-day motivational event that was led by an amazing woman. At the time I thought I went as a last-ditch effort to save my marriage, but instead it was an awakening of my soul. It was the beginning of finding out what my purpose in life was, what I wanted my life to look like and feel like. What I experienced that week with the help of this woman started to transform my life. She "sparked" a desire in me to go beyond my comfort zone and showed me it was possible to live a life of meaning and passion. She motivated me to stop playing small and do the things that made me proud and empowered.

I began to realize the choices I was making were not lifting me up: not taking care of my body, hanging around people who didn't inspire me to grow, not living in a home that supported me, and so on. I had to take a good look at what I was doing.

Since that day it has been my mission to learn what helps me thrive on a daily basis. I first had to focus on some fundamental things: eating well, drinking enough water, moving my body, doing things that I love, taking time to be grateful and making sure I contribute to this world in some way.

The simple phrase "health is your wealth" is the honest truth. Without it I was not able to thrive in my life. I also believe that "food equals mood" and when I feed my body crap that is exactly how I feel. When I was at a low point in my life I realized I had let my healthy diet go. I was not picking foods that were supporting me and I was consuming way too many sweets. Now I try for at least eighty percent whole foods (fruits, veggies, legumes, whole grains, fish) and I leave twenty percent for some wiggle room and fun.

I was also drinking too much wine and felt exhausted every day. Today I make sure I drink at least half my body weight in ounces of water to keep it cleansed and feeling vibrant. My exercise plan had fallen off and I was not moving my body on a consistent basis. I now make sure I move my body at least five times a week for thirty minutes, either by taking a walk with a friend, yoga, spin class, dance class… anything that I'm excited about. It is a must!

Another thing I realized at my most desperate and lonely point was that I had forgotten what makes me happy. I was busy making everyone else's lives go smoothly but not taking the time to do things that I enjoyed. I had forgotten the simple pleasures in life that made me smile. So I created a go-to list of all the things that make me feel alive, happy and excited about life. They include making time for girlfriends, self-care, buying myself flowers, playing music in the house, and game night with my family, to name a few.

Another important thing I have included in my daily life is making time for gratitude. I have realized that when I focus on the positive, I have a totally different perspective and enjoyment of the day. I have a variety of ways that I accomplish this. One is a gratitude journal I write in briefly every night. I could list seeing a friend, my daughter doing well in school, or even getting all green lights on the way to the store. The family dinner table has been a great place to show gratitude as well; we go around and say three things we are grateful for. And finally I have a gratitude jar on the kitchen counter for the whole family to write on a little slip of paper any time they have something happen they want to be thankful for. Making time to be grateful has truly been a game changer.

Lastly, what has brought the most meaning and purpose to me is contributing to others. When I had felt so empty inside, I couldn't think about anyone else. I now know that when I start to go to that place, giving back is what brings me out of those thoughts. Bringing some light to another human being helps me feel alive. Whether it is financial help or giving of my time, when I am in the "we instead of me" zone my life feels amazing.

My life is far from perfect but these days I know what makes me feel happy and purposeful. The changes I made in my life are ones that we can all implement, one at a time. It's eminently doable!

~Stephanie Jackson

50

Learning to Swim

The beginning and the end reach out their hands to each other.
~Chinese Proverb

I learned to swim at forty. My young daughters were taking private swim lessons and, well, one thing led to another and I found myself in the pool learning along with them. I was fearful at first but it soon became a joy to learn side by side. We cheered each other on and celebrated each little success.

One day, I was pulling myself out of the pool when I caught a woman eyeing me. She was standing by the deep end. Her two children were dressed in their swimsuits, pulling at her skirt. I sensed her surprise as she watched me, dripping wet, run to the changing area with my two little girls.

I felt my neck grow red. I had always been embarrassed by my lack of swim skills. I wondered if the woman had been noting my panicked stoke. I am sure she was shocked to see a full-grown woman going through swim drills along with young children. Wasn't I a tad overgrown for this? I know the Dora kickboard didn't help matters.

I put it out of my mind. After all, I had almost mastered the breaststroke and my swim teacher had promised to show me how to use a snorkel next week. In June I had clung to the side of the pool in the shallow end. Now, just two months later, I practiced many different strokes in the deep end. I had learned to tread water and, after much encouragement, I had done a flip turn just last week. I was proud. However, I did discuss it further with my husband over dinner.

"Maybe I should end my lessons. I'm water-safe now. I'll just let the girls continue without me."

"But, do you enjoy it?" he had asked.

Yes, of course I did. And I wanted to master the strokes.

During my next lesson, I was in the deep end and about to push off from the side of the pool to practice the crawl stroke. The staring woman made an unexpected appearance. She waved down my swim instructor to ask a quick question.

My instructor was shouting instructions to me. "Reach, pull, reach, pull."

The woman's eyes again were on me for what seemed to be a full minute. Her stare was curious and invasive. To be honest, I felt uncomfortable. I stopped swimming and clung to the side. My instructor quickly dealt with the woman and sent her on her way.

Sensing my discomfort, she said, "Michele, this is so awesome that you are doing this for you and your kids. I've taught other adults. You aren't the first one."

"I… I don't like an audience."

Especially an audience that stared. The door closed behind the woman with the probing eyes. I had hoped we wouldn't cross paths again.

I decided to not allow it to bother me. I knew I was being too sensitive. If someone wanted to stare as I swam, so be it. I was brave. I knew it. My girls knew it. That was the end of it.

About three weeks later, I was again pulling myself out of the pool after my lesson and came face to face with the staring woman. This time I was the one who stared. She folded her hands over her chest, attempting to smooth over the ruffles on her one-piece bathing suit. Her two children were on either side of her, pulling at her. She, again, looked at me with her invasive eyes, but this time I sensed she was the one who was uncomfortable.

She smiled at me shyly and then, looking at my swim teacher, said, "Do you have room for three?"

It was her awkwardness as she entered the pool that confirmed it. She stood in the shallow end and clung to the side. I knew the spot well. That had been my spot in June.

I marveled at how misunderstanding can sometimes color perceptions. When I felt judged, I was actually serving as the source of inspiration.

And amen to that.

~Michele Boom

51

Eating to Live

From the bitterness of disease man learns the sweetness of health.
~Catalan Proverb

"Your creatinine can't get any higher," warned Dr. Toral, my nephrologist, as he handed me the lab sheet with my latest abnormal kidney results — all circled in red. As he reviewed the tests, I wondered how long it would be before I'd be hooked up to a dialysis machine or waiting for a kidney transplant.

As I gathered my things, Dr. Toral gave me a stern look and admonished me once again about staying away from all dairy products, along with a list of other forbidden foods, including potatoes, bananas, peanut butter, and chocolate. In my mind, those were the four major food groups!

Before leaving his office, the receptionist handed me more paperwork for my next blood draw and sample diets that included no added salt. Why didn't she just give me a list of things I could eat? It would have been a lot easier.

I made a decision that day — as I walked across the hospital parking lot — I was going to eat to live, not live to eat!

As soon as I got home, I cleaned out the cupboards of forbidden foods, including my stash of chocolate and peanut butter. Anything that wasn't a fruit or vegetable wasn't going in my mouth — period.

Later that afternoon I called my best friend, Kathy, and asked, "Would you pray that I stick to this kidney-friendly diet? Because I think it's going to kill me."

Kathy snickered and asked, "Which one—the disease or the diet?"

"Both!"

With family and friends supporting me, I scoured the Internet for help, hints and diet information. I came across a website that listed the fifteen healthiest foods for the kidney. I knew that potassium and phosphorus had to be kept in check, but the list gave me little hope for eating some of my favorite foods.

One thing was clear: I needed to become a lover of fruits and vegetables, including red bell peppers, cauliflower, onions, apples, blueberries and red grapes—thankfully not all at the same time. I posted the list on the refrigerator door along with my new mantra: "Eat to Live!"

My husband Mark glanced at the list, sneered, and said, "Good luck with that."

Unchecked high blood pressure had placed a heavy burden on my kidneys and left me with no option than to change my eating and exercise habits. The saltshaker disappeared from the table and the sugar bowl became my herbal tea container. In one day, I had completely given up coffee, sugar, chocolate and French fries.

The following morning, my running shoes replaced my pink bunny slippers and out the door I went for a three-mile walk, which later turned into a jog—all before my green smoothie touched my lips. Even my husband joined me for my morning walks and afterward we drank a "Kidney Delight"—a blend of celery, apples, cucumbers, pineapple, fresh ginger and cinnamon. If I could make such a drastic change, anyone could.

Days turned into weeks and despair turned into hope as I began to see results from my diet and exercise program. My next blood draw was in six weeks and I was determined to have all my tests within normal limits.

When Dr. Toral called me with the results, he assured me that the lab made an error. "Your labs are completely normal and that can't possibly be right. I want you to go to an independent laboratory and have your blood re-drawn," he said emphatically.

The thought of being stuck again didn't thrill me, but I was determined to prove that prayer, exercise, and a change of diet could make a difference.

After I hung up the phone, fear started to invade my thoughts. What if the labs really weren't correct? What if kidney disease couldn't be controlled by diet and exercise, and all my hard work was for nothing? What if my kidneys were failing?

I always worked best under pressure, so I picked up the phone and dialed the number of the lab Dr. Toral had given me and made an appointment for the following week to have my blood re-tested.

After the results came back completely normal again, Dr. Toral was baffled. "I've never seen anyone's levels change for the good so quickly," he said. "Normally kidney function can't be reversed."

He got out his calculator and went through my lab tests again. Finally, I just had to ask, "Dr. Toral, do you believe in miracles?"

He paused briefly from his calculations and responded, "Yes, I believe… whatever you are doing is working, so I think you should continue doing it."

My mouth widened into a huge smile as I walked out of Dr. Toral's office and then skipped into the parking lot!

In three months, I had totally changed my eating habits, dropped two dress sizes, and people started complimenting me on my complexion. My skin actually felt different and my hair glistened for the first time in my life.

What was good for my kidneys was also good for my entire body—even my husband lost fifteen pounds and started exercising with me. Without medication, I changed the way I ate and how I lived. Hope gave me the courage to change the things I never thought were possible.

It's been almost two years since I was diagnosed with Stage 3 renal failure and now I have normal kidney function. I'm enjoying the benefits of eating to live—not living to eat.

I'm living proof that it works!

~Connie K. Pombo

52

I Left My Pride on the Beach

We don't stop playing because we grow old;
we grow old because we stop playing.
~George Bernard Shaw

"Wha did it feel like?" my husband Art asked.

"Great!" I responded. "It's like riding a bicycle; even if you haven't done it for a long time, you don't forget how.

I think I did it for the first time on a canvas-covered inflated rubber mat, in the Atlantic Ocean, when I was in grammar school.

Riding the waves, that is.

I've known how to swim for as long as I can remember. I've been told that my father took me into the warm water of the Atlantic before I learned to walk. It was my dad who taught me how to handle myself in the sea.

I loved paddling out into the surf on my rubber mat, turning, and catching a big wave. I felt as if I'd been shot out of a canon as I flew toward shore. I was fearless. I went into the water when the red warning flags were flying, along with other local kids and the lifeguards, all of us tanned dark brown, our hair bleached blond by the sun. When the surf was up, the tourists were afraid to go in the water, and we had the waves to ourselves. After my dad died, when

I was eight, swimming brought me closer to him and helped to heal my aching heart. I thrived at the beach.

My husband and I now live near the Pacific Ocean. When our children were born, it was my turn to hold their hands and pass on what I'd learned from my dad and from my own mistakes, teaching them to gauge the sets. Watch the water for a few minutes before you go in. Dive under this one, jump over that one, ride this one! No wait, there's a bigger one coming. Don't turn your back on the ocean! Pull out of the wave before you get dumped!

Boogie boards were in by the time our kids were riding the waves. Our son was just like me: fearless on his board. No wave was too big. Eventually, he moved up to a surfboard. I borrowed a boogie board from time to time, but spent most of my time in the water body surfing.

Then, in my early fifties, years of running, hiking and biking caught up with me. I started having an annoying pain in my left hip. By the time I was in my late fifties, the pain was excruciating. I couldn't sleep, had difficulty driving, and walked with a cane.

In 2003, I had my hip replaced. The surgery went well and the replacement has been a blessing. My doctor cautioned me then, and cautions me each year when I go for a checkup, that I need to take precautions to prevent dislocating my miraculous hip.

Dislocation is painful, usually requires surgery, and makes it easier to dislocate your hip in the future. No more bicycling and cross-country skiing, because I might fall at an odd angle and pop my hip out. And I had to face the truth: After the surgery, my balance was off.

The thought of getting flipped over and tossed around by a big wave scared me. I did my swimming at the Y, one-half mile or more each time.

When I do swim in the ocean, I pick my beaches with care. For my money, no beaches are better than those on Kauai, where we have vacationed for over thirty years.

My husband and I recently spent two weeks there with our son, his wife, and their two teenaged children. I swam or snorkeled every day in the calm water near the Poipu Beach public park, where even a grandmother with a hip replacement can get in and out of the water without being knocked over.

Then I'd walk to Brennecke's, a famous body surfing and boogie boarding spot, where the waves vary in size from big to huge, and watch my family in the surf. My son taught his kids everything I taught him and then some, and our grandson is fearless, just like his dad and just like I was when I was his age. What my dad taught me all those years ago had been passed down to his great-grandchildren.

One afternoon I was sitting on the beach, watching my family do something I had loved. When, I wondered, had the fearless person that I used to be disappeared? When had I become so timid?

My pity party was interrupted by my son, who ran out of the water, grabbed me by the hand and told me that he was taking me boogie boarding. He worked as a lifeguard for years when he was in school, he's a good four inches taller than I am, and I felt safe with him. My granddaughter carried the board for me and my grandson stayed near the shore to grab me in case I flipped over. I was embarrassed as they helped me into the surf. I must look like a feeble old lady, I thought.

My son handed me the boogie board and gave it a shove.

"Here you go, Mom."

I took off. I still had the moves! The old familiar thrill came back. And I did flip over and get tossed, but I didn't care how silly I looked when my grandson helped me get to my feet.

"Again!" I said, over and over.

My son was on a roll. "Let's go snorkeling in the cove," he said. We loved the cove because you were in deep water almost immediately and got to swim with fish you never saw in shallow water.

"Are you sure?" I asked. I'd given up on the cove because of the rocky entry and the waves, which made getting in and out difficult even when I was younger.

But I went. As I stood by the water with my snorkel mask and fins on, my son took me by the arms and pulled me into the water. It was just as beautiful out there as I remembered. When I was finished snorkeling, it took all three of them to get me out as the waves and currents knocked me around.

I left my pride on the beach and discovered that it's never too late to do something that makes you feel like a kid again. I'm ready for new challenges.

Anyone for the zip line?

~Josephine A. Fitzpatrick

53

On My Own

To dare is to lose one's footing momentarily.
To not dare is to lose oneself.
~Søren Kierkegaard

N o sooner had I signed the contract than I began to regret it. I hadn't been a student for nearly thirty years. At the age of fifty-something I should have been looking forward to bouncing grandchildren on my knee, not writing research papers. Yet I'd always wanted to earn a master's degree, and my company would pay if I promised to stay with them for at least two years after finishing. So why did my palms sweat once I made the commitment?

The registration form in my hand listed the first class I would take—Business Theory. I could write a book on what I didn't know about that topic. I envisioned a classroom filled with eager young minds and wondered how I could possibly compete with them.

At the university bookstore, I searched for the two textbooks required for the course. It looked more like a mall than a place to buy books. Shirts, cups, license plate holders… you name it. Every item imaginable surrounded me, each emblazoned with the university logo. The only thing I couldn't find were books. I saw a ponytailed clerk who appeared younger than either of my two children.

"Excuse me, Miss. Where are the textbooks?"

"In the basement. Over there."

She pointed toward a door in the far corner. Though her tone was courteous, her eyes held a hint of condescension. I slunk away and crept down the stairs. The neat rows of books made me feel much more at home than the shopping paradise above had done. How strange that a bookstore should showcase everything except books. I smiled at the irony and found my required texts.

At home, I flipped through the volumes and frowned. My husband Phil looked at me.

"What's wrong?"

"I'm not sure what I've gotten myself into. I wish I hadn't agreed to do this."

"Well, then don't."

It would have been easy to agree, but I pressed my lips together. The thought of being a quitter stung my pride. Yet doubts continued to haunt me. I needed to figure out why.

I knew I could do the work. Maybe not as effortlessly as I had once done, but I'd simply work harder to get the job done. I had the time. My children were grown and out on their own. Although it would be a stretch to squeeze in class and study time between a job and household tasks, I wouldn't be in school forever. I had the desire. Getting a master's degree was something I'd been thinking about for years.

So why did I still feel so nervous?

Phil interrupted my thoughts.

"Let's go out to dinner and relax."

That sounded better than any internal argument. We headed for our favorite Mexican restaurant. Over chips, salsa, and a margarita, we discussed our upcoming plans with friends and a potential weekend getaway. It felt good to talk about something other than my worries regarding school.

On the drive home we were too full of food to speak. The absence of conversation let my mind wander back to my problem. The dreaded Business Theory class was scheduled to begin in only two days. I felt just as conflicted as I had that morning and finally blurted my question out loud.

"Should I do it or not?"

Phil's voice was matter of fact. "If it's going to keep you this keyed up, I vote against it. Go out with your girlfriends instead and have a good time."

His words hit me over the head like a club.

Somehow over the years, "me" had disappeared into "we." I couldn't remember the last event that I'd attended by myself. Whether with my husband or a friend, I always had someone with me. Going out alone seemed like having peanut butter with no jelly. No wonder my brain put up barriers to school. I'd forgotten how I used to take a deep breath and march straight into a new situation. Even my first day in kindergarten, I had no problem letting go of my mother's hand to navigate my way through a sea of unfamiliar faces.

The idea that I'd become such a wimp made me squirm. I didn't care if it meant walking into a classroom of strangers without a single ally to study a topic for which I felt woefully inadequate. I knew what I had to do.

"I'm going to that class and learning Business Theory if it kills me."

Phil grinned at my determined tone.

"Somehow I suspect you'll survive."

Although it wasn't easy, I did survive. And at the end of three long years I came away from the experience with two very important credentials. I had a master's degree in Nonprofit Management and a life lesson in what I could achieve once I remembered that I didn't need to rely on anyone's strength but my own.

~Pat Wahler

Because I Can

The only person who can pull me down is myself, and
I'm not going to let myself pull me down anymore.
~C. Joybell C.

I ran in the rain today. I clocked six miles at a steady 4.5 pace. That's nothing to write home about. But I don't care. I am proud to shout it loud and clear, I ran six miles in the rain today, and I plan to run six miles again tomorrow.

You see, I am a former smoker who began a one-sided love affair with nicotine at the tender age of fifteen. After thirty-five years of self-induced abuse, I finally managed to kick my habit to the curb.

What does this have to do with running?

Transitioning from a smoker to a non-smoker was hard. Even simple things like watching a television show were taxing. I was so used to puffing a smoke while watching a favorite show that the first few times I watched television without a cigarette I almost felt abandoned by a loved one. It was hard to focus on the show. And that was just the tip of the iceberg when it came to the side effects of nicotine withdrawal. Other side effects can include headaches, fatigue, depression, fidgeting, restless hands, and intense cravings. But the most common complaint is weight gain, and that's the one I struggled with the most.

I love myself as a non-smoker, but I can't say the same about the overweight middle-aged woman I soon saw reflected in the mirror. I may be fifty-three, but I could still look and feel like a vibrant woman if I set my mind to it. So in February, I decided enough was enough and set out to regain control of my body and mind. I replaced soft drinks with water, cooked and ate healthier foods, and began to exercise.

I decided to start my exercise regimen at a local lake where a nice nature trail meanders beside the water, through the trees, and across the dam. My first day of walking was sunny and warm for February. When I arrived at the lake, I locked my car, zipped up a lightweight jacket, crammed my cellphone into my pocket, and started off at a brisk pace. After only a few feet I was winded, at the halfway mark I was sweating profusely, and by the time I reached the other end, I was convinced I was dying. My lungs burned, my chest convulsed with each short raspy breath I drew, and my legs felt like rubber. Tears streamed down my face as I leaned against the guardrail and wondered how I would ever find the strength to make it back.

Later, back at my car, I decided that I would never allow myself to become so weak again. And every day for the next four months I drove to the lake and made myself walk back and forth across the dam. By June, I could walk nine miles without stopping. My jeans became looser, my legs and stomach got firmer, but I still refused to step onto the scale.

Ecstatic about my accomplishment, I continued my daily walks and decided to see what I could accomplish next. Thus, my decision to run.

At first, I could barely run a few feet before gasping like a fish out of water. But every day I would push myself to run just a few more feet. Then one day, to my amazement, I could run a mile and still draw air into my lungs.

This elicited an intense rush like nothing I had ever experienced. I embraced the pride I felt and set out to run two miles, and then three, four, five. And it is with pride that I can now say I run six miles a day. It has been a long journey, a trying time of pain, soul searching, and meditation. But I have made it and am proud of who I have become.

So when I say I ran in the rain today, I am making a profound proclamation that I have changed my lifestyle. In a sense I am shouting to the world that I love and cherish my body the way I should have years ago.

In the beginning I ran to shed the extra pounds I had gained, and perhaps part of me hoped to reclaim some of my youth. While both of these reasons are still important to me, I now find those things are not as relevant as they once were. It delights me to say I am a healthy, happy, well-adjusted woman who no longer needs a number on a scale or a size tag in her clothing to define who she is. It's ironic that this fifty-three-year-old woman never found herself until she decided to lose her nicotine addiction.

In the past when someone asked me why I ran, I would fumble for an answer, because I was unsure of my motive. But now I know with certainty why I run, and the reason is simple: I run because I CAN!

~Sharon Rosenbaum Earls

55

Passing on the Sword

The struggle you're in today is developing the strength
you need for tomorrow. Don't give up.
~Robert Tew

Justin and I both had ADHD and severe depression. I felt like we were war buddies. He motivated me to fight for my mental health and I was finally starting to heal. I had my husband and my family for support, but they had no idea what was going on inside my head. Justin knew. I could trust his advice. I was not alone in my daily struggle for something close to normal. When he was proud of me, I was elated. He told me that I was a beautiful and talented woman despite my mental illness. We talked for hours about how we felt and how we could make each other's day just a bit brighter, to keep the window of hope open.

The day I found out that he had shot himself, I wanted to follow in his footsteps and end it all. He was far stronger than I was and he had given up. I had lost my mentor, the only person who understood. The sickness had swallowed him. I gained back the weight I had lost and stopped cleaning the house. Nothing interested me except sleep and Internet videos. I no longer cared about myself or anything except keeping my husband happy and our pets alive.

There was going to be a memorial for Justin at a convention in Canada. The organizers asked those close to him to say something. I had six months to prepare, but it was not until the week before we left that I found the words. What I wanted to do was show that he did not die in vain. He had passed on the sword to a young girl who had to continue the battle, else she would fall too. The words that I wrote and eventually spoke in front of everyone have never left me since:

If the one I looked to for strength and guidance failed, how could I have any hope? The answer is because he showed me how and I would be dishonoring his memory if I didn't keep trying. And so I do. I'm not going to let mental illness take both of us. For every successful productive day and every milestone, I flip a middle finger to ADHD and depression. Mental illness has not taken its last victim, but thanks in several parts to Justin, the next one will not be me.

I am starting to rebuild my life and making a serious effort to take back what I have lost over the years. The house is in better shape than it has been since we moved in. I am being more social and practicing my life skills. Hobbies have once again become a part of my life and I look forward to them at the end of a long workday. Pretty soon, the weight will start to come off and I might be able to volunteer at the animal shelter like I did years ago.

I wish Justin was around to teach me more, but there comes a time when I have to take the experience I have gained and become my own leader. He would be as proud of me as I am of myself.

~Sarah LM Klauda

56

The List

Happiness is like a butterfly which, when pursued,
is always beyond our grasp, but which,
if you will sit down quietly, may alight upon you.
~Author Unknown

Three weeks before my sixtieth birthday, my husband Greg announced that our marriage had "lost its spark." Never mind that we'd invested thirty-five years in each other. Never mind that we shared three children. Never mind that we had four grandchildren under the age of two and another on the way.

He wanted out.

"You get half of everything," Greg told me. "I just want a chance to try to find my soul mate before it's too late."

I declined his offer to let me stay in the spacious 1840s-era farmhouse we'd lovingly restored and in which we'd raised our family. Too much work. And too many emotional ghosts. I needed a fresh start. So, once the shock had subsided enough that I could pull myself out of bed in the mornings, I went house hunting and found a small contemporary home that felt just right.

Then I began the overwhelming task of deciding what to take with me and what to leave behind.

Some of the decisions were easy. I'd leave Greg's ugly brown recliner and take my great-grandmother's solid oak dining table. I'd take our wedding china and leave the dishes adorned with moose and elk and grizzly bears. He could have the pool table but I'd take the treadmill.

Heirlooms from separate sides of the family posed no problem. Greg would keep the antique writing desk that had belonged to his mother; I'd take the cast iron skillet that had belonged to mine. I took the Bible with my grandmother's notes scribbled in the margin; he kept the Purple Heart his father had earned in World War II. Greg's Little League baseball glove would stay; my tennis racket from junior high would come with me.

We were even able to agree on items like family photos (he kept half, I took half) and pets (I took the dog and he kept the cat).

Day by day and room by room, our possessions were split in two. It seemed almost too easy. Until that first night when I lay alone in a too-big bed in my new house. As I tossed and turned and eventually gave up hope that sleep would come, I began to understand that I had only decided which things to keep and which to let go. The really hard decisions hadn't yet been made.

And so, with tears streaming down my cheeks, I clicked on the bedside table lamp and took a pen and a notebook from the drawer.

At the top of a blank page, I wrote WHAT TO LEAVE BEHIND. The list wasn't long, but it was powerful. Anger. Resentment. Hurt. Desire for revenge. Fear, the most overwhelming emotion of all. Fear that I wasn't brave enough or smart enough or tough enough to weather this gigantic storm.

Atop the next page, I wrote WHAT TO KEEP. Try as I might, I could come up with only one item to put on the list: Happy Memories. Memories of bringing our newborn babies home from the hospital. Of the smell of wood smoke and fresh-cut Christmas trees. Of throwing hay from the barn loft to the horses waiting eagerly below. Of bicycle rides and basketball games and BB-shooting contests. Of tire swings and trampolines. Of fishing in the pond and catching nothing but snapping turtles. Of snuggling in front of the TV with a huge bowl of popcorn to share. Of Easter dresses and prom dresses and wedding dresses. I filled page after page of that notebook with happy memories.

By the time my fingers grew too stiff to grasp the pen, the sky outside my bedroom window was growing pink.

Thankfully, I was awake to witness the very first sunrise of my brand new life. A life that was sure to have its challenges and difficulties. But one which promised to be overflowing with joy.

~Jean Morris

57

Braver than Superman

Courage is not the absence of fear, but rather the judgement that
something else is more important than fear.
~Ambrose Redmoon

When I was a shy, skinny little girl, I loved going to the movies and watching my hero, Superman, fight the villains. As much as I loved Superman, I knew Superman didn't need to be brave because he was already tall and strong, a man of steel who could fly and run faster than a train. Even bullets bounced off of him. Superman had nothing to fear but Kryptonite.

On the other hand, I was a small nine-year-old who was afraid of my mother, my fourth grade teacher and the class bully Ernest Evans, who stole my lunch and hit me every chance he got.

When I grew up, I was still afraid of my mother, my boss and bullies.

I read books about courageous women who risked their lives sailing around the world, going to the Arctic, living in the jungle with gorillas and climbing Mt. Everest.

It took all the courage I had to take a bus to the mall, eat at a restaurant alone or to wear the color red.

My greatest fear was failure. What if I tried to do something and I failed? What if people laughed at me? What if I made a fool of myself?

I was such a late bloomer that I almost never bloomed at all. For years I believed a "super" man was going to save me, but I finally realized that I wasn't Lois Lane and I'd have to save myself.

It doesn't take courage to run a race you know you'll win. It takes courage to run a race you know you will lose.

I would run the race, take the chance.

I started doing things I was afraid to do. If I failed, then I would fail publicly and spectacularly. If I came in last, well, in every race someone has to be first and someone has to be last—and I'd rather be last than a spectator on the sidelines. You only fail if you don't have the courage to try.

I stopped wearing beige and started wearing red.

I always wanted to be an artist and have my own gallery. So I rented a gallery and filled it with my paintings. The first week, only two people came into the gallery and they laughed at my paintings. The second week, a woman offered me twenty dollars for the frame on one of my paintings. She didn't want the picture, only the frame. The third week, I closed the gallery. I failed and I didn't die. My failure wasn't on the six o'clock news. I survived.

A year later I tried again. I painted better paintings and the gallery was in a better location. I sold eighty of my paintings the first month. I used the money to go to Australia by myself. I rode a camel and got bitten by a wombat. It was fantastic! I'd been afraid to take a bus to the mall and now I'd flown halfway around the world alone.

I'd always wanted to travel but I'd never wanted to travel alone. I realized I couldn't sit at home waiting for a travelling companion to appear. If I wanted to see the world, I'd have to do it alone.

Each success was a victory that gave me courage to aim higher, try harder and do more. Each failure made me stronger.

I stopped saying "no" to things outside my comfort zone and started saying "YES!" to life.

If someone asked for volunteers, my hand was the first one up.

I volunteered to work in a mission in New Mexico for three months. I loved it so much I stayed two years.

I went to a rodeo and they asked for people to volunteer to ride wild burros in a race. Never mind I was twice as old as the other riders, never mind I couldn't control my burro and he went in circles and even backwards at one point. Yes, I came in last, but how many women my age can say they've ridden a wild burro in a rodeo?

I always wanted to learn to speak a different language and I took classes at the community college. I tried to learn Italian, Japanese, German and Spanish. I discovered I'm very bad at languages, but now I can say "hello" and "goodbye" and count to ten in four other languages.

I rode an elephant at a circus and drove a stagecoach at an Old West frontier town. I spent three weeks panning for gold in Colorado and found thirty-six dollars' worth. That meant I earned about seven cents an hour panning for gold. It didn't matter. I was camping in the high Rockies, sleeping under the stars and listening to coyotes howl at the moon.

I was having adventures without the help, approval or companionship of anyone.

I have some very good friends, but they are sensible, cautious, careful and saving for their retirement. They aren't interested in riding wild burros (what if you break a hip?) or sleeping in the woods (what if a bear eats you?) or knowing how to count to ten in four languages.

They shake their heads and say, "You are so strong and independent. I'd never have the nerve to do the things you do. You are so brave."

"I'm braver than Superman," I say with a smile.

Do I have regrets? Of course. Life hasn't been easy for me. Many times it has been a struggle for survival. Do I get lonely? Sometimes, but nothing is lonelier than being with the wrong person.

I've had heartbreaking, humiliating failures and I've had great victories. When all is said and done, I want to feel I've lived the fullest life possible.

I grew up on the Kansas plains and I've had a lifelong fear of water, and I never learned to swim.

Someone just asked me if I'd like to go snorkeling in Hawaii next month. I said "YES!"

I don't want to live a timid, fearful life and I refuse to "be careful."

I'm running the race!

~April Knight

Chapter
6

Time to Thrive

Help the World Thrive

58

From Living on Change to Changing the World

Only those who dare to fail greatly can ever achieve greatly.
~Robert F. Kennedy

I grew up in Spokane, Washington, where I live now. So did my brother JC and my cousin Adam. My first entrepreneurial endeavor was in the seventh grade, when I got my dad to use his membership at Costco to buy those big tubs of licorice. I'd take one, stick it in my locker and make ten cents a piece selling them at school between classes. It was my first successful business — until I was shut down by my principal.

I'd always wanted to do my own thing, and college was not it. I figured I didn't want to be a doctor or a lawyer, and there was no entrepreneur class, so when I had the opportunity to run my own business, I thought, why not try it? I never looked back.

My brother JC was a huge influence on me. He thought of starting the first kiosk business that he owned in Chicago, making key chains and license plate frames. I worked for him for six months until I knew enough to go out on my own. I got myself a cargo van, filled it with stock, and drove up to the Canadian border. Then I drove all the way down the coast to Portland, Oregon, stopping at every mall, telling them about my product and putting in applications to set up kiosks. I didn't have any money so I slept in the van. Worked out of it, too.

The first bite was from the Southcenter Mall just south of Seattle, the largest mall in Washington State. From day one it was successful, and I worked every day for three years until I could start hiring people and get a break. Eventually I had fifteen sites set up all over the country. I did that for about thirteen years, until the market got saturated and my dad got sick, when I ended up selling all of my kiosks and moving back to Spokane.

After the move, it was hard to find work and we started losing a lot of money. My cars were repossessed. I was in danger of losing my house. My brother JC was in the same predicament. My cousin Adam was having trouble, too. No one wants to be on welfare, but that's where we found ourselves, all three of us looking for jobs and barely scraping by. I had to. I had no food, two kids and my wife… I used to have a different opinion of welfare, but once I needed it and it saved me, it changed my whole perspective. It was the safety net I needed.

Then JC had his idea. He remembered 2001, when he was the meat manager at a grocery store. He decided one day to see if people would be interested in buying forty-pound cases of chicken at a lower price instead of having the store separate it out, cut it up, put it on foam trays and wrap it, which would up the cost by at least two dollars per pound. He bet if people knew what kind of money they could save, they'd definitely go for it. He put out a sign-up sheet.

Nearly 1,000 people signed up. JC ordered $250,000 worth of chicken, when his budget for everything from the market was only $90,000. They told him he had probably just blown a ton of money and probably wasn't going to be there much longer. Not only did he sell the two truckloads of chicken he had already ordered, he got enough orders that he needed another half-truckload to fulfill them! He sold more chicken than had ever happened before in the history of the company and actually ended up going on a speaking tour around all the chain's different locations. It became kind of legendary.

JC never really thought he could do that regularly, so he let it drop. When he moved to Spokane and everything was circling the drain he thought to revisit that earlier idea. We made a deal with local brokers for the chicken, and by word of mouth alone we got orders for over 850 cases of chicken. It was crazy how well it went! The economy was tanking, people were losing jobs, and we were selling chicken for $1.49 a pound. Everyone was excited, especially us now that we could pay our own bills. With that, Zaycon Foods was born.

When my brother had the idea to do "Chicken Across America," we thought he was crazy. We were comfortable staying in Spokane, but here he was suggesting we do the same thing all over the country. We sat down and thought a bit about how we could get the word out to all the people we'd need to reach to make the plan a success. My cousin Adam and I went on the Internet looking for food bloggers and coupon bloggers, sending them messages saying we'd give them forty pounds of our chicken if they promised to write about it. We didn't say what to write, just to tell the readers.

We then split up and drove around to every blogger's house—about 450 of them—to deliver cases of chicken. I drove from Miami to San Diego. It was great! Everyone blogged about it. By that time we had a website set up where people could register for events, so when we opened up the sale it was crazy! We were just watching as people signed up, one after another. In the end, we sold twenty-eight truckloads of chicken. Then we realized. How on earth were we going to deliver twenty-eight truckloads of chicken? We hadn't even thought that far! We just thought it was an awesome idea. There was no business plan. We were creating something that had never been done before. In fact, if we were the kind of people who created business plans, we would have failed because the business plan wouldn't have worked! We just had to go ahead and think on or feet.

It was stressful, but comparing the stress of being on welfare to the stress of building a company, I'd take the stress of building a company any day. To go from zero, literally zero, watching your cars being repossessed and your house about to be taken away… Going through that really humbled me and helped me understand where my priorities needed to be… I wanted to help people.

My father passed away in 2009, my mother in 2012, and I felt like there were gaping holes in my life where my parents had been. I also knew that just having "stuff" would never fill those holes. But helping people? That's the real measure of success. That's what makes me feel whole again. This company has made it possible for people all over the country to succeed in ways that might not have been possible without the extra money they save by buying their groceries from Zaycon.

We even won an award from the Post-Harvest Project for being environmentally conscious and producing zero waste, something no one thought was even possible!

In the summer of 2012, one of our bloggers asked if we would like to be on *Good Morning America*. Um, yeah we did!

They came out and filmed one of our events, and then a month later we taped an interview segment. When it aired, we had over 25,000 people come to our site to sign up. It actually crashed our server, but it was incredible. Having GMA's support really legitimized our brand, and the whole business just expanded.

More recently I started working with members of Congress to help get a paragraph added to a USDA farm bill to start a pilot program that would enable people on food stamps to use their EBT cards online, where they can get better deals for what they need. All online grocery companies will benefit from the program, but ours will be the first company to implement the change.

When you want to change things, people are so quick to tell you that you can't do it. All that does is motivate me even more. Everything you know was created by people who are no smarter than you and I, and you can influence it, you can change it. This experience has taught me that you can change things. You don't have to accept your situation.

With a little courage and a lot of goodwill, anyone can change the world.

~Mike Conrad

To see the *Good Morning America* piece about Mike and JC Conrad
and their company, use this link:
https://www.youtube.com/watch?v=BTgUj27ebCw

And to learn more about Zaycon Foods, visit www.zayconfoods.com

59

The Future Belongs to Those Who Believe

The future belongs to those who believe in the beauty of their dreams.
~Eleanor Roosevelt

I was only sixteen when my father was brutally robbed and murdered just outside the bar he owned. It was a normal morning in Camden, New Jersey and he was opening up for business as usual. That day my world changed forever.

I had always dreamed of being an actress so when I was twenty-two years old I packed my bags to move to Las Vegas with my best friend. We had met a man named Bob Kane while we were on vacation and he said he was opening a movie studio in Las Vegas. I was so certain that this was going to be my big break in the movie industry!

When we arrived my heart sank. There wasn't much of a studio at all; in fact it was just a tiny office. Then, to make matters worse, two weeks later Bob was off to Los Angeles to work on *Batman* with Bill Finger.

There I was, jobless in Las Vegas. My mother could barely make ends meet herself back in New Jersey, so I had to figure out a way to stay in Las Vegas. My spirit kicked into survival mode. I worked at a used car lot during the day, called out bingo at night at a casino, and later found a temporary job as a production coordinator for the hit show *Kojak*. They were taping several shows in Las Vegas. It was Telly Savalas who inspired me to open my own talent agency. I love helping people and creating connections, so this sounded like a fun adventure for me.

Sadly though, I couldn't even afford the three hundred dollars for a business license at the time. As luck would have it, Ellie Janssen, the wife of *The Fugitive* star David Janssen, gave me a small loan. I called my one-woman operation the Baskow Agency. I decided to work daytime as a receptionist for Bobby Morris's talent agency and share office space with him while answering his calls and mine. I was making only fifty dollars a week.

At that time in the seventies there was only one other agency in Vegas. I actually "broke the monopoly" for being the first full-service talent agency owned and operated by a Jewish woman. Unfortunately, this evolved into years of threats on my life and bullet holes in my car.

I started small. I was hired to book the principal actors for a Schmidt's beer commercial starring David Brenner. I was so proud. I remember thinking this was actually going to work! I found a whole new level of inspiration and motivation as I started to see my efforts pay off. And every dollar I earned brought me one step closer to being able to reopen my father's unsolved murder case.

Certain days it felt like it would never work out. Then doors would open and more connections would be made. Not just any connection, but the kind that lands a major business relationship for over thirty years with a company like Caesars Palace. I'll never forget getting a call from Jilly Rizzo, a famous restaurant owner in New York and a dear friend of Frank Sinatra. He asked me to meet with him and Ol' Blue Eyes to discuss my representing their protégé, Marlene Ricci. I made a friend for life that day and Frank made one call that stopped all the threats on my life.

The days turned into weeks and the weeks turned into months. Along the way I had to not only develop my business but also overcome the fear that had hung over me like a cloud since my father's murder. I spent forty-five years being afraid, even tolerating a bad marriage just so I wouldn't have to be alone. But I believe that you can't just curl up and become a victim. You have to focus on having only healthy relationships in your personal and professional life, and you need to set out to make a difference in the world.

Now the years have flown by and my life is a whirlwind of amazing stories. I wouldn't trade it for the world. I know I was destined for this line of work and my gift and purpose gets to shine every day. My career is my happy space, and as I've thrived in my own life, I've been privileged to fulfill the dreams of thousands of people in the entertainment industry.

I've also received more awards then I ever dreamed possible, from "Small Business Owner of the Year" to "Top Destination Management and Event Management Company" five years in a row. The Las Vegas Chamber of Commerce named me "Woman of the Year." I've been dubbed one of the top "star brokers in the world" as well as the "Queen of Las Vegas" on a TV show.

I've also been blessed to work with charities from all over the world raising millions of dollars for those in need. This has led me to people who have been instrumental in helping me close my father's case, including Joe Schillaci from A&E and Lenny DePaul from *Manhunters*, who I met at a charity event through my dear friend Cheryl Kagan. After Lenny and Joe have spent four years working on my dad's cold case we are extremely close to identifying the murderer.

Dad would be proud that I have continued trying to find his killer, but most of all I am personally getting closure, and for that my dad would be even prouder. Never, ever give up.

It all started on a street in Camden, New Jersey with the brutal murder of my father. I've never forgotten him and never stopped trying to solve his case. And just as he, in his small way as a bar owner, brought people together and made connections, I have carried on the tradition. It's still all about the people and acting as the bridge between them. I'm so grateful that I've been able to live a life of purpose that revolves around helping people help each other.

~Jaki Baskow

60

Reclaiming Myself

*I have found that among its other benefits, giving
liberates the soul of the giver.*
~Maya Angelou

For nine years, my sister Carla battled ovarian cancer. In some ways, it became my battle as well as I made the trip from my home in Loveland, Colorado to her home in Utah numerous times a year, often staying months at a time.

I was grateful that I had the opportunity to be with her, to support her during the grueling rounds of chemotherapy (twenty-five in all) and the inevitable sickness and weakness that followed.

In the meantime, I put much of my life on hold. I let my writing go. I asked to be released from my positions in our church. Cherished friendships withered from neglect as I focused on helping my sister.

When the disease finally claimed Carla, I was in danger of allowing it to claim me, too. So intense was my grief that I could barely function. In addition, I scarcely knew who I was anymore. So much of my life had revolved around taking care of my sister that I felt I no longer had an identity and feared falling into depression. (I suffer from chemical depression, a disease that runs in my family.)

It was time to take a stand. It was time to take care of myself.

An e-mail message early one morning pulled me from my funk. My friend Janet, the leader of the women's organization in our church, wanted me to visit a new lady in our congregation with her.

My initial reaction was to say, "No. I'm sorry. I can't." I could easily fall back on mourning as an excuse.

With the Lord's guidance, however, I found myself agreeing.

Janet arrived to pick me up at the appointed time. "I'm so glad you could go today," she said. "I really needed someone to go with me."

Someone needed me? It was exactly what I needed.

Together, Janet and I visited the lady, who eagerly welcomed us. She and I discovered we had much in common, including each having an adopted child.

This positive experience prompted me to reach out in other ways. In talking about another lady in the church, Cathy, who lived in a care facility due to the effects of a stroke, Janet expressed her concern that Cathy was lonely, receiving few visitors.

With Janet's encouragement, I volunteered to go see Cathy.

Her pleasure upon seeing me touched my heart. What I planned as a one-time visit grew to several visits a month. Upon discovering that Cathy had an insatiable sweet tooth, especially for anything chocolate, I made it a point to bring her a treat every time I went to see her.

"I love you, Jane," Cathy said at the end of one visit and reached out to hug me.

"I love you, too," I said, returning the hug, and knew that it was true. In serving her, I had learned to love her.

With the help of church leaders, we made plans to record church meetings and take the tapes to Cathy. In looking beyond myself to others who were in need, I became more involved with life and less involved with myself.

With each step, I gained confidence to take another... and another. I picked up my writing once more and began submitting stories. I started my walking and exercise program again.

My grief over my sister's passing remains, but I am reclaiming myself and, even, to my surprise, thriving, with new purpose and interests.

~Jane McBride Choate

61

What Diana Ross Taught Me

You know, you do need mentors, but in the end, you
really just need to believe in yourself.
~Diana Ross

My first real, paying job was at Bloomingdale's in Stamford, Connecticut. It was 1980, the height of the disco era, and I was a high school student. It seemed like my destiny to work there. My grandparents and other family lived near the store, and my mother had been a shopper there since it opened in the 1950s. My mother even joked that she went into labor with me there—at the time, the store had psychedelic sixties rugs that made her dizzy—and she headed right to the hospital to have me!

I worked during school breaks and such. It was a part-time sales job and I moved from department to department as needed. Some of my co-workers were pretty amazing, including a survivor of the Titanic. Marvin Traub, President of Bloomingdale's, maintained an office there. And the famed Kal Ruttenstein—the man many credit with making Bloomies exciting in that era—was often there as well.

But not only were the workers amazing, so were the customers. I met dozens of celebrities and great designers, including Carol Burnett, Lucille Ball, Ralph Lauren, Willi Smith, Paul Newman, Joanne Woodward, Jack Paar, Phil Donahue, Donna Karan—and Diana Ross.

One day, I was asked to assist the personal shopping office. This was the team that handled shopping (mostly) for the rich and famous. Clients would have a salesperson assigned to them, and we would help customers make their shopping dreams come true. The head of personal shopping pulled me aside and asked how I was around celebrities. "Fine, no problem," I told her. Which was true. I always remained calm, no matter what was going on. I was (and still am) pretty laid-back. She then asked, "Can you handle difficult customers?" Again, I said, "Fine, no problem." This was tested many times over during my years in retail, and in astounding ways, yet I maintained a Zen calm. After taking a deep breath, she said, "Okay, I'd like to introduce you to Ms. Diana Ross."

There she was. I resisted the impulse to babble about how wonderful she looked, or how amazing her songs were. I was sure she knew all that already! I got right to work. After getting lots of clothing and accessories together from around the store, on rolling racks and in carts, and getting everything to the fitting rooms, Ms. Ross and her two young daughters proceeded to try things on. As was the standard then, the salesperson would go into the fitting room too, helping customers in and out of their fashions, taking dresses over their heads, etc. Much like dressing people in the theater or for the movies, there were no boundaries. You had to get over any awkwardness fast. I probably saw dozens of celebs in their scanties (as my grandmother would have delicately put it) and it was all business all the time.

Ms. Ross tried on one dress and asked what I thought. I said something like, "It makes your butt look huge, don't get it!" She asked my opinion again when she tried on the next outfit. I told her, "Nope, your bosom is all wrong in that." I continued to bring her more and different things, until she looked as amazing as possible — and I told her so. She spent hours trying on clothes and ended up buying an *enormous* pile of clothing.

I didn't understand why anyone would have said that she was difficult. But it turned out that I was the first personal shopper to treat her properly. To the shock of everyone in the department, she hugged me and said, "You're the first person who actually told me how I looked.

Everyone else was so scared of me they just said 'You look great!' no matter what. Tim, I want to work with you again!"

So as I worked on and off at Bloomingdale's through my teen years, I'd pull together outfits for Ms. Ross. Not a bad gig. Other people were sent my way, too. The sales relationship worked beautifully, for everyone. I learned a lot about myself then, about being true to myself and my customers, about creating lasting relationships through honesty, and about making the sale — when the product is truly good for my customer.

Here's what I learned from Diana Ross:

1. Treat people like people. They are not to be oohed and ahhed over. You can't get nervous because a person is a celebrity (or rich). The customer has a goal. You have to remember what your job is and do it.

2. Be honest. If your butt looks awful in a pair of jeans, don't you want to know that before you buy them? I do. Find a way to make the selling experience real, and true, no matter what. I am not saying to be mean — far from it. In sales, you are building a relationship, and good relationships are based on honesty. If it's a difficult topic you have to bring up, put it out there. They will appreciate the honesty. Just like Ms. Ross.

3. Ask questions, show the products, ask for the sale, repeat. Overall, the story has never changed from my early days in retail, through my post-college years as a manager at Macy's, Pottery Barn, Old Navy, and Guess, to my years selling data products and services for two companies eventually acquired by Merkle, or to more recent times as a digital marketer and e-commerce leader. (I'm a start-up co-founder and CMO, a consultant, and a head of e-commerce right now.)

~Timothy Peterson

62

Take That, Universe!

Affirm the positive, visualize the positive, and expect
the positive, and your life will change accordingly.
~Author Unknown

W hat makes some people defy the odds whereas other people facing the same circumstances fall apart? Is it genetic? Is it all about attitude? I believe that, more than anything, it's our state of mind. For instance, when I wake up in a crappy mood, the first thing I do is adjust my internal language. Then I change my physiology, too, because when you stand up straight you feel better. Putting a smile on my face seems to change everything, too. It's amazing how that works.

Another major factor that affects my attitude and success is peer influence. I believe in surrounding myself with people who think positively, and most of them are dealing, or have dealt, with issues of their own.

We all have issues that we're working through, even if we don't always wear it on our faces. When I meet people for the first time, I don't have to say, "Hey, nice to meet you. You know what? I was raped and shot…." It's more appropriate to say, "Hi, my name is Courtney and I love sailing, going out and spending time with friends."

So how did I get to this positive thinking mode? I've had several setbacks in my life, wasting many years feeling I was "not enough," which led to unrestrained weight gain. I blew up to a whopping 383 pounds to be exact. I just barely functioned at that point. I would go to work, where no one would look me in the eye, where I would be bullied and eat all day. Then I'd come home and eat and hide and cry "why me," always ashamed and yet always feeling safe from the outside world. I couldn't walk or stand on my own, had to use crutches, and had many health issues: sleep apnea, diabetes and cholesterol problems. What a way to live, eh? Yet I did just that for five years. I was slowly dying. Did I really want to die? I wasn't sure.

What changed? My grandson. He came up to me and gave me a great big hug and said "I love you." No judgment, just those three simple words that I had not heard in decades. It changed everything. I changed my diet; I joined a gym and began my long journey to becoming a healthier me. I lost a total of 205 pounds! I felt success with each weigh-in. I was able to walk without those awful crutches after losing seventy-five pounds. I no longer had to wear sacks; I could fit in normal clothes and shop in normal retail stores. To top it off, people began looking me in the eye and talking to me.

I went about changing other things in my life, taking big steps by working on me from the inside, and little steps — my reaction to things, my interactions with other people — making progress along the way. Yes, life was getting better and I was on top of the world. Until I felt it was time to make some changes in my home, and then the worst day in my life happened.

I hired a handyman to paint and fix some things around my home. This man came in and took his time doing a simple task, painting my wall, asking questions about living alone and making uncomfortable remarks. He made me so frightened that I asked him to leave, turning to open the door for him. Then I felt this searing hot/cold pain in my back in two places, my knees buckled and I fell to the ground helpless to everything this man did to me.

This man shot me in the back twice. To make matters worse, as I lay on the ground dying, he raped me. I woke up in the hospital several days later very "lucky to be alive" as the nurses and doctors told me. Really! My mind was screaming at me: "Why did you lose the weight? Why did you let this guy in? Why, why, why?" I felt so defeated. All I could do was wonder what I did to deserve this.

I couldn't leave my home on my own for eight months, pitying myself and diving deep into depression. I was heavily medicated. The big question I kept asking myself was, "Should I die and just be done with this pain?" I considered it many times, but something kept stopping me. That little voice inside kept telling me I could get past this, I could succeed at anything I tried.... Finally, I decided to no longer be a victim.

I started healing bit by bit. I started believing it was not my fault, listening again to my self-help CDs, getting back in touch with people from my past. I began volunteering to crew Tony Robbins seminars, as I had in the past. I was healing, not with drugs, but by being with incredible people who themselves had overcome adversity. I started listening to what others thought of me. I started to believe I was a worthwhile person. Finally, I began to flourish.

Four years later I have a successful coaching business, helping others achieve their goals. I teach others about their state of mind, what they believe, the interpretation of the vocabulary they use on themselves, their body language, and where it can take them in life. I teach them what surrounding themselves with positive people can do in their lives and how believing in themselves can move mountains.

I am thriving; I am successful beyond my dreams in the friendships I've developed and in the business I started. I know I am loved and worthy of this love. My mantra is "I am always open and deserving to receive all that is good from the universe; I will succeed in fountains of abundance." And I have.

~Courtney Campbell

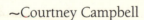

63

Thriving While Grieving

Help your brother's boat across, and your own will reach the shore.
~Hindu Proverb

A part of me felt guilty, but I knew that I needed to honor my brother by moving forward with my life's purpose. I never expected to be launching a new business and a personal development seminar one year after my younger brother suddenly passed away.

On the day Taranveer passed, my world came crashing down. Just four days prior, I had told a friend how completely happy I was for the first time ever. My parents were also strong emotionally and ready to conquer the world. Taranveer had gotten his dream job, one he had been seeking for a year.

I had moved back in with my parents three months earlier, so I had spent every day with my brother before he left for his job. He left two days after my birthday, and I was mad at him for not wishing me a happy birthday or saying Happy Father's Day to our dad.

When we said goodbye, I hugged him and told him I loved him and wished him the best. He called me a few minutes later from the car to remind me to find his speakers. That was our relationship—we were really close friends who forgave each other and went back to our dynamic relationship as siblings.

The morning we learned he had died, I was standing with my

parents and it felt like his spirit was standing beside me, telling me that we have a greater purpose and not to grieve for him too much. We decided as a family that we would celebrate him, laugh and tell his funny stories. We kept that atmosphere in our home instead of the pain and sorrow in traditional Sikh grieving households. Not following the norm, we laughed at the funeral and his pictures. Some elders of the community commented that we seemed unaffected by the death, but they didn't know we cried ourselves to sleep every night.

The year after his passing became a year of travel and self-discovery for me. I finally did the international consulting work I had always wanted to do. I was healthy and I made new friendships. I was a changed person.

Now that I had lost my identity as a sister, I had to rediscover who I was. And I had become the sole caregiver for my parents. I had to take that into consideration for all my decisions — where I wanted to live, where they would live, how I could support them as they aged and what emotional support they needed. I knew I wanted to be there to support them while they rebuilt their life.

In the Sikh culture, there were some who told my parents they had nothing left because now they didn't have a son. My parents fought back, telling everyone that their daughter was everything and more.

I had a powerful conversation with my dad, who said, "We are meant to be of greater service and contribute to our community and that is why we are facing such hardships. We need to step outside ourselves and be of service as that is how we can honor him."

As soon as my brother had passed, I had decided to have a ball hockey tournament in one year as a fun way to get everyone together, celebrate him and contribute to kids in sports. I cried each day of the tournament, but in the end knew it was the right thing to do. We contributed happiness and memories to those who attended the tournament and those who benefited from it.

I also had decided that a year after his passing, I would step up my contribution in a big way. So I launched my personal coaching company, focusing on ethnic women aligning to their passion/message by building the career and life they love.

I came forward and hosted a weekend seminar two days after what would have been Taranveer's birthday. He was always the proudest of me when I helped change people's lives. He was always telling his friends about me and all the cool things I did. I hope that he's talking about me wherever he is, saying, "That is my sister, the one who realized that living her life with purpose is more important than crying for my loss."

~Manpreet Dhillon

64

Time to Share

If you have a candle, the light won't glow any dimmer
if I light yours off of mine.
~Steven Tyler

One day while I was sitting
Feeling sorry for myself,
I started listing my laments;
Took my pen down from the shelf...

"My stringy hair so needs a perm
My clothes are old and worn;
No money to go shopping with,
I'm lonely, bored, forlorn.
No close friends to visit with
To share some times of fun,
My days are filled with dull routine
From dawn to setting sun."

But then God pricked my heart with shame
And made me think again;
He gave me something new to write
And words flowed from my pen...

"The cancer patient has no hair
And would gladly welcome yours;

Your clothes would warm the homeless one
Whose rags are thin and torn.
The money you'd go shopping with
The truly poor could use;
Would you share your wealth, my child
Or spend it as you choose?

The daily chores I've given you
Are blessings sweet and rare;
The paralyzed would love your work
And count each day as fair.
There are lonely people everywhere
Waiting for a friend.
They too, are bored and need some fun,
They're just around the bend."

And now I see things differently
I'm rich beyond compare!
I've got to run, there's someone near
...Who needs to know I care.

~Denise A. Dewald

65

Now I Know

Peace cannot be kept by force; it can only be achieved by understanding.
~Albert Einstein

It is almost twenty years later. That is how long it has taken for me to truly understand why a woman would leave a baby girl, just a few days after her birth, on a desolate, wintry street in a forlorn, bleak city called Hefei, in Anhui Province, China.

"How could a mother ever do that?" well-meaning friends and acquaintances would ask, incredulously. "Just leave a baby on the street, to freeze to death."

My response in the early days after my late husband Gregory and I first met our daughter Lili was always from my own selfish perspective. We had been desperate for a child, after years of infertility treatments, miscarriages, and two ectopic pregnancies. As far as I was concerned, that mother left the baby there for ME. Somehow, whoever she was, she knew I would be a good mother to her girl child.

"China has a one-child policy," I'd remind people. "It's against the law to have more than one child, and people need boys to work in the fields and take care of them in their old age."

"But to just leave a baby on the street?" the more persistent ones would ask. "Couldn't they take the baby to an orphanage?"

"Yes," I'd inform them, "sometimes babies were left outside orphanages. But the mothers had to run away, because if they got caught, they'd be arrested. It's against the law in China to abandon a baby."

Truth be told, we had no idea where Lili was left—in an orphanage, at a police station, or on a street. We were given a piece of paper showing the name of the street, but it was most likely fake. Some adoptive parents were given notes that were found pinned to their babies, but most were skeptical about their veracity.

"How much did you have to pay for your baby?" less tactful people would ask. After all, we were living on the Upper West Side of New York City then. I'm reminded of a wonderful article by Joan Acocella, a staff writer for *The New Yorker*, in which she attempts to explain to non-New Yorkers why New Yorkers can seem rude: "People on the bus will say, 'I have the same handbag as you. How much did you pay?'" ("My Kind of Town," *Smithsonian* magazine, May 2008)

Were Gregory and I guilty of buying a baby on the black market? We had worked with a reputable adoption agency in New York City, a pioneer in the field of international adoption. It's not like we put an ad in the newspapers in China saying we were looking to buy a baby.

But there was the matter of the thousands of dollars in cash that Gregory was instructed to bring, in a money belt, and the payoffs made by our Chinese guide to local officials. Best not to think of the darker aspects of what we were doing, or the harsh realities of life in China in 1994, pre-boom.

And Lili was never one to ask about her birth parents, unlike many adopted children. Didn't she care? Wasn't she curious?

After Gregory died from melanoma in 2007, when Lili was thirteen, I decided it would be a good idea for her to go back to China, to connect with her roots, so to speak. She was amenable to the idea, so in the summer of 2009 she went on a superb program called China Prep.

"What was it like," I asked her, "to see all those people who looked like you?"

"It was fine, Mother," she responded. "It was China, and duh, they were all Chinese!"

She is unflappable, resilient, wise. And inscrutable. She must wonder about her birth parents. She must feel like she was abandoned. She must have attachment issues. All adopted children do, the experts tell us. And she must know that girls were unwanted, discarded, in the country of her birth.

Perhaps it's for this reason that I decided, at age sixty, when Lili left for college, that my cause in life would be helping other girls born into misogynistic societies.

And boy, did I ever find one of the worst places on earth to be born a girl—Afghanistan—for my volunteer work. I signed on as a mentor with the Afghan Women's Writing Project (AWWP), founded in 2009 by American journalist Masha Hamilton. Today, 160 Afghan women across five provinces are enrolled in AWWP's workshops.

One of the young writers I mentor is Zahra, a sixteen-year-old from a Taliban-controlled province in Afghanistan. She is one of nine children, the daughter of uneducated farmers who place great value on education for their children in the face of disapproval. Here is what she wrote:

I became a feminist because I could not tolerate seeing my neighbor beat his wife. I could not listen to my teacher call me a bad girl for working on a project with boys. I could not tolerate injustice towards women. I could not see women stoned for choosing their future. I could not stand to see a man who raped a young girl walk freely in the street and not even be ashamed.

Zahra stayed at my apartment in New York City during spring break from a New England boarding school, which she currently attends on scholarship, and I was amazed at her courage. Wearing a hijab, blue jeans, a cropped blazer I bought for her at H&M, and sneakers, she looked like any high school kid on the streets of the Upper West Side.

When she showed me photos of her family back home in the wheat fields, it hit me how far she has traveled to obtain an education. She is here because she feels she can learn enough to return and help her country. There's a small group of girls like her, scattered across boarding schools in the northeast, far from home and loved ones. How do they do it?

Once when another young Afghan student, Sabira, stayed with me, she asked me to say hello to her mother back home. With zero preparation, I suddenly found myself face to face in that creepy Skype space with another mother, on the other side of the world. She is illiterate, married at a young age to a man who went to college but then had his hopes of becoming an engineer taken away by constant war. Now he works several menial jobs in order to send his daughters to school.

"Liz," Sabira told me, "she wants to thank you, for having me stay with you."

"Tell her she is very welcome," I said. "Tell her I admire her. I know how much she misses you."

It hit me then that Sabira is the same age as Lili, and this woman in black could be the same age as my child's birth mother.

And now I know. I have seen the face of a woman who could let her daughter go for a better life. I have looked into her eyes. She thanked me, when in fact I should thank her. She has given me the greatest gift of all, which is understanding.

~Elizabeth Titus

66

Finding a Way

Happiness quite unshared can scarcely be called
happiness; it has no taste.
~Charlotte Brontë

Having shared my heart and home with my fiancé for almost fifteen years, I was devastated when he informed me that he was ending our relationship and moving out of our home within twenty-four hours. I had to put my heartbreak on hold though, as I needed to focus on how I was going to buy the house from him and continue to pay for my daughter's college education while being self-employed.

After a critical analysis of my financial status, I realized that I was relatively close to being able to buy out the house that I had cherished for all those years, but was going to have difficulty meeting my daughter's college expenses. As my daughter had always been a bright and dedicated student, I did not want to impede her education, so I looked at my options. While getting a roommate wasn't my first choice, I realized that my empty guest room would be very suitable for someone who needed a temporary, comfortable living arrangement.

With much trepidation, but with a resolve to finding a way to make things work, I posted a listing for the extra room. I was pleased to find one roommate who had to move into the area to take care of his father who had stage IV liver cancer. As it turned out, the house became a sanctuary for him, as he was able to find peace in my beautiful back yard to endure the struggles he encountered during this emotionally painful time.

After his departure, my next roommate also found added benefit from my home. He was transferred to the area by his employer and arrived at my home in a state of disarray, both physically and emotionally. He was almost 100 pounds overweight, was in the middle of a divorce, and was having to assume a major responsibility in a new location for his employer.

This roommate benefitted from my guidance in helping him lose seventy-six pounds, which he has kept off for several years. In addition, my back yard also provided a soothing environment for him to work through the end of a thirty-year marriage.

While my roommates received benefits from living here, I was afforded the opportunity to pay for my daughter's education as well as focus my efforts on healing my mind and heart from the loss of my relationship.

I found the inner strength to boldly attempt an option that I might not have explored if my desperation did not motivate me. What I learned from this process was much more than I anticipated. From my first roommate, I learned about sacrifice and the power that love of a parent can give us. He left his job and his home to travel to a part of the country that he had no interest in. He literally put his life on hold so that he could be available for his father. He took a minimum-wage job to make ends meet, which afforded him the flexibility to spend as much time with his dad as possible. He conducted himself with compassion and dignity during one of the most difficult times of his life.

He taught me that while I might have been struggling, I could still choose how I wanted to behave. I could have crouched in a corner feeling sorry for myself. Or I could, like he did, face the situation realistically and let the love I had for my child guide me to deal with my circumstances with compassion and dignity.

My second roommate taught me that with determination a person could achieve great things. His commitment to his weight management and fitness program was admirable, and he did it without complaint and with consistent perseverance. He also taught me that when life gives you a new opportunity, you can choose to allow fear of the unknown to hold you back, or you can take a chance and see if there are additional benefits for you to realize.

My daughter has graduated not only from college, but also from Le Cordon Bleu in Paris and has started her own culinary business. Seeing what she has accomplished at such a young age is reward enough for the choices that I made.

In addition, my heart and spirit have not only healed but also blossomed. I have taken the time and made the commitment to myself to heal and move forward. There were times when I wondered if I had the inner strength to once again reach a place of peace, contentment, and joy in my life. I have to thank my roommates for helping guide me in this journey and my daughter for her daily reminder that with compassion, dignity, determination, and perseverance, life can be filled with the riches that matter the most.

~Judith Fitzsimmons

67

An Open Heart

The most incredible thing about miracles is that they happen.
~G.K. Chesterton

I've been told by religious leaders, mentors and most often by my parents, that in the worst of times come your biggest blessings. This couldn't be truer than in the case of my nephew, Cole.

At fifteen months of age, Cole was diagnosed with severe Ebstein's anomaly, a rare heart condition where the valve between the chambers on the right side of the heart does not work properly. This results in blood leaking backward, creating an oversized right atrium and causing the right ventricle to expand as it pumps harder and harder to push blood to the lungs. Over time, the enlarged right side of the heart weakens and heart failure develops. At the time of Cole's diagnosis, surgical interventions had been unsuccessful on other patients. The best we could hope for was that would change with time. Needless to say, my sister-in-law Shelley was devastated, as was the entire family. It seemed impossible that this outwardly thriving little boy could have a potentially fatal heart condition, and all we could do was wait.

Each year, Cole would meet with his wonderful cardiologist for an echocardiogram and, later, treadmill tests. I committed to both Cole and Shelley that I would be there for every appointment. Having worked in a hospital for years as a respiratory therapist, "medical talk" was my language and Shelley appreciated the second set of ears. The first time I saw Cole's heart as they performed the echo, I struggled to catch my breath. I knew I couldn't let Shelley see the shock on my face. Cole sensed my fear and reached out to touch my arm. With a big proud smile on his face, he said, "Aunt Linda, that's MY heart." What a blessing! I said a little prayer to myself and smiled through the rest of the exam.

Afterward I gave Cole his gift for being so brave — we went to lunch and then to a playground close to their home. For years, we repeated this scenario and Cole's condition remained basically the same, as did the limited treatment options.

In January 2008, I met Cole and Shelley at Loma Linda University Children's Hospital for Cole's annual stress test, during which he quickly tired. His electrocardiogram showed his heart beginning to fail. As I pushed back the fear and panic, I stood up and encouraged Cole to keep going, knowing his cardiologist needed him to push on so she would have all the information necessary to determine Cole's best treatment options. Finally she said, "Stop." She explained it was time to consult with a cardiothoracic surgeon. Upon hearing this, all the color left Shelley's face. I knew she was in complete shock. She has been such a rock for Cole throughout the years, and now it was my turn to step up for her.

In March 2008, my brother Charlie, Shelley, Cole and I met with Dr. Leonard Bailey, an internationally recognized authority on congenital heart surgery. Dr. Bailey explained that Cole's heart was failing and he needed surgical intervention. Dr. Bailey went on to say he had been working on a procedure to rebuild the tricuspid valve and resize the right-side chambers. He seemed very confident.

When I asked when he planned to perform the surgery, his reply was "July 8th." I was instantly relieved and took this to be a clear sign from God. That day is my favorite for many reasons — it is my baby sister's birthday, I was told I was in remission from cancer on July 8th, and several other wonderful events and blessings have happened on that date.

Surgery was scheduled, and Dr. Bailey advised us to go on as usual. This was certainly easier said than done, at least for me. For days following the appointment, I could think of nothing else. I couldn't focus or sleep. I cried a lot. I questioned my faith, just as I had done after first hearing about Cole's diagnosis years earlier. Finally, an idea came to me. If I could raise enough money for Loma Linda to benefit other children with similar conditions, maybe God would look favorably on Cole and his upcoming surgery.

So the fundraising efforts began. I organized a meeting with my co-workers, friends, and family to brainstorm how to raise lots of money in only three months. The ideas and help kept coming. We had a rummage sale, a coin drive, and a recycling drive. E-mails were sent from all over the world, from friends and from friends of friends, all pledging donations and promising to keep Cole in their prayers. We hosted a silent auction and something we called a H'Art Show. Businesses throughout Southern California, including the local professional sports teams, donated hundreds of auction items, and five local artists donated their beautiful art.

We filled my business with paintings and a huge buffet while the vacant store next door was filled with silent auction items. We turned the parking lot in front into a red-carpet reception with dozens of tables and chairs and even a red carpet. Hundreds of people attended the event and most returned the following morning for our blood drive and bone marrow registry. We were able to net 118 pints of blood and thirty-two bone marrow registrants.

Newspapers throughout Southern California came to interview Cole and wrote wonderful articles that netted additional donations for the hospital. All in all, we raised more than $27,000 in less than three months. Everyone rallied around this amazing eleven-year-old, flooding him with love and support as he went into surgery.

On Tuesday, July 8, 2008, Cole was to be the first surgery of the day. By noon, surgery hadn't begun and we were all anxious, wondering if he would have surgery that day at all. But, at approximately 1:00 p.m., he was taken back to the operating room and our family gathered in the main lobby to wait. We were given a small pager that would keep us updated as surgery progressed. We were told he had been intubated and was being "cooled," which freaked out Shelley, but I reassured her that was normal procedure and everything was at it should be.

The next page freaked me out: "We've started the procedure." All I could picture was my precious nephew's chest spread wide open. I got up and ran for the front doors, Shelley calling behind me, "Where are you going?" I quickly replied, "To get some fresh air. I'll be right outside." As I opened the doors, I was hit with 103 degrees of stifling hot air. I walked around to the side of the hospital, fell onto the grass under a shady tree and sobbed. At that moment, I realized I could have raised hundreds of thousands of dollars for the hospital and it wouldn't have been enough; it was all completely out of my control! I prayed and gave it all up to God, asking for strength to go back in and be there for Shelley and my family, whatever the outcome. After several minutes, I went back in. In an attempt to keep things light, I tried making small talk. I rubbed my very pregnant niece's feet, fetched beverages from the cafeteria, and paced.

At about the five-and-a-half-hour mark, we received a page to go to the fifth floor waiting room. Surgery was over. We all bolted for the elevators, my two brothers practically carrying my father, who walks slowly with a cane. The twelve of us piled into one elevator and my thoughts were spinning. How could surgery be over so soon? Dr. Bailey had estimated surgery would take close to seven hours; had something gone wrong? When we reached the fifth floor, Charlie, Shelley and I were escorted to a small waiting room just around the corner from the unit while the remainder of the family went to a large waiting room down the hallway.

About five minutes later, Dr. Bailey came in with a huge grin and said, "It went perfectly." I didn't comprehend or maybe believe what he had said and asked, "What do you mean? Did you have to put in a valve? Is he on an external pump? Is he okay? Will he need another surgery?" Again Dr. Bailey said, "It went perfectly. We didn't use a valve. I don't know if he'll ever need another surgery. He's okay and you can go see him in a couple of minutes. He's fine." Shelley screamed, Charlie jumped up and hugged Dr. Bailey, lifting his feet off the ground. All the while I was frozen to my chair, trying to take it all in. It was a miracle!

The rest of the family came running up the hallway after hearing

Shelley scream. Finally, I got up and shouted, "He's OKAY! It went PERFECTLY!" My family, all crying happy tears, took turns hugging Dr. Bailey as I leaned against the wall, looking at the picture hanging just outside the small waiting room. I must have seen it before, but never really saw it. It was a surgical team performing surgery on a child with a silhouette behind the surgeon — God's hand on the hand of the surgeon, performing a miracle.

Today, Cole is eighteen years old. He graduated from high school this year and is a thriving, healthy, strong, six-foot-two young man with his whole life ahead of him.

~Linda M. Johnson

68

A Boost to My Confidence

All glory comes from daring to begin.
~Eugene F. Ware

I had been invited by my principal to attend an educational convention where the guest speaker was Grace Corrigan, whose daughter Christa McAuliffe was the first teacher to be sent into space. During the lunch, I reflected on that tragic moment on January 28, 1986 when Space Shuttle Challenger exploded only a minute into its journey, with no survivors. On this day, Mrs. Corrigan would speak not of how her daughter died, but how she lived.

Not wanting to miss a second of her presentation, I slipped out to the ladies' room before the program. On my return, I walked past another large, empty banquet room. The door was open and I saw a gray-haired woman, small in stature, sitting alone.

Worried that she might be sick or lost, I inquired, "Are you okay?"

Lifting her head and smiling she said, "Come on in. I'm fine, just gathering my thoughts." She had me to sit down and right away she asked my name, but refrained from giving me hers. Within a matter of minutes we were carrying on a conversation like we'd known each other for years... more of her inquiring and me responding.

Interestingly, for the past few months I had been contemplating returning to college to complete my degree. It had been almost thirty-five years since I had walked the halls of higher education. In record time, I expressed my fear of being too old for the challenge. After about twenty minutes she kindly excused herself, but not without parting words of wisdom. Looking at me with a grin and a pat on my hand, she quietly said, "Cindy, it's a big world out there. Don't let time pass you by. Go for that knowledge you are searching for in life!" After giving me a big hug, she left the room, never having given me her name.

I was overwhelmed with inspiration. Feeling as if an angel had been sent from the heavens to encourage me, my confidence and resolve were recharged.

Returning to the conference, I began explaining the chance meeting to my principal. Finally, the MC introduced the guest speaker. Climbing the stairs was a gray-haired woman, small in stature. I choked up as I recognized my angel. Somehow, my path had crossed with Grace Corrigan's, and now I was positive what my future would hold.

Within a few weeks, this fifty-two-year-old mother of four and grandmother of twelve was enrolled in a Women's External Degree program. As I continued my full-time job as an elementary tutor, the road was not easy. I'd be remiss if I didn't confess there were moments I was tempted to give up.

However, with the constant support of family and friends, I graduated in three years with academic honors. A few months later, I received a congratulatory note along with a photo of the Challenger crew from Grace wishing me luck on my future endeavors and reminding me to always keep the door open for my next adventure. My discovery? One is never too old to pursue a new dream… I'm living proof!

~Cindy L. Ely

69

Love Is Not Pain

Be careful to leave your sons well instructed rather
than rich, for the hopes of the instructed are better
than the wealth of the ignorant.

~Epictetus

H e pulled out the rifle, pointed the barrel right at my
face, and shouted profanities. I only had a few seconds
to react. I did the unimaginable. I cried and begged
him to forgive me. The only thought that entered my
mind was, "What would my son do if he lost his parents in a murder-
suicide?"

Those few seconds felt like a lifetime. Though the gun turned
out to be not loaded, that day has been deeply ingrained in my mind
forever. It was the day I would never look at my husband the same
way again, and yet, it would take me nearly seven more years to finally
leave him.

That life-altering event occurred one beautiful, sunny day in the
summer of 1996. We were a young couple with a beautiful toddler.
It was meant to be a day spent with my husband's family, barbecu-
ing and fishing at the park. The day turned dark quickly because of
our miscommunication. He had issues with anger management and
my issues as a codependent lover perpetuated our roller coaster of
a marriage. He often overreacted and overexpressed himself while I
suppressed my true feelings and stayed quiet. When we were doing

well as a couple, we were madly in love. When we struggled, it was toxic and life threatening.

I replayed in my head, so many times, how we got to a place of such bitterness and resentment. Perhaps marrying at age sixteen, before completely maturing, played a huge factor in our crumbling marriage. Or, perhaps I had been taught that unconditional love meant enduring any and all pain that comes with it. Whatever the case, I knew that something did not sit right with me and that I had to explore this burning flame flickering inside my gut.

As much as I despised him for treating me with disrespect, I realized that I co-created that situation because I stayed silent for so long. My husband often told me I provoked the abuse. Though I logically knew that wasn't true, I hadn't developed a strong enough belief system to disagree with him. In fact, I subscribed to his beliefs and began second-guessing my own. I didn't want to be rude. I wanted to be the better person. Therefore, I subjected myself to years of suppressed thoughts and unexpressed feelings and made myself sick to my stomach.

One fall evening in 2002, I had my first epiphany. Nearly six years after pointing that rifle at me, my husband went away for a weekend of deer hunting with his friends. I vividly recall that chilly fall afternoon, secretly fantasizing about my life without him. I imagined waking up every day excited to live on my own terms and finally having my own voice without his criticism and dictatorship. By 2003, the flames flickering inside my gut became unbearable. When I asked my older brother what that meant, he told me, "You're yearning for more." Though I didn't know what more was, I just knew that I had to start my journey of self-discovery and had to trust I would figure it out when I did. Unlearning twenty-six years of conditioned behavior is extremely difficult to do. However, it wasn't impossible.

Having the innate inclination to please others, I immediately thought of my little boy and asked myself, "What kind of role model do I want to be for my son?" My little boy was only ten when my husband and I divorced in 2003. That little angel of mine taught me one of the most profound lessons in my life when he shared with me,

"Mom, I'm sad about the divorce, but you taught me that I have to stand up for myself when people put me down."

I thought that being unconditionally loving and strong as a wife, mother, and daughter meant bending over backwards and being able to endure the worst pain. I finally learned that love does not have to include pain, and that taking the high road means that you show others the kind of respect you expect for yourself, not letting other people treat you badly. I learned that you have permission to use your voice.

I had my voice all along, but I didn't know I could use it. It took a ten-year marriage of me getting it wrong, and the wisdom from my ten-year-old son to remind me that I have permission to use my voice. Now I carry this new belief with me, that I am good enough, as I dedicate my life and work as a coach, speaker and writer. Today I help other women speak up, stand out, and change their world.

~Berni Xiong

Chapter
7

Time to Thrive

It's Time to Reinvent Yourself

70

From Breakdown to Breakthrough

It's your place in the world; it's your life.
Go on and do all you can with it, and make it the life you want to live.
~Mae Jemison

I spent eighteen years in Corporate America in publishing and marketing. On the outside, I looked highly successful and accomplished. My friends thought I had it "all," and were often annoyed when they'd hear me share how challenging I felt my life was.

I worked hard, made all the "right" choices, and rose to the level of Vice President, earning great money, recognition and apparent reward. But on the inside, I wasn't successful—far from it. While I adored my family life and children, I was unhappy, sick and unfulfilled professionally for many years, and as I approached forty, these bumps in my work life turned into full-blown crises. In the last years of my corporate journey, I experienced twelve serious crises, including gender discrimination, sexual harassment, zero work-life balance, chronic illness (a painful, debilitating infection of the trachea that reappeared every three months for four years), and most challenging of all, the agonizing feeling that I was wasting my entire professional life on work that offered no value to anyone.

I attempted for several years to find a new path, but despite my efforts and thousands of dollars in therapy, working with a career counselor, and taking fruitless career assessment tests and evaluations, I remained utterly stuck. I simply could not figure out how to apply my talents and skills in a different direction that would be emotionally fulfilling as well as financially rewarding. With two small children, I needed to contribute substantially to our family's finances. I struggled inwardly to understand why I continued to face so many challenges in my professional life. I knew I was smart and dedicated, so why was it all so wrong? No matter what new path I explored, I couldn't find a way to use my talents toward something meaningful.

In my thirties, I had experienced my first painful wake-up call when my dear friend Lillian died of cancer. Right before she died, she pulled me close and whispered in my ear, "Kathy, *please* don't waste it. Don't waste your time. Just shine." I felt a terribly deep pain and regret, and such a sense of loss, yet my breakdown moment still didn't come. I didn't move forward or make a change, primarily because I was deathly afraid of what I'd lose (power, money, self-esteem).

But then, one month after moving to a more affluent town and a bigger home in Connecticut (meaning greater financial burdens and worries), 9/11 occurred. And one month after that, I faced a brutal layoff. During the first week after I was laid off, I got up each morning at the same time I always had, snuck out, and drove around aimlessly, dressed in my suit and high heels, desperately trying to regroup. I didn't know who I was without my corporate VP identity. I felt like a complete loser and a failure, and I just couldn't let anyone know. I kept my layoff a secret from everyone but my husband. Finally, I realized I could not simply go out and get another corporate job—that professional identity was dead for me.

The next week, I had a session with my spiritual psychotherapist, and was in his office crying, sharing how devastated and shocked I was at being let go. He said, "I know this feels like the worst crisis you've ever faced, but from where I sit, this is the first moment of your adult life you can actually choose who you want to be in the world. Now, Kathy, *who* do you want to be?"

That one question was a life-changer for me. Before I knew what was coming out of my mouth, I cried, "I want to do what you do—help people, and not hurt others and not be hurt!" From that discussion and our subsequent work together, I explored becoming a marriage and family therapist and a career coach.

After conducting online research, interviewing therapists and department heads at several universities, and determining it was an exciting direction for me, I enrolled in Fairfield University two months later to pursue my master's degree in Marriage and Family Therapy. I also learned about coaching a year later and pursued training in that as well. I promised myself then that no matter what happened, I would take control of my professional life and align it with what I truly valued and believed. Somehow, in those intensely painful times of reevaluation and reckoning, I awakened and found new energy and purpose. While contemplating the master's program, I read over the curriculum, and said to myself, "I'm so drawn to this material. I've just got to learn about it. I don't care what happens in the end — I just want to learn about this material and find a way to use it." It turns out that the therapeutic training was the single most transformative experience I'd ever undergone.

After becoming a therapist and launching my own therapy practice, I worked with clients dealing with the darkest forms of human experience, including rape, incest, pedophilia, drug addiction, alcoholism, depression, suicidality and even attempted murder. I learned how to hold a loving space with another who was in deep pain, and find compassion in my heart for even the harshest human behaviors. While the training and experience were indeed life changing, I had another breakthrough moment when a female client called me to share that she was going to wrap her car around a tree and kill herself that moment. We got her the help she needed to stabilize her, but once again, I had to face the harsh reality that this professional identity of therapist didn't fit with how I wanted to offer my professional talents in the world. I was ashamed to admit that, and thought, "What kind of a healer are you that you want to leave the therapy profession?" But I decided to make myself right instead of always doubting my deepest instincts. I decided to honor my belief that I needed yet another change, and this time I didn't falter or hesitate.

I found the missing piece in 2006 as I delivered workshops to women around Connecticut about how we can learn to thrive through change. After the talks, women would line up to speak with me — some with tears in their eyes, some shaking, saying, "Kathy, I felt like you were telling my story. I don't have anywhere else to turn, but I'm facing all the crises you experienced in corporate life, and I really need help." From these talks, I conducted research that revealed that seven out of ten mid-career working women were as unfulfilled and miserable in their careers as I had been, and fifty percent had no idea what to do about it.

A switch was flipped. I was shocked and distressed at the magnitude of the problem for working women today, and I realized then that the serious challenges I had faced in my corporate life represented the challenges of hundreds of thousands of other women around the globe. I decided then and there that I had to be part of the solution.

I wanted to help working women and emerging female leaders overcome their challenges in the business world, and lead their lives more powerfully and passionately. I wanted to do my part to help move the needle on women's leadership globally. And I wanted to elevate these challenges to the national conversation, and help women speak up and stand out.

At forty-two, I suddenly found a calling and a purpose that I felt was missing for my entire professional life. It wasn't easy by any stretch to reinvent myself (twice), but the misery I felt for eighteen years before my reinventions was my motivator. I decided to turn my "mess into a message" and help other women bypass the twelve "hidden" crises I had faced in my work life. I started my business, Ellia Communications, which offers programs, resources, coaching and training all dedicated to this purpose, and I conducted a year-long national research study on professional women overcoming crisis (which culminated in my book *Breakdown, Breakthrough*). With this new direction, and building my own business, I finally felt that all the dots were connecting. Everything I had loved to do as a young adult, and everything I had learned in my corporate life and therapy and coaching training were being utilized in a way that felt right, true, and aligned with what I passionately cared about.

The result of my journey is that, at fifty-four, I'm working in my own business, writing, coaching, speaking and training inspiring, amazing women who long for more passion, power and purpose in their work, and who wish to play bigger and make an impact in the world and their communities. This work feels like the answer to my deepest, most perplexing life question—"What am I here on this planet at this time to do, contribute and leave behind?"

As one who was so lost but climbed back from a professional abyss, I know there is a way back from breakdown. Often this lowest point in our lives is exactly what paves the way for a true breakthrough, if we'll let it.

As Maria Nemeth, the inspiring author of the powerful book *The Energy of Money*, shares: "We are all happiest when we are demonstrating in physical reality what we know to be true about ourselves, when we are giving form to our Life's Intentions in a way that contributes to others."

Now that, to me, is a life well lived, with amazing success and happiness. The question I'd like to leave you with is this: Can this, finally, be YOUR time to shine?

~Kathy Caprino

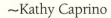

71

A Future to Step Into

We must be willing to get rid of the life we've planned,
so as to have the life that is waiting for us.
~Joseph Campbell

I had always envisioned the "Golden Years" as a time in our lives when my wife Lynn and I would have the free time to explore the country in our custom motorhome, going from place to place like two leaves in the wind. This was not a "bucket list fantasy." This was a well thought out season-of-life game plan.

Lynn and I had met thirty years before and instantly became best friends, soul mates and later, husband and wife. Lynn was an artist and photographer. She was as wonderful as wonderful can be and allowed each day of her life to unfold as magic moments.

I was a young attorney at that time, building my practice in the Midwest. Lynn would come with me to the law library on weekends and was my cheerleader and confidante. About seventeen years into my law practice I was offered a once in a lifetime opportunity to become the CEO/President and General Counsel of a company that is America's leader in the field of self-help and peak performance strategies. This opportunity required that we move to Southern California. This was such an exciting time for us both.

This new role brought us the opportunity to travel the world together and to experience a lifestyle we previously would not have imagined.

We found our dream home in a beach community, and with our six dogs and two parrots lived every day experiencing the joy and happiness of our life together.

And then Lynn was diagnosed with a medical condition that changed the course of our life. This disease had the ruthlessness of a home invasion robbery. The cancer had metastasized throughout her body. We approached it scientifically, medically, spiritually and with tenacious abandon. It was devastating for me to know that each day was one day closer to her end. For the entire year we were side by side during the ineffective yet hopeful regime of treatments.

On January 16, 2011, Lynn passed away with the same style and grace that she lived her life. On that day I joined 7,500 other Americans who also lost a loved one.

It was Friday, January 21, 2011 and the last of about twenty people were leaving our home. Father John, our parish priest, lingered behind and hugged me. He said: "Hang in there, this is God's will, may her memory be eternal."

As I watched his car pull away, I closed the door. I heard a new kind of silence and looked around. All of the dogs had circled me as if by design and we froze together in the moment.

This was going to be a time to thrive or a time to be smothered by the dark clouds of grief and despair.

We did not have children. We did, however, have a close community of friends who all stepped in and reached out to me in wonderful ways. Hospice introduced me to grief counseling and a counselor met with me weekly with assurances that the deep physical and mental pain of this journey would ease with time.

I realized that friends and associates were without words. Some disappeared from the radar. I was forgiving of that and was clear that this journey was mine alone.

Grief has a life of its own. We have all had our disappointments and loss of others. I was totally unprepared for this.

During the following year I went through the motions of work and life. I stayed close to home, and the dogs and parrots became my nuclear family. I did very little to our home other than find worthwhile places to donate Lynn's things.

I decided to take up poker and began to commute back and forth to Las Vegas. Poker gave me an opportunity to keep my mind engaged and to socialize in a new way. Eight weeks after learning the game, I played in my first World Series of Poker. Little did I realize that my time to thrive was unfolding in front of me and the healing process that protects us was in full swing.

Without a design or conscious game plan, my life was changing. It was little steps and I barely noticed it myself. On the first anniversary of Lynn's passing I was at the cemetery for my weekly visit. I can barely describe what occurred, which was a feeling of lightness and euphoria. I could hear the wisp of what I sensed was the dark cloud catching a wind and beginning to disburse. I felt guilty that I was feeling lighter.

The following week I was in Vegas. By chance and circumstance I met a woman who has become a great friend and companion. I got a stunning high-rise condo on the Las Vegas strip and began to split my time between Las Vegas and California. For the next two years I began to spend nearly all of my time in Vegas, experiencing a lifestyle change that I had never dared to dream.

Back in California there was unfinished business. The home I shared with Lynn remained untouched. I also still had a full-time high-pressure job to maintain. Somehow I made it all work. I had a house sitter and housekeeper take care of my home and my pets around the clock. This went on for three years. I would go back and forth for visits. The house was full of memories of Lynn and me and I would fast-track back to Vegas. My job could be supported virtually and I had a stellar team at the home office dealing with day-to-day matters. Where there is a will, there is a way.

I closed my eyes to the fact that something had to give. Of course what I was avoiding was letting go of my house and my pets and thirty-one years of the most wonderful memories. In my mind, that would somehow end my relationship with Lynn and I simply was not able to fathom that.

It was approaching the third anniversary of Lynn's passing. My poker coach, Kenna James, put it on the line. He said, "Poker and life have many similarities. You can only lose what you are attached to and until you can give up those attachments the game will control you instead of you controlling the game." Something deep inside me began to stir.

That month I returned to California. I got our home ready to list. With the help of Gale, a dear family friend, I found homes for all my pets. What a heartache that was. I realized that to thrive I needed to let go of it all. I made a decision to begin my life all over and to invent a new future.

I got rid of everything I owned. I sold six Harleys, my motorhome, all my cars, all my furniture, collectables — everything went.

The house was impeccable, and on the first day it was listed I had six full offers.

It closed on Lynn's birthday. I went to the cemetery and there were no clouds. I knew Lynn was orchestrating things. It was all too smooth and effortless to be coincidence.

I bought a new Corvette Stingray and returned to Vegas with only my clothes and a box of photos.

I then met with the Chairman of the great company that had given me such opportunity for the past two decades and we agreed on and announced my formal retirement.

Yes, I gave it all up.

I am a private kind of guy. I decided to share this story because I want anyone who finds themselves in these circumstances to know that life is guided. You unfold the future — the future does not unfold you.

There is such a thing as a time to thrive.

~Sam Georges

72

A Ham Is Born

You will do foolish things, but do them with enthusiasm.
~Sidonie Gabrielle Colette

My son Levi went off to college and never looked back. Yeah, I know, I should have been happy that he was independent and doing so well. But when even my very subtle reminders about the nineteen hours of labor I endured to bring him into this world failed to get him to phone home, I realized it was time to get on with my own life.

The day-to-day part of raising a kid was done. All that creative energy, all that passion, all that focus—they had to go somewhere.

And then.

Our family joke is that I have always been Lucy to my husband Bill's Ricky—the wacky redhead who is always trying to get into her husband's shows. Bill sings, acts and writes musical theater. Levi has inherited his gifts. I, however, hadn't appeared on stage since my remarkable debut as Aunt Polly in my sixth grade production of *Tom Sawyer*. Whenever Bill produced or performed in a show, I pretended to campaign for a role. "Why can't I play Othello? I'd be brilliant!"

Now that my days weren't full of have-you-done-your-homework, have-you-written-your-college-essays, get-off-the-computer-and-go-to-sleep hysteria, I thought maybe I shouldn't pretend anymore. Why not give acting a shot?

Bill challenged me: Our local theater, Curtain Call, was doing

Waiting in the Wings by Noël Coward. Set in a home for retired actresses, it had a large need for "women of a certain age." "If you audition, I will too and we can do it together," Bill offered. It was put up or shut up time.

I'd given lectures and readings, and had always felt comfortable on stage. I'm pretty good at feeling a mood and getting an audience to come with me. But that was me as me, saying my own thoughts. Could I assume the role of someone else? Could this aged brain actually retain lines? I read the play and saw a teeny tiny part that lasted a whole three pages. I could audition for that. "Sure, what the hey," I said.

Flash forward and guess what? I was cast. Initially I was sure they did so because they knew it was the only way they'd get brilliant Bill. (He made it clear that we were a package deal.) But I was cast in a much larger role than the teeny tiny one. I was Almina, an eighty-five-year-old obese former vaudevillian. Huh.

Bill and I were out together every weekday night at rehearsals for two months. When 7 p.m. rolled around, we both thought, "Uck, we're too tired to go out." But once we got there, we were energized by the creative process and the camaraderie of the cast. I felt as if I were back in college—making friends, laughing, discovering, and gossiping. I loved the inside jokes. I liked challenging myself to get inside someone else's skin.

I had few lines but for some reason was on stage the entire time. I couldn't figure out what I was supposed to be doing. "Do whatever you feel like," said the director. "I'll pull you back if it doesn't work." Wha? On the Internet, I found one review of a former production that said Almina stole the show every time she was on. Okay, I thought, she was doing something out there. It was up to me to find it and go for it.

At first I did a little mugging and sighing and eye rolling. The director said nothing. So I went broader: I hid food in my purse and pockets and stuffed my face constantly, actually making a bit of sorting through jellybeans. For the Christmas scene, I took a bird ornament and fashioned it into a barrette for my hair. (We were performing in a dinner theater in the round. During one performance, the ornament took a swan dive into a patron's dinner. I turned around and asked, "Can I have my birdie back?") By the final performance, I had become fearless. I was singing, dancing, pretending to sleep and snore, shamelessly scene stealing. This is what used to be referred to as "making stupid." Directed to take a small drink of rum, I grabbed the whole bottle and pretended to guzzle it. I did everything short of roll on the floor and pull my dress up over my head.

A ham was born. (Did I mention that the bows were my favorite part? Yay for me! Everyone clap for me!) Was I great? No, but was I really kind of okay? Yes. And did I enjoy it? Oh, yeah. While seasoned trained actresses in the cast were practically throwing up before every performance, I calmly did crossword puzzles.

I no longer sit home, waiting for Levi to call to fill me in on what's going on in the world. I am finding out for myself. Although I still can't believe how fast parenthood flies, from the umbilical cord dropping off to your kid dropping off laundry on his way to somewhere else, I have learned that the empty nest can actually be a blessing. It gives me time to find out who I am when I am not Levi's mom. And apparently, there are many different "me's" who are waiting to make their entrance.

Do it again? I already have. (I believe audiences are still talking about my definitive Sarah the Cook in *The Man Who Came to Dinner*.) I have learned to sing and dance—at the same time, mind you—for *Fiddler on the Roof*. The head of the company has talked to me about upcoming productions that call for over-the-top comedy. Or as he so delicately puts it, "whacked-out nut jobs." I've never been so complimented.

~Beth Levine

73

Taking a Chance on Me

Do one thing every day that scares you.
~Eleanor Roosevelt

I fell into teaching with a thud, landing on my feet and not quite knowing what hit me. As a writer accustomed to quiet, alone time, the idea of being in charge of a classroom filled with twenty-five students was at once daunting and exhilarating. When I was first asked to teach a full-credit college English course, I brushed it off with a resounding: "Teaching? Who me?"

Years before, when my husband Mort was alive, he had on numerous occasions suggested I give teaching a try. "You'll love it," he said. "Take a risk."

Ensconced in my writing, with enough work to keep busy full time, the last thing I wanted was an intrusion on my silent literary life. Now, years later, his words still resonated in my head: "Take a risk."

Shortly after Mort's death, and mostly as a tribute to him, I interviewed for a teaching position at a local college. To my surprise, I was hired. I thanked the head of the department, secretly thinking she had made a terrible mistake. "Along with the necessary credentials, we also like our professors to have other interests," she said. "The fact that you're a writer will add a different dimension to the course."

I was told I could design my own syllabus while using the textbook as a guide. Aside from following the standard requirements, I had free rein to be as creative as I wanted, the bait that ultimately lured me in. And so began my agonizing attempt at putting together a course curriculum based partly on my own ingenuity and partly on the textbook.

I became a stranger in a strange land, embarking on a surprising journey. Since that time, I have traveled hundreds of academic miles. I began as a novice and grew into the role, teaching myself how to teach, and expanding my knowledge with each passing semester.

But in the end, it was the students themselves who taught me. Bolstered by their enthusiasm and motivated by their trust in me, I took their lead. Slowly, without realizing it, I became the best version of myself in ways I had never known before.

The student body was diverse in terms of primary language, ethnicity, and lifestyle. I taught kids with emotional and academic problems, some with learning disabilities, and many who were on the verge of making bad decisions. Often, I was able to redirect their thinking. I taught ex-cons, recovering alcoholics and drug addicts, a police officer, construction workers, an auto-body mechanic, nurses, a horse breeder, actors, an acrobat, a dancer, budding filmmakers, artists, floral arrangers and young mothers and dads who worked two jobs while simultaneously taking college courses. I had students who had flunked out of Ivy League colleges and for whom this course was a last chance to prove themselves. I administered harsh reality through fair grades, and I rewarded those who kept at it until the end.

The papers that were turned in became revelations on myriad subjects, and through their writing I became educated, too, and my consciousness was raised. Students from third-world countries wrote about their childhoods in distant lands. Those from homes where education was not readily available or encouraged walked away with diplomas—pioneers all—moving on to substantial jobs and solid futures so alien from their humble beginnings.

A Vietnamese student from my first class keeps in touch. He had struggled with English, but he managed, through hard work and extra tutoring, to graduate and move on to a career in accounting. Now he is married with three young children. On graduation day, I was invited to attend a Vietnamese banquet hosted by his family in his honor. They welcomed me into their home and introduced me to culinary delicacies I had never before tasted. We still remain friends.

I have received gifts from foreign students: a sari from an Indian girl, a silver goblet from China, a gold star from Russia, a shawl from Peru, homemade bread from a culinary arts major, a Japanese kimono, French perfume, a handbag from Haiti, a plaid Scottish tam, a French beret, a pencil drawing of me, a poem, and a photograph taken in Mali by a West African student. A girl from Dublin taught me the Irish jig. A dancer from Colombia gave me a pair of silver ballet slippers. Numerous trinkets of sentimental value adorn the shelves of my home—all artifacts of my students' devotion and pride in jobs well done… for us all.

Through these years, I provided hugs, shook many hands, polished my sense of humor and went that extra mile for a kid who thought he wouldn't make it, but who tackled the job head-on. He walked down the aisle at graduation, his shoulders high, en route to his diploma. I have seen skills develop and essays take shape from wobbly writers who suddenly had an epiphany and "got it." And then there were those days when the job was overwhelming and beyond my grasp—days when my efforts went unappreciated and it all seemed so futile. It was on such an afternoon that a student handed in a paper that surprised me by its brilliance, and the cloud of hopelessness was lifted. It all came together once more, as one large, grand piece of tapestry, gnarled on the underside, but smoothly sewn together on the front so that all the pieces fit neatly into place.

And so, I heeded Mort's advice: "Take a risk." And in doing so, I continued to persevere and thrive. I write my humor column, now in its twenty-ninth year, and have published my second novel and am completing a third. I have watched my grandchildren, who bring magic into my life, grow from infants to teenagers. And, I became a Professor of English. One year, I was awarded Teacher of the Year, an honor bestowed upon me by the student body, with a plaque that reads: "For imparting wisdom with contagious enthusiasm." It is, to date, my most treasured acquisition.

Above all, I took a chance on me. As a result, I grew as a person and as a teacher. I also like to think I made Mort proud.

~Judith Marks-White

74

A Life by Design

Don't confuse your path with your destination,
just because it's stormy now, doesn't mean you aren't headed for sunshine.
~Author Unknown

irst my neck itched. Then I broke into hives. In what seemed like seconds, I was gasping for air. In a panic, I frantically looked for my life-saving EpiPen, only to note the terrified eyes of my two-year-old son witnessing my struggle. I stared into his frightened eyes, and told myself I couldn't die. As I injected my thigh with the epinephrine, I was vividly connected with the concept of second chances. I felt tremendous gratitude for the gift of life. It was then that everything changed for me.

It was determined years before that I suffered from stress-induced idiopathic anaphylactic shock. The very fancy name denoted that, in my case, stress could really kill me on the spot. Why couldn't my body pick something a bit more manageable like peanuts or penicillin? I could have certainly done a good job at avoiding those. But stress? That seemed so impossible to manage. How do you control what life throws at you? What felt like an ominous curse turned out to be my biggest blessing.

During the months leading up to that fateful night, I became painfully aware that life was so much more than a struggle to merely survive. I don't mean literal survival like "a saber tooth tiger is about to eat me." However, my brain couldn't distinguish the dangerous imaginary tiger from my own self-imposed limiting beliefs. Beliefs that chased and cornered me into a life not fully lived. The concept of thriving appeared so unachievable while in survival mode.

The year was 2008. To say my life was upside down is a huge understatement. It seemed like I was facing the culmination of all my poor decisions and unresolved issues from the past. The events in my life mirrored the economic chaos and depression of the time, and I found myself doubting I had the strength to pull myself through. Within a matter of months I was overwhelmed by a roller coaster of life experiences. First, I went through a divorce. Shortly after, the company I worked for closed its doors and declared bankruptcy. I lost the house I had purchased with my life savings, and found myself both collecting unemployment and incurring credit card debt to support myself and my young son. I can't quite describe the horror of doubting my ability to care and provide for my amazing child.

How could my life have hit such a low point? Depression took over, and I found myself unable to do more than the bare minimum to care for my son. There were days my only activities revolved around him, and the rest of the time was spent feeling either sorry or angry with myself. I knew my son deserved so much more, yet the fear of not being enough paralyzed me. Intellectually I knew I had to get out of my "funk," but emotionally I felt I didn't have the resources to do so.

And then I saw my son's terrified eyes on that life-changing night, intuitively understanding the seriousness of the situation…. It became crystal clear that the solution was to master my inner world, instead of allowing my external world to literally leave me gasping for air. The path to transitioning from an unfulfilled life to a thriving one was always available. I just hadn't seen it before.

Suddenly, I was incredibly aware that all the resources I needed were inside me, just waiting to be accessed. The belief in my own power propelled me to decide, once and for all, to be the creator of my own life. With unwavering certainty, I decided that I would do whatever was necessary to turn my life around. Ensuring I was mentally, emotionally, and physically capable of not just providing, but fully caring, for my son became a must. I would choose to unequivocally create and live life to the fullest. I would work on becoming the best version of myself, and to leave my son a legacy only possible through leading by example.

Tapping into that deep desire allowed me to give myself permission to thrive despite all circumstances. And so I did. Within a few months, life began to transform. I started my own business, which now has been soaring for six years. I paid off all my debt, purchased a beautiful home, and started investing in my financial freedom. Most importantly, I did the inner work necessary to truly become the person I was seeking to find. The journey led me to the love of my life. We married and had a beautiful baby girl, and my boy and I finally got to experience the family, the love, and the life we so deserved.

The panic and vulnerability I saw when I stared into my son's eyes on that powerful night gave me the gift of leverage. I was more compelled to do for him than for myself. The willingness to embark on a deep personal development journey gave me the courage to take full responsibility for what had shown up in my life. Furthermore, it provided me with the belief that I was capable of changing, overcoming, and deliberately creating whatever I wanted, needed, or desired. Leaving the past behind allowed me to be present and open to acquire the emotional and psychological strategies to truly live by design.

Now when I look at the EpiPen I keep at my bedside table, I'm reminded of how powerful I am, and how adversity is an incredible teacher. After experiencing a total of ten life-threatening episodes, I am elated to share that, after that blessed night, the only thing that takes my breath away is the life and the love all around me.

~Marcia Castro-Rosenberg

75

Endings
Can Be Beginnings

Every story has an end but in life every ending is just a new beginning.
~Uptown Girls

I still clearly remember the night when my dad gathered our family in the living room. After nearly eleven months of unemployment, we could sense what this meant. Even though my dad usually had a way with words, he skirted around saying what we knew was coming. Finally, he said it: "I accepted a new job." And in turn, I had to accept my fate.

I blurted out the obvious question, "Where?" Before my father could finish saying "Austin, Texas," I had burst into tears, practically inconsolable. I would have to completely start over, which was less than ideal for a sophomore in high school. My crying continued well into the night.

After that I was done. Not another tear fell.

Following that December night I became numb, withdrawing into myself in an attempt to make leaving seem painless. While my dad commuted back and forth between California and Texas, my sister and I were allowed to finish out the school year, leaving me with six months to sabotage my relationships with people who cared about me. As a result I felt detached, almost as though I was living a double life while I kept this secret from my friends and others around me. I was consumed with self-pity, questioning the purpose of engaging in the world around me since I knew I was leaving. However, somewhere along the way of counting down the days in anticipation of the end, I found myself counting down the days in anticipation of the beginning.

Suddenly I stopped feeling sorry for myself. I decided to take charge of my life and add some certainty to my unclear future. I diligently researched high schools and neighborhoods, and in return my parents gave me a say in where we would begin the search for our new home in the Austin area. Once we purchased our new house, I could see my future unfolding before me. With knowledge comes power. I did not have to become a victim of my circumstance, but instead a victor. I could take this clean slate and use it as an opportunity for self-improvement.

My self-improvement began by emulating confidence. My end goal was to become proactive and independent, which at the time seemed overwhelming. I knew the only way to achieve this was by taking baby steps, so I e-mailed the tennis coach at my new high school and inquired about trying out for the team. The seemingly simple e-mail soon turned into a conversation as he put my mind at ease, reassuring me that I was "coming to a great school and tennis community," and my prospective team was looking forward to having me.

The interaction could not have gone better. Little did I know that would set the course for my "new and improved" life. My coach had gone on to inform the team of my arrival. Within the week, I was communicating with a redheaded girl on the varsity team named Danielle who had reached out to me via Twitter. It dawned on me that the only things she knew about me came from an Instagram account and a horribly outdated Facebook profile. This was my chance to put my clean slate to use. I could assume the role of the confident girl I wanted to be. For the first time I felt like I was in control, because for so long I had let other people, whether friends or unacquainted peers, control me. This was my time.

More than six months after my family packed up our cars and drove to what I had come to view as my promised land, I have never felt more "me." I successfully threw myself into everything I possibly could, enjoying the process of uncovering what I truly did and didn't like, not what my peers dictated I *should* like.

At my old school I would have never given math club a second thought, even though I was fairly skilled in the subject. However, it was a new school, a new me, and I decided to challenge myself and join Mu Alpha Theta, a mathematics honor society. Shocking as it may be, I actually enjoyed being a "mathlete," but even more shocking to me was the fact that no one teased me for my decision. It seemed as though everyone around me had already realized that they should "live and let live."

It was then that I realized the judgments I perceived from others were, in actuality, nonexistent. The perceived ridicule was purely something I allowed myself to fear, and moving gave me the freedom to see that I decide what shapes me. The courage and confidence I had sought had been there all along, simply waiting beneath my insecurities to finally surface when the time was right.

The night I learned I was going to move, the person I used to be evaporated with my last tears. The debilitating dread of what I thought was the end was replaced by anticipation for a new beginning. While every new beginning contains an element of fear, it also contains an element of promise.

~Brianna Mears

76

Letting Charlie Go

You will never change your life until you change something you do daily.
~John C. Maxwell

W ell, the divorce is final! Let me explain. I spent twenty-five years in an oppressive, controlling, stifling, and demoralizing relationship with "my other half." By other half, I mean two hundred and fifty pounds of extra body weight. It had somehow taken on a life of its own and eventually took away mine in the process. Let's call that other half Charlie.

Charlie was a gleeful soul at first. We spent lots of time together and had fun eating and drinking to our hearts' content, loosening our belts as they became tighter and tighter. Charlie's philosophy was always "Go big or go home," and boy oh boy did we live by that principle. We did everything to the extreme—extra-large pizzas smothered in extra cheese, double quarter pounders with cheese… supersized, please.

As time went on, we began spending all of our time together. Charlie became so possessive. It got to the point where he would not let me leave the house. I could not see my friends or visit with my family. We stayed home all the time. We did not go on dates—no movies, carnivals, or concerts. "We have a big screen TV," he said. "What else do we need?" Like the devil, he seduced me into staying home and accommodating his needs, and he was oh so needy!

I became mournful and miserable. My life had no meaning or purpose. My purpose had become feeding Charlie, my captor. Don't get me wrong, he gave me things too—anxiety, paranoia, high blood pressure, depression. In return, I gave him my health, my happiness, and my freedom. There came a day when I felt I might suffocate myself with Charlie. I could see my life slipping away. I looked at him with loathing as we sat in silence and stuffed ourselves to the point of intoxication. We were indeed a toxic couple.

One night, I asked him for a trial separation. Oh, he fought like the dickens to hold onto me, playing head games and mental manipulation. I fought back. I joined Weight Watchers, began walking, went back to school and slowly began taking my life back.

Charlie continued to hang around, to hold on, tempt, and entice. As I became stronger and healthier, I saw less and less of him. So today, I declare my independence! My divorce is final! Charlie, my "other half," who is most certainly not my better half, is officially gone and out of my life. He won't be back. Goodbye and good riddance. I realize today, that I only held on because I was afraid to let go.

~Alana Marie

Nowhere to Go But Up

*If you have made mistakes, even serious ones, there is
always another chance for you. What we call failure is
not the falling down, but the staying down.*

~Mary Pickford

As my car sputtered to a stop in front of my mother's house, I took a deep breath, reclined the seat, and slowly exhaled. I closed my eyes, in part because pure exhaustion had taken over, and in equal part because I wanted to stem the flow of tears.

How had I arrived here? Three weeks earlier, I owned a successful restaurant, lived in a beautiful home on a tree-lined street, drove a brand-new car, and had plenty of money in my pocket. Now it was all gone. The business was shattered, the bank account emptied, the vehicle repossessed, and the house gone when it became abundantly clear that making the next payment was a laughable prospect.

At twenty-five years old, I found myself sitting in front of my mother's home, slouched down in a rusting 1984 Volkswagen Rabbit, jobless, homeless, penniless, and seemingly out of options.

Too ashamed to walk up the steps, I sat alone with my thoughts. "Why me?" I asked no one. "What did I do to deserve this? I worked hard, I treated people well, and yet, through a series of cruel twists, everything I thought was mine was gone in a flash."

In the weeks to come, I found myself dodging creditors, preparing to file for bankruptcy, and struggling to land menial kitchen jobs. After a few days in my old bedroom, a friend took me in, and I spent countless nights tossing and turning on a mattress lying on the floor of a spare bedroom, wondering how one person could be hit with such bad luck. That had to be what it was, right? Just a messy series of events, all linked to the worst luck a man could imagine?

But luck had nothing to do with the sad state my life was in. The failed business, the broken lease, repossessed car and empty bank account could all be traced back to my own unspeakably poor choices.

Coming to the realization that I alone was responsible for my life wasn't easy—or quick. It took most of a summer spent living off of others before I fully embraced the tired cliché that I really did have no one to blame but myself. It seemed as though at every fork in the road of my life, I had gone the wrong way. Those wrong turns had left me penniless, depressed, alone, and with no real end in sight to my misery. But eventually, driven more by desperation than inspiration, I decided it was time to stop waiting for my life to change and go change it myself.

It began with getting my own place again. It was small and slightly depressing, but it met two key criteria—it came furnished and I could pay by the week. It was a small first step, but one that I knew was crucial if I was indeed going to rebuild my life. With two jobs and my Rabbit still holding on, despite the fact that if you lifted the floor mat on the passenger side you could see clear through to the ground, I was surviving, which, sadly, was more than I could have said for myself three months earlier.

My bank account was still embarrassingly empty, but at least it wasn't overdrawn. I was sleeping in my own bed (albeit under a blanket left by the previous renter) and I slowly began to see the tiniest glint of light at the end of the tunnel.

With a few dollars in my pocket and a place to call my own, I embarked on what for a poor, nearly destitute guy was the scariest of all propositions—I asked a girl out on a date. That may not sound like much, but the date had to be within walking distance, given that if she sat in my car, her feet would go through to the ground. Then too, it had to be an inexpensive date, as I was broke.

That date—a walk to the library and drinks and *Scrabble* at a local coffee shop—was, I say with absolute certainty, the turning point in my comeback. For all of the questionable choices I had made, this was the defining moment. As we sat and talked, I laid my entire gruesome existence on the table. I held nothing back. I was as me as I could be, and at the end of the day a funny thing happened; she asked for a second date.

That girl from the library and I just celebrated our fifteenth wedding anniversary. The rusted-out Rabbit is gone, replaced by an SUV with two car seats in the back for our beautiful, healthy, amazing children. A house in the suburbs, complete with a bed covered in my own blankets, has replaced the rent-by-the-week apartment. The late nights working as a fry cook are no more, as I earn my living as a marketing director and an author. The bank account that once began with a red number is now supplemented with a retirement account and enough cash to enjoy a dinner out with my family, a vacation in Myrtle Beach, and most importantly, peace of mind.

As I look around at all that I have in my life, two things keep me grounded and working harder than ever. First, I never forget the pain I felt that day, parked in front of my mother's house, when my life had, by any reasonable person's assessment, hit rock bottom. And second, I remind myself that as hard as I have worked to rebuild my life, I truly believe that the best is yet to come.

~Matt Chandler

Taking a Chance on Life

*Grieving is a necessary passage and a difficult
transition to finally letting go of sorrow—
it is not a permanent rest stop.*
~Dodinsky

Paul and I had married young and lived happily ever after, as they say. We had produced three wonderful children, and we lived in a beautiful home in suburbia with careers we loved. We had truly achieved the American dream.

Life came crashing down on a cold December evening in 2010 when my soul mate and husband of forty-plus years dropped dead of a heart attack. "We shocked him three times, but we're sorry. We did all we could," the doctor reported sympathetically.

How would I cope without my rock, the love of my life, the guy who always called me "babe"? I was about to find out how hard life could be.

The days following were a blur. My three kids, their spouses and the grown grandchildren moved in for a week while we planned the funeral. I cried myself to sleep every night and slept alone for the first time in decades.

We buried Paul in the pouring rain a week before Christmas. The skies were a fitting dark gray as we trudged to the burial site in our boots and jeans. We were a little group of nine lost souls. My parents, husband's parents, my sister and extended family had all passed away years before. I had never felt so alone.

The kids and I bought a Christmas tree and new ornaments, trying our very best to act merry. I couldn't bear to bring out the old ornaments that Paul and I had accumulated over our many years of marriage. I vowed to never like Christmas again. We cried, we laughed, but mostly everyone just tried to cope. And then they all left.

I spent New Year's Eve alone for the first time. I was terrified of this new lonely life. I had been with Paul daily for so many years. Panic and anxiety filled my days, and weird dreams filled my nights. I awoke every morning at four.

The first year was filled with bereavement groups, friends dropping in or calling, kids visiting on weekends, finding a grief therapist, and living from day to day. Barely eating, losing weight, crying until my eyes were swollen shut, I was a shell of a person. But somehow I kept going. There were all the firsts: first Christmas without Paul, first birthday, first wedding anniversary, first Mother's Day, Father's Day. On and on they came, crashing against me. Going back to Sunday church, I found my faith again and this helped me immensely.

I went to lunch and dinner with everyone and anyone I could find. I tried to stay busy and not be alone. That didn't work either; I just couldn't outrun the grief. Finally, tired and weary, I started staying home more.

Every time I wanted to throw in the towel, I made myself do something hard to keep moving forward. I took off my wedding ring and cried all day. I got rid of his clothes and sobbed when I smelled his cologne. I yearned for his touch and turned over all his pictures on the credenza. I shut down our joint accounts and rearranged our bedroom furniture. I bought his gravestone as a birthday present for him and took him flowers from his garden when it was laid. I bought an ornate cross for my living room on the first anniversary of his death. The kids and I gathered for dinner at his favorite Italian bistro and told stories about him. I had buttons printed with his photo and his favorite saying: "Drive Fast, Take Chances." This was his way of saying live life to the fullest.

I was trying, but I hated my new life.

There were many days I prayed to die but suicide was never a viable option. I knew Paul wouldn't want me to give up, and I had a small group of dedicated friends and our kids rooting for me.

Years two and three were when the reality of my loss hit hard. The feeling of Paul being there was fading but taking its place was a huge chasm of loneliness. I spent time talking to my friends and family on the phone, sometimes crying out in pain, "I am so lonely!"

Nothing filled the hole. I had to remind myself that Paul was a huge part of my life and you don't get over grief, you get through it. You learn to live with the pain and accept the loss as your new normal. I was either going to give up and die or decide to live. I was down but not out.

As the fourth anniversary of Paul's death approached, I sat down and had a heart-to-heart with myself. Paul would have wanted me to live life to the fullest just as his favorite saying had stated. I had come so far from that first year and now I was determined to live life with meaning, not just exist. A new stronger me was emerging and I liked her.

I joined an art group and a widow/widowers meet-up. I am writing a book on my experiences to help others who have lost a spouse. I started teaching a writing class for senior citizens at Cal State Long Beach. I'm now signed up to teach every year and I love it. Helping other seniors realize their writing dreams is very rewarding.

As I enter year five I am excited about the future. I thank God that Paul and I had so many wonderful years together, but I am also thankful that I found a new stronger me. I can hear Paul saying, "Drive fast, take chances, and you go, girl!"

~Sallie A. Rodman

79

Countryfied Chick

There are shortcuts to happiness, and dancing is one of them.
~Vicki Baum

I t was a typical Friday night, me on the bed in my finest gray flannel pajamas, popcorn at the ready while a murder mystery blared on the TV. My husband, on the other hand, was stationed comfortably on the rather inappropriately named love seat in the living room, wearing a faded Sasquatch T-shirt, TV tray filled with potato chips and Vienna sausage, absorbed in a monster show he'd recorded earlier on the DVR. Very romantic.

The next week, my husband announced he'd be going out of state for a few months for work. Following his departure, I caught the Country Music Awards on TV. Those women looked so beautiful. A couple of days later, I received an e-mail announcing some upcoming continuing ed classes at the nearby community college. One in particular caught my eye—line dancing. I must have been inspired by the awards show, so I said what the heck and I signed up.

Now, I was nervous. What had I done? I was in my fifties and hadn't danced since disco was in, decades ago. To say I was anxious would be an understatement.

I imagined my teacher would look like a country western star. Instead, he was a little on the short side, pudgy with snow-white hair, and wore glasses. If it had been December, I would have jumped on his lap and given him my Christmas list. Instead, I decided to let this jolly elf show me what he knew about country line dancing. And, to my surprise, it was quite a bit. In spite of outward appearances, the guy had some moves.

The class was comprised of eighteen mostly menopausal ladies and two brave guys. Our instructor asked each of us to go around the room, sharing why we wanted to learn country line dancing. The younger man, a twenty-something my son's age, was there to learn some moves to impress the ladies at the honky-tonks. The older gentleman, closer to my age, was there so he could take his wife out dancing on their anniversary. How sweet. The rest of the middle-aged mamas were there to learn something new, get some exercise, and have some fun at the same time.

The class was only supposed to last an hour, but we were enjoying ourselves so much that we went over by thirty minutes. I hadn't laughed, or sweat, so much in years. I couldn't wait for the next class.

In between classes, our teacher posted the dance steps on YouTube so we could practice, which I did for nearly an hour every day. It was so much fun, the time flew by. Little by little, my jeans started loosening, and I needed to buy a smaller size. Of course, you can't do country line dancing without wearing cowboy boots, so I bought a pair of those too.

During the sessions, we learned all sorts of dances, like Tush Push and Wobble. My husband was coming home soon, and I was eager to show off my new dance moves. When he finally arrived, the delighted look on his face said it all. He couldn't take his eyes off me, told me I looked great, and asked what I'd been up to since he'd been away. Instead of telling him, I demonstrated my best moves.

As he unpacked, I noticed a new pair of red and black size fourteen cowboy boots. Apparently, my husband had been learning some dance moves of his own. That Friday night, we went out dancing. Friday nights were never the same again.

~Tamara Moran-Smith

80

Small Business Dreams

Forget the risk and take the fall, if it's what you want,
then it's worth it all.
~Author Unknown

L
ike a lot of people, I've always wanted to be self-employed, but I was afraid to make the leap. Everything I had read about starting a small business suggested I should have a whole lot of money in the bank before I even considered striking out on my own. Three kids, my own college loans, and several medical mishaps over the years had certainly not allowed for *that.*

I'd had jobs I liked, but somehow I'd never been satisfied. Teaching school had been fulfilling for about ten years, but then the luster had faded. Careers as a college instructor and corporate training designer had begun to tarnish eventually, too.

One boring day at the office, I made a list of all the technical skills I'd acquired over the years in my jobs and as a freelancer. The list was substantial. But I considered my dreams of self-employment an unlikely scenario, and the list went back in my drawer, only to emerge the next time I got the corporate blues. As I continued to work at various tasks and learn new things on the job, my list grew.

Eventually, the little list stopped growing and blossomed instead into a full-blown business plan.

One autumn evening, I showed the plan to my husband while we were out having dinner.

"It looks feasible," he said. "Maybe some day."

I swallowed my disappointment. What did I *think* he would say? "Sure, hon, go ahead. We have no money saved, but just quit your job and give this a go. The worst thing that can happen is we'll lose the house."

The next day I went back to work, and the list went back in the drawer.

And then it happened: I got greedy.

I had a perfectly good job at a perfectly good company. A decent salary. A great boss. But another perfectly good company offered me more money, more vacation time, more everything.

And just like that—with one swoop of my pen—I undertook a role for which I was not fully prepared. For more than thirty years, I had been the quick learner, the independent worker, the self-starter. And here I was, in my early fifties, with multiple careers behind me—at a new job—not able to catch on or fit in.

Now what?

Looking back, I realize it wasn't that I couldn't still learn just as fast as I ever had; it was that I had entered a corporate environment where lifelong employees had developed a climate and lingo so specific to their company and industry that newcomers felt more like outsiders than part of the team. If I had done my homework, I would have known this was a poor move.

Still, I now had to make a decision. Stay put and pretend that I "got it"? Financial common sense would suggest that I do just that, no matter how miserable it made me.

But I've never had a lot of common sense when it comes to following my heart or my head. My heart always wins.

And this time my heart won in more ways than one: when I again brought out my little business plan during dinner, I was reminded just how much my husband of over thirty years loves me. "I believe in you," he said.

More powerful words were never spoken.

I launched my small business, which provides editorial and design services, a few weeks later. It hasn't been easy. I found out quickly that self-employment and "flexible lifestyle" are not synonymous. I work many more hours now than I did when in the employ of others. And money is inconsistent. Some days are good, and some days I still search the want ads and question the wisdom of my decision.

No guarantees exist that my business will continue to grow or even maintain its current momentum. But no guarantees exist either that another employer wouldn't lay me off or that I wouldn't find myself in a bad job situation again. I took a risk and faced my doubt head on. I made the choice to *believe* in myself.

And that's a risk worth taking.

~Dianna Graveman

81

Dream Life through Freedom

The guardian angels of life sometimes fly so high as to be beyond our sight,
but they are always looking down upon us.
~Jean Paul Richter

"We've got a Code Blue. CODE BLUE!" blared over the intercom in the ICU of Stony Brook Hospital. My brother and I were huddled in the hallway twenty feet away, holding each other and trying very hard not to cry. We knew it was for our mom. We had just been holding her hands minutes earlier, me holding her left, and James holding her right, when her heart stopped.

The doctors said it wouldn't be long after they stopped the medicine that was keeping her body alive, and yet it was still shockingly fast. I knew she was already gone—she had said goodbye to me earlier when I had been in that dreamlike state between being awake and asleep on my flight from Las Vegas to New York. She had told me she loved me and to be strong. In fact, I wasn't expecting her to still be alive when we landed. She had had nine heart attacks in ten hours. Mom was always a fighter. But I knew that "she" was gone. They were keeping her body alive for us to say goodbye.

My mother had been sick for years—suffering from diabetes, heart disease, obesity, and three different types of arthritis. In the end she died from liver failure. Too many Tylenols for her arthritis—apparently you can't take twenty-plus a day—a complete overdose no one caught because they were too busy looking at the "big diseases." Ironically, she was in her best health in the years after my father passed away. He had died almost four years earlier after a nine-day battle with prostate cancer. He was diagnosed and unexpectedly died of the disease before anyone had even figured out a treatment plan. He said he had never wanted to be an old man who faded away and got weak. To our disappointment and anguish, he got his wish.

Losing both parents before the age of forty was daunting to say the least. I was at war with our family—emotions were brought up and resentments that had percolated for years shot to the surface. Things I never knew about my parents or my grandparents came to light as the weight of being executor of five family estates was placed on my shoulders. I tried to grieve as best as I could while still trying to keep everything together. It wasn't fun. At the end of it all, half of my family had disappeared. I was left with a nice nest egg, but only half a family, no parents and no place to go "home" to anymore.

After two years of battles, it was finally over. I was finally able to grieve. One day, I looked to the sky and said out loud, "Okay Mom, what's next?" Instead of being scared or uncertain, it was a strangely freeing question. I had moved to Las Vegas years earlier on a complete whim, throwing away years of building a successful marketing career to follow my dream of being a singer. Was it selfish to ask for more? To ask my mom for a new dream? To ask what's next?

Within the next few months, weird things started to happen. Right before my dad died, I had started following the teachings of both Tony Robbins and *The Secret*—getting the movie a year before it was publicly released—and started keeping a gratitude journal. For years nothing seemed to happen, no real changes in my life. But after the day I asked my mom what was next, little by little everything in my journal started to come true, as if by magic!

I was able to live in Las Vegas and summer in Long Island like I had wanted to since I was a child. I started to travel the world—sometimes winning free trips! I wanted to move from my apartment to a new home, and my best friend, who was a real estate agent, drove by a new development that was building the exact home I had envisioned years before. I was able to buy it—and at a discounted price. The original owners who had commissioned my house surprisingly bowed out while the structure was already under construction. I even rescued the exact dog I had envisioned as being a part of my life—a pure bundle of love.

Even though I loved being a singer on the Las Vegas Strip, I had actually wanted to leave my job for some time. It had always been a place of negativity—a place where management didn't seem to value us as individuals. It was hard to put on a show and make people happy when management would cut me down almost every day. I had no idea what the next step would be. But I wanted something new. What that "new" was, I had no idea.

I took the summer off to finally work out my grief and plan my future. When I returned to work, I was told I had been fired but never given a reason. Searching for new employment and facing nothing but dead ends, I wandered into a Meetup group and found my life's purpose—voice acting. I could act, perform, create my own schedule, travel, make a good income, and still have time to volunteer and teach. My "tribe" of fellow voice actors became my new friends and replaced the family I had lost—giving back to me tenfold all that I gave to them, a group of like-minded people who put others before themselves.

Lastly, my greatest blessing was when I returned home from my mom's funeral, and my best friend informed me she was pregnant with her first child. That little girl is the complete light of my life. I can't walk into a room without her dropping everything to rush to me with a giant hug. I honestly believe my mom sent this angel child to me.

They say when God closes a door he opens a window and that everything happens for a reason. My parents gave me the freedom to achieve every dream I ever thought of and ones I didn't even know I had until they came true. I miss my parents every day and I wish they were here. But I know they have had a hand in this—and that they continue to allow me to thrive and send me blessings every day.

~Andrea Hadhazy

Chapter
8

Time to Thrive

It's Time to Pursue Your Dreams

82

100 Pairs of Shoes

All growth is a leap in the dark, a spontaneous
unpremeditated act without benefit of experience.
~Henry Miller

T he 100 pairs of shoes were the first things to go. Next were the 200 pieces of clothing, many with designer labels and some never worn. Soon after were the thousands of photos, the twelve cases of books and an entire filing cabinet of personal papers. Reams of coloured paper and pencils were put aside for the local primary school. I then piled up tens of thousands of dollars worth of personal development material that had taken me on a thousand journeys over thirty years, but no longer seemed relevant. My entire office and twenty-six years as a businesswoman were reduced to one cardboard box.

Significantly, I decided to trash every diary and journal I had written since the age of twelve. While they were a record of my deep emotional life, I felt the person they would go to after my demise, my only son, shouldn't have the emotional or physical burden of storing them. In the end, they were the easiest to dispatch.

Sitting on my garage floor sorting through this stuff made me reflect on the past forty years of my life. There were beautiful times and innocent times and I contemplated why I needed to leave Melbourne and Australia. I think the innocence left when I got my divorce. So as I threw out things I'd once held dear, mementos of my life, it felt strangely distant. Not sad, not melancholic, no feelings of "I wish it was still like that" as I sifted through twenty-one years of marriage, motherhood and almost three decades of business. Instead, it felt truly exciting to go through my past selecting what should go and what should stay.

In the end I took 100 large black garbage bags to the tip and have never looked back.

My decision to leave home came all of a sudden. I'd just finished a television interview: It was Valentine's Day and I was talking about Internet dating following the success of my recently published book. I knew then I didn't want to be known as the "Dating Queen," and I knew I was over living in Australia.

My twenty-year-old son had just headed overseas and it was the first time in twenty-five years I was free from cooking nightly dinners. I'd left my husband five years earlier over his infidelity.

But that was the past and now my thoughts were of me. I had no more responsibilities and I could either stay where I was, learn to play bridge and golf, and enter God's waiting room or do what truly made me feel alive: travel.

I rented my house, put eighteen dozen bottles of wine in storage, along with my convertible Mercedes. My beloved cat Polyester went to my ex-husband's first ex-wife, my art and possessions went into a storage container, and at sixty-four I took off for the unknown with nothing more than a suitcase, a laptop and a one-way ticket.

The amazing thing was I didn't care where I landed. I didn't need to know where I would live — it could be London, Paris, Rome or somewhere else. I didn't need to know in advance. I needed to feel where was right.

This was a time to move out of my head and into my heart. This was a time to indulge all my senses; no longer needing to hold a life together that had truly passed its use-by date.

I began to really thrive and be excited by living in a state of uncertainty that came with a promise of so much more. It felt freeing and liberating not having a plan. There was only my daily decision to live in joy.

And that was easy. I love culture, art, history, and architecture.

I was in London with its 250 galleries and museums. I adopted the hashtag #galleriesandlunch and life took off!

No longer being a businesswoman, a wife, a whatever I'd said about myself in the past when meeting new people, I decided to adopt the identity of "The Invitation."

All of a sudden I was being invited to functions at embassies and gorgeous homes. I forged friendships and relationships with an amazing assortment of new people and enjoyed spending time with friends I had known for years.

There were films, dinners, lunches, art, museums, music, and culture of all sorts. There were tempting projects on offer, but the minute I realised I was evaluating them with my head I said no. When they pulled at my heartstrings, I said yes and threw myself into them.

Life was good. Life was actually outstanding. When people asked whether I missed my possessions, my books, my art, my car, my whatever, I can honestly say I replied, "No, not in the slightest." I had three things to do most days, starting from morning and ending at midnight. I was totally in love, with London and my life in it.

The only thing that was missing was in fact love. But since I'd been in a loveless marriage for so long and that ended now seven and a half years ago, I guess I'd learned to live without that too and still be happy.

So what do they say happens when you're not looking but simply enjoying your life? Suddenly the partner of your dreams crosses your path. And yes, he did. A gorgeous, caring, kind, passionate man just dropped in two days after I sent the message to the universe that I wanted him.

I was sixty-seven-and-a-half years old; I was living in a rented flat 12,000 miles from "home;" I had none of my possessions with me, no car to drive, no longer a business to occupy my time and no daily, weekly or monthly schedule. I'd chosen to launch into the void, and here I was in wonderful London living in total joy.

I'd always loved Rod Stewart's rendition of "Never Give Up On A Dream," and now I was living it. Taking that risk, leaving certainty and boredom behind, leaving Australia with just a suitcase and a laptop gave me the ultimate prize of love and happiness.

And I never once missed those 100 pairs of shoes!

~Dr. Buzz McCarthy

A Story of Love and Teeth

You are never too old to set another goal or to dream a new dream.
~C.S. Lewis

When I'm asked what it's like to be married to a dentist, my first response is glib: I get teased for being the only parent who sends her kid to a sleepover without a toothbrush, I co-carry a school debt load as big as a mortgage, and I'm expected to have perfect teeth and even better breath—which, in my experience, is not always possible.

But then there's the response that's not glib, but heartfelt—as true as anything I've ever believed: I can't separate my particular dentist guy from his dentist job, for together they make him the person I'm married to.

My particular dentist guy, Mick, was once an unfulfilled twenty-eight-year-old manufacturing and plastics engineer who drew computerized sketches of an airplane's wing rivets for a prominent aerospace corporation. A couple of years later, he designed water ski and wakeboard bindings for world-class athletes. Cool enough, to be sure, but that same engineer guy would come home disappointed that he'd sat at a machine all day and had spoken to only one or two other human beings—about nothing that meant anything to him.

Then Mick got laid off, just days before planes were used as bombs to take down the Twin Towers. He spent six months searching for engineering work — mostly in his underwear at the computer — while I taught college courses part-time and we shared caring for our infant and toddler. Desperate, Mick eventually took up work with a contractor, installing hardwood floors and painting trim for another few months.

Somewhere in there, though, he observed his younger brother at work as a new dentist. Mick sat in the operatory and watched carefully. He saw how the mouth was the gateway to health for the rest of the body. He watched his brother's hands move in intricate and detailed ways in a small space. He listened to the care, banter, and concern communicated between patient and dentist. In short, he immediately saw how he, too, could use his head, his hands, and his heart — by being a dentist.

Initially, he didn't say anything about what that visit meant to him. But I'll never forget the rainy day he pulled our old VW Vanagon off the highway and cut the engine. He unfastened his seatbelt and turned toward me, his voice shaking. "I think I want to be a dentist."

I shivered.

Then I nodded my head like crazy — I knew he could do it, and I knew he'd be good at it. I also knew he was brave to want it, which added yet another layer of love for him in my heart. There in the van, he told me he'd considered dentistry in high school, but thought the road too long and possibly too hard. However, after watching his brother go through dental school, he reflected on how four years passed no matter what. Time passes whether or not you're doing what you want. Why not take a risk and make sure you do something meaningful while the time passes?

Looking at our two kids, oblivious in their car seats, Mick said, "I want to leave them a legacy they can be proud of. I want to leave a legacy of pursuing dreams — even if they seem really, really challenging."

So Mick returned to college at thirty-three, taking three full years of prerequisite classes from the school where he'd graduated seven years earlier. For the first few months we wondered what we'd gotten ourselves into. We were on public assistance, my part-time contract work at a college an hour and a half away was finally up, and we were out of money. I remember standing in the kitchen taking a phone interview for an airport shuttle job, with my toddler squeezing my knees and my baby sticking a Cheerio she'd found on the floor in her mouth. I was scared, I could barely concentrate, and I couldn't stand the thought of random hours driving an airport bus.

That interview, and another for a résumé-writing service, went horribly. We trusted our persistence would pay off, though, and put the word out to all our friends that we each needed work. Our friends were excited for us, even envious at times, and they looked out for us, the way people will when they want to be part of something big.

Eventually, I got a miraculous call to interview for teaching a full course load at the university. I started a week later. Mick started a part-time job making dentures that same month.

Carefully balancing my job, Mick's job, childcare, and Mick's student load, we made it into the final quarter of prerequisites. Mick scored high on the Dental Aptitude Test, filled out fifteen dental school applications, wrote a killer statement of intent (thank me very much), and earned himself a seat in the only three-year program in the nation.

After a mighty garage sale where we sold everything we could think to sell, mostly wakeboards Mick had acquired, we packed up our three- and four-year-old kids and moved to San Francisco for a life of school, loans, and part-time work.

Dental school was challenging and scary. We were still on public assistance and I worked part-time as a preschool teacher — so I could bring my kids. I managed all childcare, healthcare, and household work in order for Mick to give 100 percent to his studies, which often felt laced with elusive requirements as he bartered and traded patients with other students to drum up crown work, root canals, and fillings.

It was really hard. But it was really worth it.

Now Mick's a dentist, one who's just ironic enough to enjoy saying it's time to go to the dentist when it's "tooth hurty," and who comes home from work deeply moved by the work he's done and the lives he's encountered. He never tells me names or places, but his eyes often water as he tells me about hardship, victory, silliness, or gratitude he's seen or experienced in the mouths or lives of his patients. He never got that fulfillment as an engineer.

So when Mick leans against the kitchen counter, a new dentist at age forty-one, talking to me passionately about his work, I appreciate this particular guy who loves his particular job. I hold onto the memories of hardship and risk—because they make this all the sweeter—and I hone in on his lovely, if slightly imperfect teeth and his occasionally bad breath. Because, well, sometimes you just can't have it all. But with a lot of determination, you can come pretty close.

~Anjie Reynolds

Your Sweater Is Awesome

A desire to be in charge of our own lives, a need for control, is born in each of us. It is essential to our mental health, and our success, that we take control.
~Robert F. Bennett

As a young child, I understood that my mother, from the moment I was born, had laid out my path. My path was straight, forged from steel and lined with barbed wire. I was not to deviate from nor question my path.

Make-up, short shorts, tight jeans, high heels or low-cut tops were not part of the approved ensemble. Boys were most definitely not allowed. On this path I would be an obedient daughter, student and member of the church. I would go to college, marry a good boy from the church, have children and settle down in some nameless Midwestern town.

For eleven and a half years I followed these rules and met all expectations. I was an excellent student, I practiced hard for my piano lessons, I visited my two approved friends, and I went to church, where I had to stifle my questions. At my church, we were taught the following:

1. Science was false.
2. The Bible was truth verbatim.

3. Premarital sex was an abominable sin.
4. The end of the world was imminent and preparation was required by all.

Outwardly, I accepted these teachings. I tried to fit into the awkward youth group gatherings and become an active, productive member of the congregation by serving lukewarm coffee in the food kitchen. Inwardly, I was confused because the rest of the world seemed to be doing just fine believing in modern science, engaging in premarital sex and not waiting around for the world to end. I felt I was hovering on the fringes of fully living.

On the cusp of my graduation from high school, I met a boy. It happened at my part-time job, amid harsh fluorescent lights, surrounded by racks of clothing and the scents of mingled perfumes from the cosmetic counter.

"Your sweater is awesome."

My eyes lifted to meet the blue stare of a tall, handsome boy with long, straight pale blond hair. He was dressed in a dark suit and colorful socks.

"Thanks."

He dipped his head in acknowledgment, grinned and walked confidently into the break room. With that seemingly trivial first exchange, I felt a sense of possibility and optimism. I was not sure what would happen, but I knew I had come to a bend in my otherwise straight path.

We began dating immediately, almost without conscious thought or spoken agreement. Being with him felt dangerous, freeing and exciting. He was confident, sophisticated, well educated, and intelligent. We took breaks together at the mall food court, laughing over limp Taco Bell and sticky tabletops. On his days off work, he dressed in black T-shirts with ripped jeans, drank alcohol, cursed and played electric bass. His friends were down-to-earth, non-judgmental and genuinely friendly, a far cry from the people I grew up with at church. He introduced me to new genres of music, such as the surprisingly lyrical metal band Tool and the experimental ramblings of Michael

Gira. He taught me to appreciate the metaphysical art of Salvador Dali, showed me indie films like *Garden State* and racy comedies like *Super Troopers*, and helped me enjoy new experiences. I was eighteen, he was twenty-one, and we were inseparable.

I brought him to meet my parents after a month of dating. They hated him on sight. The tension was palpable. I felt waves of judgment radiating from my mother as she questioned him the way a detective might interrogate a criminal. My throat was dry and my hands were slick with sweat as I contemplated the results of this disastrous meeting. In the aftermath, I was forbidden to see him again based on the sole fact that he was a treacherous speed bump in my carefully paved future. It was during this first meeting that I believe I made the unconscious choice to go against my rigid upbringing and make my own decisions.

Secretly, Andrew and I continued to date. With each lie and fabrication, I felt my protective bubble disintegrate and allow me to glimpse the freedom that every teenager longs for. I went to loud, outrageous parties, the bass pumping through my body. I stayed out past 9 p.m., driving around in his huge baby blue Buick LeSabre, feeling the cool night air snake through my hair and give me a shivering thrill. I made new friends, went to my first non-Christian rock concert and drank my first alcoholic beverage. I even committed the aforementioned abominable sin. I reveled in the feeling of truly belonging to someone and something.

Eventually, one hasty lie caused the entire house of cards to crumble around us. I can still feel the punch glancing off the side of my head as I sat at the dining room table in front of my mother, forced to disclose my intimate experiences in front of my family and youth pastor. Time slowed to a crawl as I was immobilized by shame, anger, hurt and final disillusionment. As if through a fog, I heard my brother call me a whore and saw my youth pastor convulsively clutch his worn brown leather Bible as he looked at me with disappointment and disgust. I will never forget the moment I saw my mother decide that I was tainted by my relationship with Andrew. In her eyes, I was ruined. My life as a sheltered, supported dependent ended that day. My parents turned me out of the house into the proverbial unknown. My car was taken and sold, my college funding stopped. I had nowhere to go but into the arms of the boy who had showed me a glimpse of how rich life could be.

Perhaps I was immature in how I chose to handle that fortuitous summer after graduation, or perhaps it needed to happen for me to realize that the weight of my predetermined future was slowly crushing me. On some level, I understood my need for rebellion and experimentation. I felt fleeting flutters of guilt as my previous "good girl" persona made herself known. But deep down, I yearned for the ability to be my own person and make my own choices, for good or bad, without fear of judgment from those professing to love me unconditionally. Andrew showed me that it was okay to fail and that it was okay to have my own opinions and ask questions.

For many years, I could not recall certain events of this time. The confused feelings of guilt, shame, freedom, and love were like tangled threads, too intertwined for me to examine them individually. Later, I was able to separate them and grow to understand how each thread was important to my personal development.

I keep the "awesome sweater" in the back of my closet as a memento of the quirky pick-up line that was the beginning of a new future. Sometimes I take it out, put it on and become the oppressed eighteen-year-old girl I once was. As I look in the mirror and see the moth holes and unraveling hem that belies its age, I wonder how different my life would be if I had chosen to wear something else that day. Meeting that boy eight years ago was the catalyst that changed me as a person and gave me the strength and ability to deviate from my path.

That boy has now been my husband of six years, and because of him, I am able to see how different the world is outside of the bubble made from religious judgment, rigid rules and fear. To this day, I still struggle with my personal views on religion and reconciliation with my family. As a new mother, I can only hope that my daughter grows up free to believe and experience what she wants. May she find acceptance in being herself, formulate her own beliefs, and love whomever she chooses.

~Emily Oman

Fort

*If we are ever to enjoy life, now is the time—
not tomorrow, nor next year, nor in some future life after we have died.
Today should always be our most wonderful day!*
~Thomas Dreier

Her nickname was Fort. She was my cousin's daughter, she was in her late twenties, and she had stage IV breast cancer. If there was ever a case to be filed in the "Life Isn't Fair" folder, this was it.

As Melissa (her real name), battled cancer, her nickname seemed most appropriate. She was a fort indeed. She seemed strong, impenetrable and she held up during the battle of overcoming cancer. Like all forts, she was a little battered after the wars, but somehow she remained standing. She fought that cancer for five years before it finally beat her.

Those around Fort were consumed with grief, anger and frustration. How could someone so young and vibrant be taken away so early? Many people around Fort seemed to question why such a horrible thing could happen. They felt sorry for Fort. They felt sorry for themselves. No one seemed to handle Melissa's cancer or death very well. No one, that is, except Melissa herself.

Melissa "Fort" Fortener tackled both her cancer and impending death with an amazing attitude. She appreciated each day she had in her last five years. Though she understood that her life could be shortened, she lived it to the fullest. Each day, she kept a big smile on her face and a wicked sense of humor by her side. Fort even started a daily blog, so she could chronicle her battle with cancer and inspire others. Guess what? That blog worked!

Fort shared her wit and her wisdom. She shared the pain of chemotherapy and the battles she endured with health insurance companies. On her blog, she also showed everyone how much fun life could be. The theme of her blog seemed to be "live each day to the fullest, because it can be your last."

Fort shared her feelings about every topic and she did it because she didn't want to regret leaving something behind.

Her blog, which was filled with humorous and articulate revelations, inspired me. I realized if I kept putting my dreams off until tomorrow, my tomorrow might never come. So six months prior to turning fifty, I told myself to "start writing." I vowed to have no regrets. I wrote story after story. I wrote short poems and long poems. I wrote short stories, some real and some fictional. Some of my writing was sad; some was funny. Some of what I wrote was deep and introspective and some was just plain dumb and nonsensical. There were days when I didn't want to write, but then I thought of Fort. She wrote when she was in pain and near death. If she could write in that condition, then I could certainly make the effort.

Finally, I took another page from Fort's playbook. I gained courage! After all, she had shown plenty of it. I had written lots of stories and it was time to share them. Writing is very personal, so sharing what you've written is sometimes difficult. But I shared. First I shared stories with family and friends. Then I shared with colleagues and acquaintances. Finally I gained the courage to send some stories to magazines and publishers.

Now, three years later, I've had articles published in national magazines. I have short stories in best-selling inspirational books and I have also published a children's book that has been released worldwide. I'm not stating this to brag, I'm stating this because I'm thankful. If Fort had not inspired me, I might have never attempted to be a published author. I always loved writing and always dreamed of being a published writer, but two things always stopped me: fear and procrastination. I learned from Fort that you have to tackle life without fear. I also learned from Fort that life can be too short. I could not let my procrastination keep me from my destination.

I wish I could thank Fort for inspiring me. Her words and her attitude were fantastic even at the darkest time in her short life. Thankfully, those words and that positive attitude rubbed off on me. It made me start writing and motivated me to chase my unfulfilled dream. Now when the time comes for my life to end, I can go with no regrets. Just like Fort did!

~David Warren

86

But You Were Just a Cop

I love writing. I love the swirl and swing of words as they
tangle with human emotions.
~James A. Michener

I used to dream of being a writer, of possessing the talent and ability to cohesively convert my thoughts to words on paper, and then offering my pieces to the public for their personal reading consumption. Oh yeah, I dreamed of being a writer all right — if only I had the talent and the ability.

But despite my shortcomings, I somehow succeeded. And surprisingly — at least to some — the seeds for my eventual success were sown courtesy of my former career in law enforcement. But long before I could hope to become any kind of writer, and even before my cop career commenced, writing and I would have to be formally introduced.

The C that I'd received for my required freshman writing course in college should have put me on notice that I wasn't a writer, but somehow, it didn't. While my instructor might have assumed that my failure to comprehend the essentials of proper sentence structure and effective writing techniques clearly demonstrated that I had no business entertaining any thoughts of writing, I apparently missed that memo. Shortly after concluding the course, I decided to write a book.

I'd noticed a paperback belonging to my younger sister — a light-weight literary precursor to what would be categorized today as Young

Adult. After giving it a quick read, I concluded that it amounted to little more than trash. But then, an epiphany: If this was what kids were reading, and if this was what paperback publishers were printing, I could write this stuff. I mean, how hard could it be?

As it turned out, trash writing was harder than I thought, and so I asked a friend for help. Wayne, like me, had absolutely no knowledge of the writing process, but he had one qualification that surpassed my own: He'd received a B in our writing class. Wayne agreed to co-author my masterpiece. And so, with only a storyline to follow, we got down to the business of writing a tale about a couple of crazy kids spending a crazy summer together on the Jersey Shore. It was going to be real trashy and it was going to be a monster!

Our completed manuscript actually caught the attention of a few publishers, but in the end, real life trumped our part-time literary endeavors. Wayne became an accountant and I became a cop. Marriages and kids soon followed, and suddenly our trashy monster was forgotten—banished to an old briefcase—handed a life sentence with little chance of parole.

Several years later, I was seated at the dais of a banquet hall stage about to share my thoughts concerning current family values. I was speaking at this conference as a result of my background as a police detective who specialized in juvenile and family matters. I delivered my prepared remarks, which included several personal stories relevant to the topic. Afterward, during the applause, I noticed some audience members were smiling while others were crying. Their responses caught me off guard.

Later, while still considering the audience reaction, I thought about the power of words and wondered if I could take some of the key elements from my speech and incorporate them into a short essay. The idea of using words to make people laugh and cry while still delivering the intended message intrigued me. That night I wrote a rather mundane piece about my son kissing me goodnight. When finished I wrote a second—this time about my daughter. And when I was done with that, I wondered if either was good enough to be published.

Some magazine editors wondered this as well. I'd sent both essays to various publications, and received several rejection notices in return. I began questioning whether anyone would ever be interested in reading the kind of personal pieces I was now writing.

As it turned out, somebody was.

One afternoon I received an acceptance notice, and a few days later, another. My essay about my son kissing me goodnight would eventually appear in several publications—including a Chicken Soup for the Soul book! The piece about my daughter was also published. And just like that, I was a writer!

I've written lots of pieces since then—many of which have also been published. And these days, when people who are familiar with my background want to talk to me about my writing, some still feel the need to mention, "But you were just a cop," as if my previous profession should negate my ability to string together a few sentences into a publication-worthy piece.

But to be honest, I credit my former career with affording numerous opportunities to speak publicly, thus necessitating the need to craft relevant speeches that were both entertaining and informative—the old "make them laugh and cry while still delivering the intended message" format that I still use today. Had I not been a cop, it's doubtful that I'd be sharing my thoughts through my writings today.

I still dream of being a writer, except now I dream of being a better one. It's become a passion and I'm humbled to know that people are sometimes moved by my writing—which, by the way, may someday include a trashy novella for teenagers. You never know! Until then, I'll just continue offering the reading public my scribbled thoughts—the products of a not especially talented, grade C, writing ex-cop. Imagine that!

~Stephen Rusiniak

87

Seeing the World

Life begins at the end of your comfort zone.
~Author Unknown

M y friends and I chatted at my kitchen table. "You've got to see these pictures of my trip," one of them said as she rummaged in her purse for her smartphone. I gave a shy smile. Inside, dark thoughts swirled. How I wished I could see them and how I wanted to be independent and free to travel as she did. Secretly, I cursed the retinal disease that took my eyesight and kept me at home.

I hid my disappointment behind another fake smile. "You guys will have to describe them to me," I said. "I sure wish I could travel like you."

"You can," she said. "Airlines have assistance for the blind."

Assistance? Not the kind I needed. I first needed help in overcoming my apprehension of going anywhere alone. And I also needed to learn to have enough boldness to ask for help.

For a long time, I went to bed with that desire in my heart and that sense of helplessness in my mind. I prayed for freedom and I asked God for solutions.

Months later, He answered me by giving me boldness. "It's been years," my cousin said in Spanish when she called on the phone from Bolivia. "You need to come and visit."

I couldn't pass up a chance to go back home. I didn't want to miss that opportunity. That visit was a desire I'd tucked deep in my heart for years.

My sons were old enough to stay with their dad and the airline ticket for me was affordable. Although I had no excuses to pass up the trip, I had one hurdle to overcome — fear.

Determined to fight that insecurity, I took the first step. I swallowed hard and picked up the phone. I dialed directory assistance and contacted an airline. I requested a round-trip ticket from Orlando to La Paz, Bolivia.

"Anything else?" the airline representative asked.

I took a deep breath. "Yes," I said. "I'm blind and wonder if you would have anyone to help me navigate through the airport?"

"Yes, ma'am," she said. "Just a moment, please."

My muscles stiffened. I wasn't as bold and secure as I thought. But there was no turning back now. Everything about the idea scared me — the international flight and all of the uncertainty. The risk I'd end up somewhere else. The possibility I'd trip or fall, lose my luggage, or need something and have no one to ask. All the possibilities ran through my head.

Traveling alone for the blind should be banned, I thought.

The rep came back on the phone. "I have it all arranged," she said in a matter-of-fact tone. "Is there anything else?"

That was my clue. Her voice, pleasant and calm, told me they'd dealt with blind people before. The help they provided seemed to be part of their routine. And that's when I vowed that my sense of adventure would also become part of my life's routine.

I removed fear from my itinerary. Instead, I packed courage, trust in God and lots of boldness.

Once in the airport, I sharpened my hearing to take in the action around me and to listen to announcements. I then heard the announcement to board the plane.

When I arrived in La Paz, my cousin and I hugged and hugged at the reunion. We relished every moment during my visit to my hometown. And eventually, the trips that followed turned airplanes and airports into familiar settings for me.

Years later, sharing my story of moving from "fear to faith" with audiences also became a familiar activity. Like an airplane on a runway, my career as an inspirational speaker took off. Dozens of trips all around the world continue to fill my calendar.

My routine seldom changes. I kiss my husband goodbye at curbside. With excitement in my heart, I hand my ID to the airline representative when I get to the counter. Then the fun begins. I wait for the escort assigned to me. And holding his arm with one hand, I carry the white cane with the other as we walk across the airport. Engaged in conversation, we follow the exercise through security and head to my gate with ease.

But sometimes, with no extra effort, I land in trouble. On one occasion, a flight attendant guided me by the arm to my seat inside the plane. She stopped. "Here's your seat," she said.

"Thank you," I said as I stretched my arm and held onto the back of the seat. As I did, I noticed the object I was holding onto began to move. And that's when I realized it wasn't the seat I was gripping, but a man's bald head.

Embarrassed? Perhaps a little, but I quickly add those incidents to the humorous stories I later share with my audiences.

When arriving at my destination, someone assigned by the organization I'll be speaking to is usually waiting for me. I've never met him or her before, but after a few moments of chatting, he or she becomes my friend. Everyone I encounter usually does—the person seated beside me on the plane, the hotel clerk, and even housekeeping staff become friends for the moment. Some even open their hearts and share intimate, painful details of their lives. And other folks I meet become lasting friends.

Most are curious. "Are you totally blind?" they ask when I first meet them. "Were you born blind?"

That begins a warm conversation in which I relate details of the retinal hereditary disease. But I emphasize the advantages of being blind: I don't judge anyone on appearance. Everyone is beautiful to me. When I look outside, it's always sunny. And in the morning when

I glance in the mirror, in my mind, I look pretty good. No bad hair days for me.

My trips have taken me from self-pity to security and from complacency to passion. Unlike my friend with her smartphone, I carry images in my heart of the vibrant places I've been. I store images of friends I've met and who've added to my joy. And in the photo album of my heart, I include not only kind gestures from those I meet, but the beautiful opportunities to show others how to see the best of life.

~Janet Perez Eckles

88

Breaking the Mold

You conceive your world in your mind
and then you create it with your hands.
~Chris Widener

G azing out my office window, my eyes fixed on the woman moving slowly down the sidewalk. It appeared the weight of the world rested on her shoulders. The methodical shuffle and the frown lines on her face seemed to signify a joyless life and hidden sadness.

I sensed she knew I was watching when she stopped abruptly and turned toward me. Uneasiness gripped me as the sun cast her shadow's outline across the desk. When I momentarily gazed into her sad eyes, I saw a reflection of myself. She turned and shuffled away, leaving her image to haunt me.

That evening, as I told my husband Chris about my encounter with the sidewalk woman, I struggled to hold back tears. I described the overwhelming emptiness I felt when our eyes had locked.

Sensing my precarious emotional state, my husband asked cautiously, "You work downtown and see countless street people every day. What was it about this sidewalk woman that disturbs you to the point of tears?"

In a barely audible voice, I whispered, "I saw my future. That sidewalk woman is me if I don't change the course of my life in ways that will nourish and nurture my happiness."

With trepidation, Chris asked, "What changes do you need for that to happen?"

His voice reflected his fear that I might be about to ask for a divorce or confess to marital infidelity. I grasped his hands in mine and released the words I had longed to say aloud for the last few years: "I am going to quit my job."

I don't know who felt a greater sense of relief, my husband or me.

Generally, when a person gives a "quit my job" proclamation, it's followed by a plan of action. I had none. My business degree had landed me at a downtown city hospital with a job that provided a good income and coveted health care benefits. The Monday through Friday workweek and thirty-six days of paid time off were added perks. To the average worker, this was a dream job—no nights or weekends, and a pension plan with union job security. Yet for me, it was a prison sentence.

I had allowed my entrepreneurial and creative spirit to be suppressed by the mundane routine of shuffling papers and punching in and out at a time clock. After fifteen years, I finally found the courage to relinquish job security for happiness. I applied for early retirement. Looking back, I can't help but wonder if the sidewalk woman was really an angel in disguise and not just a chance encounter.

It is amazing how fast you can draft a business plan when you don't have a paycheck. When I worked at the hospital, I had put together gift baskets to be auctioned or sold at fundraiser events. Many of the baskets were filled with bath and body products, and over time I began to make my own in an effort to increase the profit margin.

I started to purchase lotion and shower gel in bulk containers and then colored, scented, bottled and labeled the product from home. It wasn't long before I added decorative soaps to the product line. I searched the Internet to find specialty molds to cast my soaps, and eventually stumbled upon a website that offered custom-made soap and chocolate molds. Bingo! My creativity went wild as I looked at all the ready-made designs available, not to mention what I could create myself.

I acquired a domain name and uploaded all my finished bath

products to the website. The proverbial saying, "Build it and they will come" never happened; so I changed my strategy. Instead of selling ready-made product, which was quite labor intensive, I would target the "do-it-yourself" market. I channeled my energy into developing a unique line of soap molds for anyone to make their own bars of soap.

The mold maker at the company I discovered online began to create my mold designs, and wholesale accounts were set up with various vendors to purchase soap bases, dyes and fragrance oils. Soap-making tutorials became my trademark in this new and upcoming industry. Others would soon follow, but I knew I was the pioneer.

It all proved to be a good marketing move; I had an immediate increase in sales. It was empowering and intoxicating to finally have some control over my life and the direction of my future, but my income wasn't self-sustaining.

I registered for classes in HTML at the local university to become skilled in the infrastructure of website design. Upon completion of the courses, a local school district hired me to set up their website, which provided income to continue growing my soap-making business. In my mind, no side job was too small if it brought me closer to my business goal.

My friendship with the owner of Mold Market continued to grow and our shared Christian faith further deepened that business relationship. It was a solid partnership of skills; he casted the molds and I marketed my designs. Three years later, I purchased Mold Market with a ten-year contract for exclusive rights to my mold maker's services.

That partnership and friendship continues to this day. My company offers 300-plus unique soap and chocolate molds with distributorships around the globe. That encounter with the sidewalk woman forever changed the direction of my life and inspired me to step out in faith and believe in myself.

We only get one chance at life. Now I get to mold mine to order.

~Denise Marks

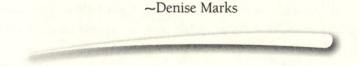

Music Lessons

Music gives a soul to the universe, wings to the mind,
flight to the imagination, and life to everything.
~Plato

I picked our gray cat off the top of our piano and gave her a hug. "That's an expensive perch for a cat," I said out loud.

She head-butted my chin and wiggled out of my arms back to her favorite place — the top of our piano. It gave her a good view of the entire living room, the kitchen, and the back yard.

My husband and I had purchased the piano so our son and daughter could take piano lessons.

I had a secret dream of my own that I did not share with anyone. One day I wanted to learn to play the piano.

I had taken lessons for a short time in elementary school, until my military dad received orders for reassignment, and our piano could not be included in our household shipment. Over the years, the time to play the piano hadn't been right — there had been no place for a large musical instrument, or we didn't have the money for lessons.

I did pursue my love of music and learned to play the flute in junior high school. I made the high school marching band. I enjoyed the performances and the support from others who loved music as I did, but still I had dreamt of sitting on a piano bench and performing.

But as I dusted that piano on that fateful day, I knew it was now or never. I could either try to make the dream come true, or I could forget it once and for all. I lifted the keyboard cover and stroked the keys. I played a few scales I remembered, and the piano sounded as good as it had when it was new.

The next day at church I passed our bulletin board. It listed items for sale, odd jobs, and at the bottom, someone was offering piano lessons.

My voice trembled when I called the number the next day.

The lady who answered had a kind voice as she answered my questions. When she learned that I was the student she hesitated. She had never taught an adult learner, but she was willing to try if I was.

Fortunately, the lessons would begin that week, because I soon began making excuses to myself as to why it was not a good time. I had a full-time job, I had family responsibilities, and I had signed up for a class to update my computer skills. Perhaps I needed to wait until my schedule cleared a little.

I timidly knocked on her door the day of my lesson, half hoping she would not answer. But she did answer and introduced herself as Melody.

What a wonderful name for a music teacher.

When the lesson ended, Melody opened the door to her next student, a six-year-old boy bubbling with enthusiasm.

Melody introduced us and told me his name was Jeff.

"I'm going to learn to play the piano," he told me. No doubts or insecurities got in his way.

His enthusiasm was contagious, and on my way home I whispered, "I'm going to learn to play the piano."

I wasn't a star pupil. I didn't have instant recall on how to read music. I could only read treble clef music since I had played the flute for six years. Reading the treble clef came easy, but playing the bass clef was a struggle. Getting both hands to cooperate was difficult and then she introduced me to the pedal. Maybe I had bitten off more than I could chew.

Melody scolded me for not practicing enough. She had told me at the start that thirty minutes a day should be enough for me, but now she told me that I should increase it to an hour a day.

An hour a day? How would I ever find the time?

I remembered some encouragement I had received from a friend when I started the piano lessons.

I had mumbled, "I don't know if I can find the time."

She had said, "If it's important to you, you don't find time, you make it."

That's what I had to do now. I had to look at my schedule to see where I could make time. Getting up early and practicing wasn't an option; I would wake the whole household. The same was true if I practiced late at night. But then I realized I was practicing when I got home from work, so I only had to add another thirty minutes to that time. I had been watching television before I fixed dinner. I enjoyed the thirty-minute television show but I could turn that into practice time instead.

The next obstacle occurred the following week, when Melody told me I would need to participate in the December recital. Each student would play one selection of a familiar song as well as a Christmas carol, and we had to play by memory. There was no way I could do that. I would have one month to memorize two pieces and I hadn't even seen them yet. I hadn't had to memorize anything in years.

"It's the customary way," Melody said. "And even Jeff is memorizing the pieces he is playing."

Well if a six-year-old was up to the task, surely I could do that.

I practiced the two pieces, and even took the music to work so I could memorize them on my lunch break. It worked! I was able to commit the two pieces to memory.

On the day of the recital, Jeff was the first one up and he played flawlessly. The audience applauded as he bowed.

I was next. As I sat at the piano and took a deep breath, I glanced at my husband. He smiled at me and gave me a thumbs-up. But would the rest of the audience think I was foolish for performing in a children's recital? I placed my fingers on the keys and my memory took over. It was just me and the piano. I wasn't aware of anyone else there. I stayed seated for a few moments at the end.

There was no sound from the audience until one of the men said, "Amen."

Then the audience applauded. But the applause didn't matter. What mattered was that I had followed my dream and I hadn't quit when things got difficult.

~Mary Ann Hayhurst

90

A Student of Life

What lies behind us and what lies before us are tiny
matters compared to what lies within us.
~Ralph Waldo Emerson

I wasn't born a brilliant student. My learning disability, auditory processing disorder, made it nearly impossible to become an outstanding student. Still, throughout my testing, teachers found that I had a special gift—the gift of writing. While I scored poorly in most school subjects, I had nearly perfect written papers and exemplary spelling and grammar skills.

This phenomenon excited both my parents and elementary teachers as they encouraged me to continue with my writing. I often received journals on special occasions such as birthdays or Christmas. Each new journal excited me. Throughout elementary school, middle school, and eventually high school, I already had a dream. Unlike most students, lost, wondering where they'll attend college or what subject they'll major in, I already knew that I wanted to become a writer.

Unfortunately, despite my outstanding grades in advanced English, science and math were holding me back from attending a university where I could pursue my writing career. I'm just not the student type, is what I constantly told myself, but this wouldn't matter to colleges. All they cared about were grades, right?

To achieve my goal of attending a university, I enrolled for two years at a local community college. I started getting my general education classes out of the way during my senior year of high school in order to get ahead, reassuring myself that I would only be attending a community college for two years.

Although I struggled with my math and science classes, often retaking them multiple times, I achieved my goal and it was time to apply to the UC system. I wanted to attend one of the top universities in California — the University of California, Los Angeles, or less likely, the University of California, Berkeley.

A number of colleges accepted me, but then UCLA's letter came: "We regret to inform you…" I didn't need to read the rest of the letter. As tears rushed down my face, I lost hope that Berkeley, the last school that I would hear from, would accept me. If I couldn't get into UCLA, how on earth would I be accepted to Berkeley?

The last day of April arrived — the deadline to hear back from all the public universities in California. No, I didn't have butterflies. This feeling was too painful to be mere butterflies. My stomach was caught in a torturous knot. I knew this would make or break my educational career, determining where my writing skills would be developed.

As my family and I reached our cabin in Lake Tahoe to begin our summer of fun, my phone buzzed. It was an e-mail from the administration of UC Berkeley. My mother and father reassured me that no matter what happened, they were proud of how hard I had worked these past two years. My hands trembling, I opened the e-mail to read, "Congratulations!"

Orientation came just a few short months later. While incoming students took a seat, the head of administration welcomed us to our new home in bear territory. "I'm sure most of you are thinking this was a mistake. Believe me; you're meant to be here." As he continued his speech, he explained that every school is looking for the right fit. Berkeley administrators were looking for students with a unique story to tell.

In my essay I had explained my difficulties in school and how I had overcome my learning disability, which as a result, opened a whole new world to me. I had fought my disability through my passion for writing, all the while exploring what life had to offer. I had been one of a handful of students chosen to study abroad in Germany at the end of high school and I had begun studying under a talented Bay Area photographer while developing my own photography skills. I wasn't the right fit for UCLA, but I was the right fit for Berkeley. They wanted students with passion; students who had fought adversity and overcome it; students with a voice.

As a recent graduate, I've been published by a local publication, worked at two magazines, created my own website, and continue to develop my skills as a writer and photographer. Although I struggle with the writing process from time to time, I still aspire to become an author in the near future. Whenever I'm in doubt I remember the words that reassured me that day at orientation. I am a woman with a unique story, a woman with a voice, and one day, I plan to share it with the world.

~Chelsea DuHaime

91

Fear of Falling

Four wheels move the body. Two wheels move the soul.
~Author Unknown

"Thank you for not running me over," I said as I lay bruised and bloodied in the intersection with my mangled bike on top of me. The man looking down at me had just hit me with his car and I was thanking him for not running me over. In reality I was thanking him for not destroying my goal of proving my independence. I was planning a bike trip in the Canadian Rocky Mountains. I was both terrified and thrilled at the challenge.

Biking in the Rockies wasn't the typical midwestern middle-age mom jaunt, but I had to prove to myself that I was more than just a typical middle-age woman. I had a great life, but something was missing. I needed to explore the part of me that was independent from my husband and kids. When a friend mentioned going on a bike trip together, I enthusiastically signed up. The fact that I hadn't done anything like it before was part of the allure.

Living in the flat Chicago area, I was anxious about my stamina cycling uphill and terrified about speed going down. My biggest fear was hitting the ground after I'd hurtled down a mountain road out of control.

Three weeks before the trip I was biking on a paved path that runs between a busy street and a channel. Cross streets with traffic lights disrupt the route every half mile. I saw the green light as I approached the intersection. As I was crossing I glanced to my left and saw a car rushing toward me. There wasn't time for me to move out of the way. The car smacked me, I struck the ground and the car stopped.

"I'm sorry," said the man who hit me.

I was bruised, but hadn't broken any bones. I was still focused on "I'm going to bike the Rockies."

"Thank you for stopping and not running me over," I said. "Didn't you see the red light?"

"Yes, but I went anyway," he said.

His response was so unexpected that I asked again. "Didn't you see that you had a red light?"

He repeated, "Yes, but I went anyway."

I thanked the man again for stopping. I was aware of how incongruous it was. He ran the red light and hit me and I kept thanking him for not running me over. All I could concentrate on was that I was still going to be able to leave my comfort zone and bike the Rockies.

The man was concerned about the blood flowing from the superficial cuts on my arms and legs. I was aware of pain in other parts of my body — where his car hit my arm and hip; where my torso twisted and hit my bike; where the gears cut into my leg, where my anklebone smacked the pavement. Biking gloves saved my hands from being pierced by the stones on the street, but my left hand ached. My helmet softened the impact to my head.

"I'm okay. My son can pick me up," I said. I wanted to say "Thank you for not killing me. Now go away and get out of my life. I need to bike the Rockies."

The man said he'd pay for the bike repairs, gave me his name and phone number and left me standing on the side of the road.

The next day I left the repair estimate on the man's answering machine and asked him to call me. He didn't call. Had he decided that he shouldn't have given me his name? Shouldn't have admitted guilt? Was he afraid I was going to sue? Had he forgotten about the accident? Had he been driving drunk?

Now I regretted that none of the bystanders had taken the initiative to call the police. I wanted the man to get a ticket. I wanted him to go to court and admit that he ran a red light and hit me. I wanted it to be on his driving record. I was still focused on biking the Rockies, but now I was mad at myself for letting the man off so easy.

I speculated about the man's reaction if my three sons—two of them 6'3", one in his police uniform—knocked on his door and said, "You hurt our mommy." I wondered how he would have responded to my phone message if I had mentioned that I was a lawyer.

The man cheerfully answered when I called again and said, "I'll mail a check." He didn't ask, "How are you?" Why hadn't he called me back? Did he tell anyone he hit a lady on a bike? Did it affect him at all? Did he respond to his friends asking, "What's new?" with "I ran a red light and hit a lady on a bike?" Did he continue, "No one called the police and she thanked me for stopping and not running her over?"

I focused on the freedom I felt in being hit by a car but still being able to go on my trip. The multi-colored bruises on my arms and legs were wonderful conversation openers. When I said that I was hit by a car, I felt compelled to explain to everyone—family, friends, acquaintances, strangers—that I didn't do anything wrong. A man ran a red light.

When I picked my bike up from the store I forced myself to go for a ride. My arm and leg throbbed each time they were jarred when I rode over an imperfection in the street. I approached intersections with apprehension and looked at every car as a potential enemy. I also felt a bizarre sense of freedom in knowing that even if I did everything right, I couldn't control what happened to me.

Three weeks later I rode my bike in the Rockies. Most of the time I was cycling on long mountain roads with rare cross streets, so I didn't have to worry about being hit at an intersection. Vehicles could only strike me from behind or sideswipe me. I would stay to the side of the road, but there was nothing more I could do about it. Each time I heard the roar of a heavily loaded logging truck approaching I anticipated the aroma of freshly cut wood that I'd enjoy as it passed. I inhaled deeply and enjoyed the smell as I struggled to maintain my balance so that I wouldn't be blown off the road by the backdraft. With my elbows bent close to my side and my head down, I picked up speed as I hurtled down the mountain roads. The speed was exhilarating. I knew what it felt like to fall off a bike and hit the pavement. I'd done it and survived. The man who hit me had liberated me. He released me from my fear of falling.

I was free and independent as I soared down the mountain roads, no longer afraid.

~Karen Gray-Keeler

My Everest

What you get by achieving your goals is not as important
as what you become by achieving your goals.
~Henry David Thoreau

It was October and I was at a bookstore to hear the author and mountain climber Heidi Howkins. She looked intense. "Mountaineering is a life-or-death situation," she explained. "And I have to be ready for whatever challenge I may face. I take it seriously." Heidi proceeded to read and comment from her newly released book entitled *K2, One Woman's Quest for the Summit.*

Her obvious excitement built as she continued: "K2 is a deadly mountain. Only five women had made the summit and all died either on the way down or in subsequent climbing accidents. I wanted to summit that mountain!"

In her two prior attempts on K2, Howkins had seen climbers swept away by avalanches and had seen frozen bodies along the trail. And yet K2 kept calling her.

I had never been a particularly daring person. I had attempted many things in my life, but never felt I had mastered any of them: knitting, sewing, skiing, scrapbooking, rafting, running, foreign languages, sailing, water skiing and the litany goes on, without ever reaching perfection in any of them. I was about to turn sixty and become a grandmother, too.

I needed to prove something to myself. I raised my hand and asked, "How does one actually get started?" The author turned her full attention to my question and replied, "Love of mountains and the sense of accomplishment in achieving goals." I thought to myself: Hey, I'm there, I have always loved mountains, read every book I could get my hands on about mountain adventures, flew over Mount Everest in Nepal, went to see the IMAX films on Everest and Eiger, not once but three times! I am there; I can do this… maybe.

After the book signing session was over, I was able to speak personally with Heidi. "Do you think a woman my age could ever achieve a personal goal of actually climbing a mountain?" I timidly asked, thinking she might laugh at such a preposterous question. She looked directly at me and said, "Follow your heart and achieve your goal. Climb your personal Everest, but do it with the most knowledge, planning, training and professional guidance that you can find!" She wrote inspirational words in my copy of her book, smiled and said, "You go for it, girl!" I left that evening filled with inspiration and determination.

I thought to myself, "I have my goal. Now I have to achieve it!" I even knew which mountain I wanted to climb. It was in my back yard and a source, for many years, of great family memories. I had skied, summer camped, snowshoed and photographed that mountain many times: It would have to be Mount Hood. Heading home from downtown Portland that evening my mind was reeling. I walked in the door to my house and abruptly announced, "I am going to climb Mount Hood!" My husband raised his eyebrows as he often did when I made one of my pronouncements, and said, "Really, now wash up, dinner is ready!"

I began my research right after dinner. A community college featured an adventure course in the spring. Starting in early May, a mountaineering course designed for first time climbers was being offered. It was perfect. All I had to do was get in the best physical condition I could achieve in the next six months. I was not a novice in physical conditioning as I had always had a gym membership and used it at least once a week. I felt reasonably certain I could intensify that routine and achieve greater cardio and endurance conditioning.

Months passed. When I wasn't on a treadmill or pumping weights at the gym, I was running the hills around our neighborhood. By early May, I felt I was ready to learn the climbing techniques. I enrolled in the one-day "snow school," which taught the intricacies of climbing as part of a rope team and using an ice axe for self-arrest. There were six of us in this class, and I was filled with anxiety as I realized I was old enough to be the mother of my classmates, who would become my climbing partners. What in the world had I been thinking?

Dave, the instructor, a middle-aged, rugged and gruff individual, began to speak. "In essence, I will be asking you to carry a fifteen-pound backpack with gear, wear a heavy pair of boots and walk on varied slope angles for six to eight hours, much of which will be during the night. In addition, we're going to diminish the amount of available oxygen along the way." Dave proceeded to say, "Not all of you will be physically able to summit. You need to be honest at all times so that you do not jeopardize the safety of the group. We will be roped together." My heart sank, as I was certain that speech was directed at me.

Dave continued, "Mount Hood, Oregon's highest summit at 11,240 feet, is a volcano. It is considered a technical climb with crevasses, ice and falling rocks. It is a mountain where weather can change without warning signs. 157 climbers have lost their lives on Mount Hood!" Why did he have to say that?

It was May 25th and it was time. We would start to climb at midnight. There was no visibility beyond the direct arc of our headlamps. By starting at midnight, we would be off the mountain before the sun melted the high walls of ice on the upper slopes. We roped into two teams of three and started to climb. We climbed and climbed, at first with no more effort than climbing stairs, but gradually getting more breathless as the altitude increased.

Dave kept repeating his mantra: "One foot in front of the other in a very slow pace." He also kept asking me "Are you with us? Are you pacing yourself?" He must have been concerned about my abilities but it was starting to irritate me. All the faces around me displayed a mask of extreme fatigue and I knew mine was no exception, probably more obvious because of my age. It was almost dawn; we climbed at a pitch that seemed wildly steep, perhaps forty-five degrees. We negotiated around rocks, crevasses and large chunks of ice.

Resting briefly, we noticed a hot, sulfur odor escaping from a nearby fumarole; a reminder that Mount Hood is an active volcano! I no longer paid attention to the complaints of fellow climbers who were verbalizing their every discomfort. I was cold too, but my hunger had been replaced with raw nerves. I had to pull deep within myself to focus! The air was definitely thinner and it was harder and harder to take deep breaths. No longer did our team chat endlessly. There was an eerie silence. Only our crampons could be heard crunching on the frozen ground. Would this ever end? I told myself to keep moving and squelched my doubts.

I pictured the mountain, where we might be on its flanks and how close we were to the summit. Someone yelled, "We're at the Pearly Gates"—a narrow icy and extremely dangerous gully. A small slit of sun was breaking though the darkness of the night. We continued to climb, and then we suddenly stopped climbing. There were no more places to climb! We were there!

I stepped onto the peak's windblown summit, more than two miles above sea level! Lights from faraway places twinkled magically. Incredible! Exhilarating! I had done it! The view was magnificent!

A sudden strong gust of cold wind served as an abrupt reality check. And then, I thought to my very weary self, "I have to get down from here!"

~Shirley Deck

Chapter
9

Time to Thrive

Make Time for Your Relationships

93

You Should

Every day is a new beginning. Treat it that way.
Stay away from what might have been, and look at what can be.
~Marsha Petrie Sue

All of my life I have been guided by those two small words: you should. Many times those two words guided and served me, but they also hamstrung me and boxed me in a corner. In March 2013, I'd had enough and retired from my well-paid corporate job at age forty-eight with two children approaching college age. This after a lifetime of being responsible and doing the things I "should" do.

My parents and all the other people who were telling me what I should do did so with the best intentions. And for the most part, all of that guidance served me well. But there comes a time when you have to stop doing what "you should" do and follow your gut instead.

Thirteen years ago, I was in a bad marriage, mourning the passing of my mother, managing an intense career in a large corporation, and raising two daughters with limited support from my husband. One Saturday morning, I was trying to get the girls (two and four years old) fed, dressed and ready for our day. I was cooking breakfast when my back seized up, forcing me to stop and lie down on the cold tile floor in the kitchen with my two girls walking around me and asking what was wrong. It's said that if you have pain in your back, it is because you have no support. I wish I could say that was the day I decided to make some changes in my life, but it wasn't.

Ten years passed, and I had remarried, still in the newlywed stage with the man of my dreams. But I was challenged with raising two teenaged girls, moving into a new home, learning how to blend our families, and leading the charge on a thirty-two million dollar business deal that required I leave my home in Maryland each week for Cheyenne, Wyoming. I was exhausted!

The straw that broke the camel's back was my younger brother's failing health. He unexpectedly required open-heart surgery. Naturally, as the older sister, I should have been the one to care for him. My husband and I invited him to move in with us so that I could help him recover. He moved in and for six weeks I changed the bandages on the machine that kept his heart pumping, prepared meals, changed bedpans and ensured that he had everything he needed and wanted.

With my brother so near death, it made me stop and think. How much more could I put on my plate? If I didn't devote my full attention to his recovery, wouldn't I always regret it? With my girls in high school didn't they need my guidance more than ever? When was I going to have a chance to breathe? Would I ever actually spend quality time with my new husband? When was my time? What did I really want to be when I grew up? What did I want to be remembered for?

I chatted with my husband and he agreed I should take a leave of absence from my job. The next day I went to talk to my manager, who gave me his full support. I felt as though the weight of the world was off my shoulders. It took a couple of weeks to wrap up projects, but I immediately felt less stress than I had in a long time. One of the first days of leave was spent preparing a healthy after-school snack for my girls and then hanging out for an hour on the trampoline in the back yard. We were just lying there looking up at the beautiful sky. It felt amazing to be able to take the time, with nothing more pressing ahead of me that day than preparing dinner.

So how did I spend my year? After getting my brother on his feet and on the heart transplant list, I spent a lot of time on meal prep and cooking for my family; I was able to chat with and coach my girls (and their friends) every time something came up at school or in life; I gave my husband time that wasn't rushed or squeezed in between activities.

I think most importantly I gave time to myself. I rested, read, watched movies, and traveled to many events in various cities, all in pursuit of furthering my skills in coaching, women's empowerment, speaking, and leadership. These had long been my areas of interest. I now had the time to discover and apply all that I had learned.

I also had time to connect with friends who weren't local. If I had to sum it up, I would say that I filled my soul. And, yes, there were times that I felt a twinge of guilt for leaving my family at home, but I knew in my heart that all of my investments would serve my family in the long run. The most valuable lesson I learned was that I should take care of myself if I wanted to be better at taking care of my family.

In a few weeks I will return to my corporate position. I feel very fortunate that I have experienced the gift of time, as my girls will soon be off to university. I feel thankful for the opportunity for my limited retirement at a young and healthy point in my life. I also know there are many new areas of interest that I will pursue soon and that I have many gifts to share. I am so happy that I took a break from what "I should" be doing and nurtured my soul.

~Allyson Ward

94

First Sheep!

Rejoice with your family in the beautiful land of life!
~*Albert Einstein*

It was early morning, still pitch-black outside. Despite being exhausted and hoping to sleep in, we had already been awake for a while. Jetlag can be brutal, especially on a long winter night.

Jonah, our ten-year-old, sat bundled up in fleece pajamas and warm wool blankets. His nose was pressed right up against the inside of the large, cold, damp window—eyes wide open, trying not to even blink. He was waiting patiently, resolutely, for the first sign of sunrise—straining to see the first sheep.

We knew they were out there. Even if we hadn't seen the flock yesterday morning, it would have been a safe bet that there were some nearby. New Zealand boasts a sheep population of about forty million.

"That's more sheep than people!" my husband Geno reminded our boys daily.

This two-night rental cottage was surrounded by rolling green hills and vast quantities of lush farmland. We'd arrived after dark on the first night so Geno, the first one out of bed the following morning, had caught us all off guard when he exclaimed, "First sheep!" as the sun's rays woke us, presenting the sheep grazing in the idyllic countryside.

Jonah had been flustered, proclaiming in adamant frustration,

"That's not fair!" So on the second morning he was determined to get first-sheep for the day.

I'm not exactly sure how the first-sheep game started, but we'd been playing it since we'd arrived in New Zealand. Traveling via car each day, staying somewhere new almost every night, searching for and calling out "first sheep" had become a favorite pastime.

Each first-sheep was rewarded with a point. Points were cumulative for the trip and Geno was currently in the lead, with Jonah a close second. I was third, though to be fair I'd had much more success in the first-cow game—which, to my chagrin, nobody else seemed to want to play.

Joshua, our thirteen-year-old and fourth participant, claimed disinterest in the game as soon as it became clear that he wasn't going to win. He was the only one of us still sound asleep in bed.

It was cold, cold, cold. The house was heated by a mere three space heaters—one for each bedroom and one for the living area. Geno had already turned on the toaster oven, leaving its little door open in a last-ditch attempt to heat up the kitchen.

In a couple of hours, we'd be on the road again—on our way to see the glaciers farther south. We'd also see plenty of sheep today, of course, but the first of those would be right here from the windows of this cottage.

Jonah eventually got that day's first-sheep and we all enjoyed another spectacular rural sunrise.

The first-sheep game grew even sillier as our trip went on. It evolved, as new games are prone to do, particularly in the hands of competitive people. Many other animals were added. First-sheep, then first-cow, first-horse, first-bison, first-chicken, first-deer, first-goose, first-dog and even first-penguin. No animal escaped our attention.

We laughed as each new animal was spotted—arguing over whether that particular animal officially "counted." Typically, whoever spotted the new animal argued that it did. Everyone else was firmly opposed to that animal's inclusion in the game. There were usually protests and an attitude of forced outrage.

We drove hundreds of miles over the course of two weeks. We saw many, many sheep, along with plenty of other breathtaking slices of nature—the stunning lakes, the rivers, the mountains, the countryside, the coastlines. We visited national parks, hiked, took photos, went for boating excursions, built snowmen, ate fish and chips, and skied. We spent some amazing family time together.

No stress, no pressure, just fun. Just love. Just us.

This was a pretty drastic change from our lives in the Northern Hemisphere. We'd left home on the first day of summer vacation, traveling directly away from the pressures of work and school overload, sports schedules, housework, errands and never enough time for the four of us to simply enjoy being together.

After a couple of long flights, we arrived in New Zealand's winter with suitcases full of fleece, down, and wool. We rented a car and began following our vague notion of an itinerary that would—hopefully—place us back in Auckland on time for our flights back home.

As the first-sheep game attests, we like to "win" in our family. I was raised with an anything-that-is-worth-doing-is-worth-doing-well ethic, and my husband is one of life's overachievers. I suppose it isn't shocking that our kids have learned our competitive behaviors. We generally expect them to perform to the best of their abilities—and, because they are capable, bright kids, our expectations are high. When they were little, we never, ever let them beat us at board games unless it was legit, nor are we fans of youth sports teams with an everyone-gets-a-trophy mentality. I want my kids to work hard, to compete, and to earn their achievements.

Reflecting back on our time in New Zealand, what strikes me most is the realization of how soon our kids will be grown, that life is insanely short, that it is all happening right now—this minute. It is so easy to get sucked into the day-to-day of work, school, sports, errands, housework, family obligations, and a million other tasks. Sometimes, we need to step outside of our daily circumstances to experience life's deeper meanings.

I wonder if my boys will enjoy traveling with us in the future? Will we all be healthy enough to hike through gorgeous national parks? Will we maintain the financial resources to take these extended, exotic vacations? Will we always love each other, and enjoy being together, the way we do now?

Sometimes, you need to make time for randomness. On the last day of vacation, as we were driving toward the airport, Geno shouted out with absolute jubilation, "Llama! First llama!"

I didn't actually see the llama, which seemed like the most unlikely animal possible. Jonah vaguely agreed that he saw "something," and Joshua was laughing too hard to give his opinion. Although I honestly don't think Geno could have made that up, that doesn't stop me from giving him a hard time every time he mentions this particular victory—which is more often than you'd expect.

So I usually say something like, "Whatever. I won first-cow!"

"That doesn't count," he'll respond.

"It counts more than first-llama!"

"No, it doesn't. There's only first-sheep and first-llama."

"I don't think you even saw a llama!"

If the kids are around, they'll light up and jump into the conversation. In the end, we are all laughing.

Although New Zealand may have done nothing for my competitive nature, I do know that the thousands of miles (and thousands of sheep!) of our adventures certainly offered a new perspective on the importance of enjoying my family every day, not just on vacation days.

Nonetheless, I'm still looking forward to our next big trip. Ireland? Brazil? Alaska? Wherever we go, I'm totally claiming first-unicorn. I can already hear my family's lively laughter.

~Lisa Pawlak

95

The Hourglass

*You must have been warned against letting the golden
hours slip by; but some of them are golden only
because we let them slip by.*

~J.M. Barrie

I was raised in New York, but I was a child out of sync with a city that moved at manic speed. "Hurry up, Deirdre" might have been my name. I was not slow, indeed I was one of the fastest on the track team, but I was easily distracted by life's incidental moments. The cooing of pigeons would draw me away from tying my shoe and toward the preening birds on my window ledge. On my way to school, I'd get so wrapped up in a conversation I was overhearing on the crowded L train that I'd miss my stop. I could sit on my building stoop and find a hundred things to absorb me: the line of ants making their way across the cement; an old, stooped woman pushing a cart with her scruffy dog at her side. People thought my head was in the clouds; I was considered spacey, but actually my mind was preoccupied—not by dreams or clouds—but by the minute details of ordinary life.

And then I grew up. At twenty-two I learned a lesson: "Time is money" said one of my first bosses. Time could not be wasted on gazing at patterns of light on the ceiling, or idle chitchat in the employee kitchen. I could no longer linger on my way to work to watch the shrieking kids run through the sprinklers, nor stop to converse with

Mrs. Timoney on her way to church. Time is money and money pays the bills.

I was forced to conform to the rules of the land of responsible adults. Focus on your goals; make lists; get things accomplished. Subway rides were now opportunities to regroup and make to-do lists: "pay gas bill ASAP," "fax Mr. Gruen."

Getting married meant lists for me—and lists for him. I devised a system (thanks to yellow sticky notes) to keep order in my household. "I love you," I posted on the bathroom mirror smack in the center for my husband to see as he shaved, "and please remember to take the cat to the vet." Nothing would ever be forgotten.

Children came along and then technology. My lists that had once been on colorful Post-its all over the house could now be organized in my computer and phone. A "bing" would alert me to a parent-teacher conference, an orthodontist appointment, or a deadline at work.

When my father got sick, the list became three-tiered as "Parents" were added. Bing! "Bring Dad to the VA hospital for blood work." Bing! "Hire a housekeeper." Flying back and forth from Los Angeles to New York took more structuring of time. And dragging a toddler around with an elderly man in a wheelchair took some maneuvering on the streets of Manhattan.

When my dad died suddenly after a perfectly non-eventful hip surgery, life could not slow down. Mourning a father I loved so dearly and yet having children to look after and a mother who was beyond sad left me putting aside my own grief for a more convenient time. More lists were made. I felt satisfaction in getting my son to the asthma specialist, writing and mailing thank you cards, paying the hospital bills, picking up Mom's medication and burying my father, all in a timely manner.

The day before I was to return home to Los Angles and my neatly scheduled life, I awoke at 4 a.m. to hear my mother mumbling in the living room.

"Mom? What are you doing?"

She was sitting on the couch holding two remotes in her hand, confused.

"I can't seem to turn off the DVD player. See, the little light is still on."

"It's 4 a.m."

"Your father always turned it off before going to bed. He always did."

"It doesn't matter, Mom."

I did not recognize at the time that her respect for my father's rules—however insignificant to me—was a way to keep things the way they'd always been, a way to deny that my dad was dead.

She sighed and put the remotes down. Life and DVD remotes were too much for her now.

"Sit down, Deirdre." She lifted her hand to mine.

"Mom, I'm so tired."

"How about if I make us some tea?" she suggested.

When I was a child, my mother would make us tea. It tasted so good because of all the milk and sugar, combined with the feeling of being taken care of. I wanted that now; I wanted a mom who could make all the decisions. But I could not allow myself to say yes, because in two and a half hours my toddler son would be up and the day would be long and—as I quickly calculated in my head—the shuttle to the airport would be coming at nine, I'd have to take him out to run in the playground beforehand, and there was a layover in Chicago. Could I finish my work and entertain a two-year-old at O'Hare?

"Tomorrow Mom, I promise."

I went to bed, but she did not. She sat on the couch, the remotes again in her hands.

The time for me to sit down with my mom did not come. The next day, my mother did not get up. What had gone unnoticed while my father was dying was my mother's weakening lungs from a prior illness. I pushed her in the same wheelchair my father had used, with my son toddling beside me, to the hospital, where the doctor whispered not unkindly in my ear, "I don't think your mother will be leaving the hospital."

"Not ever?" I asked, not comprehending.

My mother died three weeks after my father.

Now, almost six years later I am haunted by her words, "Sit down, Deirdre."

I regret not sitting down on the lumpy couch beside my mom, I regret not taking her slim, fragile hand in my own, I regret not waiting with her and watching the darkness move into the pale of the morning. And I regret not asking her all the questions I'd been saving to ask when time permitted. For time is elusive. And moments only come and go and then... they're gone forever.

The days are still hectic. I still make my lists, but now I take time to examine the tide pools at the beach, to pause from my work and listen to my daughter's story for the umpteenth time, to try and understand what my son is speaking about when he talks about *Avatar* and the difference between an Earthbender and a Waterbender, and to spend time in the garden... simply watching the butterflies dance. Time is not money. Time is life itself.

~Deirdre Higgins

Fuel

*Love is a symbol of eternity. It wipes out all sense of time,
destroying all memory of a beginning and all fear of an end.*
~Madame de Stael

Ten years ago my world was rocked. I was twenty when I got the devastating news. My cousin was killed in a car accident. It was horrific. We were closer than most cousins. He was like a brother to me. It tore my heart out and turned my world upside down. How was it fair to take someone so young? He was only twenty-four years old!

My cousin's death made me question everything. There were little things like whether it was safe to drive, and there were bigger questions: Why was he taken from us? Why was God punishing us? Was I next? What is life? What is the purpose? Is it all worth it?

I was already in a stage of life where I was trying to figure it all out. I was sad and depressed, angry and confused. It was the most difficult time in my life.

And then, four years later, I changed in the most unexpected way. My younger sister Kate, only nineteen years old, was diagnosed with cancer. C-A-N-C-E-R. That word hits you like a ton of bricks. The long, hard struggle begins and you watch this disease take a toll on your loved one, yourself and everyone around you. My sister was the one I had turned to for help in tough situations. Now it was my turn to help her. What do you do when your loved one is in a tough situation? You watch and you pray. You experience every doctor visit as if it were your own. You take the news—the good and the bad—as if it were your news. You sit next to her while the poisonous chemo trickles into her body drip by drip. You hold her hair—until it all falls out—as she vomits every color of the rainbow. You wipe her tears, and yours, when the pain is so overwhelming that it all doesn't seem worth it anymore. You do it all, every day, for five and a half years.

Until one day, after three remissions, three transplants and countless hospital stays, it got even worse. We landed in the emergency room and were faced with a lot of medical terminology and none of it was good. The very treatment that was to save my sister was killing her. She could no longer breathe on her own and needed life support. She could only communicate by writing things. She was there, still fighting. And so were we. But it was hard to hide the emotion. We were all scared. We were told on two different occasions that she would die within the next forty-eight hours. But she did not. That's not to say we did not have scares, but she did not die. She was with us.

My sister was the most positive person I have ever known. She found the good in any situation, even this one. She loved life no matter how hard it got. She showed us that through the power of love she could get through anything life threw at her. It was only in tiny moments that she would show her fear—fear of the pain to come, fear of the road that lay ahead and, truthfully, fear of the end. We all feared it.

Just when I thought I could not cry anymore, that dreadful day came. I watched her take her last breath as I held her hand, tears rolling down my cheeks. To watch someone you love pass away is something you never forget. It seems to stop the world from spinning, first in the moment of loss, but then many more times in the days, months and years ahead.

Losing a sister is devastating and tragic. It truly changes your life forever. I miss her every day but I also thank her every day. I thank her for showing me the importance of love. Because of her, I realize now how blessed I am. I know that sounds crazy but it is not. It's enlightenment. In losing my cousin years ago, I questioned everything and in my questioning, I kept coming back to one simple concept.

Love deeply. Whether someone lives five years or one hundred years, their loved ones always wish for just one more day with them. It is never long enough.

Realizing this changed my life. I approached the world completely differently after that. While my sister was sick, I loved her and everyone else as though each day was my last. I am able to look at my life now and realize how truly special it is and how lucky I am. I have a bond with my family that is so amazingly strong and beautiful. I have found a love that will give me gifts I could have never imagined possible.

Learning how to love so deeply is priceless. That simple fact is what fuels me. I thrive because I allow myself to love deeply, every day. Nurture that love — for family, friends, strangers, and yourself. Be grateful for its existence because you have just found your fuel to thrive.

~Kristin Doney

97

The Muscle Car

Here's to freedom, cheers to art. Here's to having an
excellent adventure and may the stopping never start.
~Jason Mraz

I have been married for forty-six years. People ask, "How do you and Bob do it?" There are the obvious answers—trust, consideration, honesty, patience and respect. But mostly, I think it's because we have taken advantage of some unexpected opportunities and just had fun. Recently, for example, our relationship was enhanced by an automobile accident when my car was "crunched" by an attendant at a "free" valet service. I decided to rent a car for five days—a Camaro.

We had, of course, heard about them since they came out. My sister had a green '72 Camaro and loved it. My daughter always wanted one with the flame effect—she never got it. I asked Enterprise if there was a black one with red flames trimmed with gold on the hood, but they said that was a little high-end for them. So I took a 2015 black Camaro—a bit more subdued, but we liked it.

We were driving "the car of youthful dreams." I knew it was going to be fun the first time I stepped on the gas. We seemed to explode down the road.

What did we think of it? Well, first Bob and I had to get in it and we were not sure we could. Both septuagenarians, we've lost lots of flexibility, but we were ready for an adventure.

The roof was low, the seats narrow, and windows so long and

slender they seemed almost non-existent. Eventually we learned to enter it by simultaneously bending, swinging, and dropping. We got pretty good at it.

Vision from the interior was difficult, but the mirrors were terrific and so were the large doors. Closing them needed someone with seven-foot long arms, but nothing is perfect. By driving fast, we managed to look almost like we belonged in a Camaro. By the time admiring observers realized how old we were, we were gone.

San Diego County is about the size of Connecticut. Its mountains, over 6,000 feet high, are just forty-five miles from the silvery beaches of Coronado and La Jolla. We tried to cover as much of the county as we could.

On our first day, Bob and I drove up to Julian, a charming nineteenth-century gold mining town. The mountain road wound past pine and oak trees, boulders, fields, and cattle, all a blur as the tires clung to the curves in our "muscle car." The motor's roar was rich and low, the sound of strength; the pipes in back rumbled, pushing the vehicle forward with a surge of speed reminiscent of a black jaguar lunging at prey.

We strolled Julian's wooden walks and dirt paths on the side of the main street. There are no large grocery stores, no fast-food places, and only one service station; but it is crammed with restaurants and a wide variety of small stores for shopping. We selected Romano's, a longtime center for Italian food and community get-togethers.

On the way home, as the shadows lengthened in the afternoon's setting sun, we reflected on the variety and beauty of the valleys and mountains. The car hugged the road as we made our way to Interstate 8 and home. Our first adventure was over; but we were not finished.

We drove all week — the mountains; La Jolla with its tricky traffic; downtown San Diego. We toured, we shopped, we visited renowned restaurants.

There was the fun, excitement, and challenge that two elderly, long-married people can have but seldom do. There are always routines and schedules, but there are also new opportunities. When those opportunities arise, take them — at any age.

The long-term advantage Bob and I gained from that Camaro? We did not argue or bicker once during that week—even as Bob gave me vague and dubious directions through the mid-day crowded downtown traffic. As long as you are active and curious, and have a good sense of humor, you are not too old to speed down life's highway. We enjoyed each other as much as we did that Camaro.

~Janet Bower

98

A New Kind of Life

Being a mother is not about what you gave up to have
a child, but what you've gained from having one.
~Sunny Gupta

W hen my son was grown, it was hard on me. I knew he would still need me, but not in the same way. It took me a long time to work through the fact that there would be no more babies. No more snuggling under a blanket, pretending to be bears in a cave. No more saving the day with clear tape and a hot glue gun. No more feeling the weight of my sleeping child in my arms. It felt like a part of me, the biggest part, was lost, and I grieved for that loss.

One morning, after I had finally come to terms with all this, I was driving to work. Suddenly, I was struck with a horrible case of the stomach flu. I went from singing along with the radio to nearly debilitating nausea. I couldn't believe how sick I felt. I hadn't felt so bad in… in… twenty years…. No way! That would be impossible. After all, my husband had undergone a vasectomy a few years earlier. I was in my mid-forties. He was nearly sixty. It was ridiculous to even imagine such a thing. Yet as the morning dragged on, along with my misery, I began to feel something else—hope.

Several months later, as my friends were welcoming grandchildren, I was waddling around. Throughout the entire pregnancy, one set of memories kept threatening my happiness. It was the memories of having to leave my sweet little boy at day care and crying all the way to work. I dreaded that more than anything. I was a college-educated career woman who had always dreamed of being a stay-at-home mom. I knew the disappointment of missing a field trip or performance. I knew the agony of not being able to personally care for a sick child, and the sadness of not being together during holiday and summer vacations. I said to my husband, "I don't know how we are going to survive, but I absolutely will not work full-time and go through that again."

Twenty-one years and three days after the first time I became a mom, we welcomed our baby girl into the world. And just as I had promised, I cut my hours in half. At first, that seemed acceptable. It wasn't the dream, but it was something. As she grew and became more active, my work-at-home husband began to find it impossible to work at home while watching her. Money became tighter. I battled my instinct to go back to work full-time. I have always been a provider, so for me to simply leave it to someone else felt unnatural. At one point my college-age son came to me and asked, "Mom, are we going to become homeless?" "I don't know," I told him honestly, "but I'm not leaving her."

We struggled through six months of super low-budget life, and then my husband was offered a full-time job. It was demanding and high stress. "The only way I can accept this," he said to me, "is if you quit your job and take care of her full-time." We had less than twenty-four hours to make a decision. The next morning was surreal. After all those years of wishing, I gave my two-week notice and became a stay-at-home mom. For me, it was a miracle.

Making the transition from two incomes to one, especially without prior planning, was jolting. It meant sacrifices by everyone in our family. We lost our health insurance. Car repairs became terrifying. Indulgences like salon visits, expensive face creams, dining out and even the occasional cup of fancy coffee disappeared from our lives. My son wondered if he would be able to finish college. Sometimes, our situation looked so bleak, my family must have thought I had gone crazy. But I held on to our baby and the belief that the time for my dream had come. As the financial storm raged around us, I learned to sew the baby pants I had no money to buy. I discovered a food and household item salvage in my community. I learned to make bread, pizza dough and even homemade pretzels. I washed and reused sandwich bags. I stayed home and conserved gas. And I started to write, selling freelance copy where I could. My son began working between classes to help with the bills. Slowly, cautiously, life went on.

I would be lying if I said being a stay-at-home mom was everything I had imagined. It took a while to realize that we could have fun without funds. Holidays and birthdays were the biggest reality check. But the little things became causes for celebration, and the celebrations became organic rather than commercial.

In time, a new kind of homegrown happy, creative lifestyle developed for our whole family. We're starting to realize that my being at home full-time is a luxury for all of us. When my husband needs to talk at 4:00 a.m., I'm available to listen. When my son texts me with an invitation to join him for a midnight snack in the kitchen, now I can accept. When our baby girl is fussy and just wants to be held all day, I do just that. It's not glamorous, but it's beautiful, this new life we share.

~Edie Schmidt

The Dad Who
Dropped Out

*A truly rich man is one whose children run into his
arms when his hands are empty.*
~Author Unknown

I n winter, I often walk in a nearby park during lunchtime. The
park is quiet, as few have the time to enjoy the winter sun on
weekdays. The two people that often break my solitude there
are a middle-aged father with his little daughter. She's in her
school uniform, pigtailed hair with red ribbons tied neatly around
the ends. The father looks like he has all the time in the world—he
refuses to hurry along the jogging path; instead he matches his pace
with that of the little girl. Sometimes when I see them, they're eating
oranges. Sometimes they're lolling lazily in the sun, laughing and
chatting.

Since I walk solo, I often have little better to do than speculate
about people I pass. How does the man find time in the middle of the
day to play in the sunny park with his daughter? He certainly doesn't
look unemployed. What sort of job must he have that gives him the
flexibility to walk in the park in the middle of the day?

A few days ago, the child caught me looking at them and smiled
at me. I smiled back. Yesterday, I threw a ball that had strayed from
them in my direction. And today, we finally sat on the rocks and had
a little chat.

"You must enjoy the park very much to come here so often," I said.

The father nodded. "We love coming here... there's no park near where we live and little Guddi enjoys playing here while we wait for her mother to get free from work," he said.

The child's school was next door, as was his place of work, a private business where he was an accountant.

I couldn't help myself. I just had to ask.

"How," I asked curiously, "do you manage to leave your office every day in the middle of the day?"

The story that the father, Satyendra Dubey, told me showed me how if we dig underneath the surface, even ordinary people's lives can seem quite extraordinary.

"I used to be no different from any of those thousands of office workers scurrying to work every morning in chartered buses," he began.

His wife (a teacher in a government school) and he were comfortably off but rarely managed time off for leisure. Their daily routine consisted of dropping their child at school, going to work, picking her up from daycare and going to bed exhausted.

One morning, on his way to work, Dubey was hit by a bus. "I awoke in the hospital, unaware of the extent of my injuries, afraid I was going to die," he said. "As I waited in that cold room for my wife to reach me, a terrifying thought crossed my mind. 'How would my daughter, then only four, remember me if I died that day? Would she think of me as a stern man who worked very hard? Or more uncharitably, as a father who had little time for her?'"

As he lay there, racked by pain, he realized that his child would probably not have many happy memories of just "being" with her father.

Dubey made a full recovery from his accident, but something in him had changed. "I started having recurring dreams about floating high up in the air, watching people like myself turn into little ants scurrying mindlessly from office to home," he said. "High above them, I could see that few of them were actually enjoying any bits of their lives. They seemed too busy trying to go from one day to the next!" he reflected. In the quiet of the night when he lay awake after one such dream, he resolved to be different.

The day he went back to work, Dubey used the excuse of his recent accident to take some time off at lunch. He picked up his daughter from school and took her to the park. The child was hesitant; she'd never seen this strange side to her dad.

At first the father and daughter didn't quite know what to do with each other. Then, slowly, they evolved a set of shared activities they enjoyed together. "We talk, play, laugh and sometimes just sit silently. Our time together in the park is the best part of the day for me!" he said. "Now, when my wife finishes work early afternoon and comes to take Guddi home, I feel quite bereft. And then, I return to the office."

"Is it easy," I asked, "to take time off every day?"

He smiled. "My co-workers work much longer hours than I do. I know they'll probably get better postings and promotions. But are these things really important in the larger scheme of things? I'm happy I stopped to think about this instead of blindly going on and on...."

It was actually a very small change he'd made to his life, he said, but it amazed him every day to see the difference it made to his life. "It brings me so much joy that I can't believe why others haven't thought of doing the same thing," he said simply.

I got up to resume my long-forgotten walk, unexpectedly happy after hearing his story. When I passed them again that day, they were having a race. Just as he was about to win, Dubey noticed that Guddi's energy was flagging a little. Immediately, he bent to tie his shoelaces while the child triumphantly sailed past the finish line, laughing gleefully. As she lay down on the grass next to him, I couldn't help but smile as I thought about the man who'd dropped out of the race, only to see how much nicer a slow walk in the sun was.

~Geetanjali Krishna

The Strength of No

I encourage people to remember that "no" is a complete sentence.
~Gavin de Becker

All my life I heard yes, yes, yes. Any time a patient needed my dad he would go to his optometrist office no matter what time of the day it was. He would make sure breakfast was always made for my brother and me, but he would leave the house immediately to take care of whoever had called him. If a volunteer organization needed him, he was there. Any time they would ask him to help with something, it was "How high do I need to jump?"

Dad was a huge role model for me. He appeared to always be fulfilled and happy. So I tried to do the same thing, "be everything to everyone."

Amazing, right?

The part I never saw was what I witnessed when he was on his deathbed, truly exhausted. Because he had always said yes to everyone except himself. He had been sick for fifteen years but never told us, pretending that everything was fine.

My dad's need for love and acceptance from the external world was so strong that it drained him in many areas of his life. As much as he loved my mom, she wanted to support him and not deny him his wish to be the "ultimate giver." She was always the strong woman, and she never spoke up about how he was living his life. She just wore this mask and took it. So that was another thing I modeled—being strong. Give and be strong.

As an adult, I continued the cycle—giving and giving, even to people who did not appreciate my giving.

Why did I do it? What made me say yes all the time?

And what did saying no really mean to me?

It took some time to figure it out.

All my life I have been a pleaser. I love to make people happy. I used to do ANYTHING and EVERYTHING for ANYONE who needed me! That is what life is about, right? At least that's what I thought when I modeled myself after my generous, loving, altruistic father, who pleased everyone at the expense of his own health and happiness.

I remember the day… the day I finally said "No." That was the day I grew up. A little girl trapped in a forty-five-year-old body became a woman who truly understood her worth that day. I could still help people and have purpose and do what I was here to do in the world, but not at my personal expense or the expense of my children.

Here's what was happening in my life the day I grew up. I had just gone through a divorce, my kids' dad had moved to California from Las Vegas where we lived, I was driving my kids to three different schools every day, and sometimes I had more month than money. I was working hard to support us, but not at the expense of my kids. I was committed to being there for them no matter what.

I was stretched thin!

So that day, I was working at my desk, going on conference call after conference call, attending meeting after meeting. I was rocking it! Then I looked over at my phone and a longtime friend was calling. We talked for about fifteen minutes, just small talk, and I could sense she was getting ready for "the ask." And there it was: "Oh and by the way… do you know someone who can help me with this or can you help me plan this…"

I remember catching myself… the old me, the one who was a pleaser no matter how much extra work it was for me, or how much it would distract me from my mission. I would always just do what I was asked. But this time I took a deep breath and said, "I'm sorry but I just have to say no. I need to focus on my kids and my work."

I felt this sense of power like never before. I didn't worry about whether she would get upset. Instead, I really looked at my values and what was most important was for me to thrive and for my kids to thrive.

That day I got clear. Really clear. I learned that being a martyr is not good at all, and it is NOT what we are supposed to do. In the end, it benefits no one.

Honestly, that was the best call of my life. Ever since, I have set boundaries for what I will and won't do, and also for what I will stand for and not sell out to.

Now I make sure to take care of the relationships that matter to me, and that means keeping myself in top form. Watching the most successful people in the world, I noticed there were certain things that they did, one being to stick to the routines that worked for them. So every Sunday night at six, no matter where I am in the world, I sit myself down and plan my week. I look at what needs to happen that week and what resources I need to access to make that happen.

And every morning, I wake up and I say, "Today is going to be the BEST day of my life." It might sound silly, but it really works and it sets me up for the day.

I also make sure that I stay true to my ideals and that I work with people I respect.

I'm creating a new role model for my children, building on what I learned from my father, but taking it up one more level to make sure that my priority remains myself and my children. It's like they say on the airplane—"put your oxygen mask on first." You can't give what you don't have.

~Loren Slocum Lahav

Carving Out
Some Work-Life
Balance

*By working faithfully eight hours a day you may
eventually get to be boss and work twelve hours a day.*
~Robert Frost

There are two main themes running through this book:
1) Make sure you take the time to thrive every day; and
2) It's your time to thrive, so if you need to change your
job, your home, your life, get to it.

And then, even if you are doing something you love, it shouldn't
be all that you do. That's a lesson I have had to learn in my own job
at Chicken Soup for the Soul. My husband and I had just become
empty nesters when we took on the challenge of running this amazing
company. We had been working from home—he on various business
ventures, and I on several corporate board memberships—so when
the last child went off to college it should have been our time to scale
back our workloads, do some traveling, and enjoy ourselves.

But no. Crazy us. We had learned earlier that year that Chicken
Soup for the Soul was for sale by its founders, Jack Canfield, Mark
Victor Hansen and his ex-wife Patty Hansen. We loved everything that
Chicken Soup for the Soul stood for and we thought that we could
take the company to the next level, bringing the books back to their

old level of popularity and relevance, and expanding into additional areas where we could add value to people's lives.

We and our business partners, mostly friends and family members, became the proud new owners of Chicken Soup for the Soul. I had read 100 of the old Chicken Soup for the Soul books in preparation for the acquisition, and I knew exactly what I wanted to do as author, editor-in-chief and publisher when we took over. It was like Chicken Soup for the Soul had been inside me all along waiting to come out.

Thus, at ages fifty-five and fifty, respectively, my husband and I returned to the world of full-time work, just when we should have been planning our exit strategy! He became CEO and I became Publisher. It has been non-stop excitement ever since. The first "excitement" was that we managed to time our purchase perfectly for the start of the deepest recession since the Great Depression, one that led to Borders going bankrupt, independent bookstores closing, and consumers scaling back on discretionary purchases. But we survived that, managing to redesign our books and increase our sales and have a number of bestsellers among the 120 new titles that we have published since mid-2008. My husband, as CEO, has put together a team in the non-book part of our business that has updated our popular pet food products, launched a line of food for people, and started a TV and movie production business.

What we hadn't expected was that this would become an all-consuming endeavor and that we would work virtually every day. I'm writing this on a Saturday night at ten o'clock, for example. We love what we do, but we have to make some boundaries so that work doesn't take over absolutely everything.

There is a saying that in order to be happy you should return to what you loved doing when you were ten years old. When I was ten I loved to walk in the acres of woods behind our house, write stories just for fun, and read books. And now I have a job where I read and write every day, I go for long walks in the nature preserve near my house, and I still squeeze in a little time reading books that I did not have to edit. So despite the fact that I am working seven days a week and am constantly in crisis mode, I am truly doing what I have always loved doing.

My husband and I have to be particularly careful that we don't let work take over every aspect of our lives. Here's how we do it. If you saw any of the Harry Potter movies or read the books, you'll remember that the evil wizard Voldemort was so terrifying that everyone but the equally powerful wizard Harry Potter called him "He-Who-Must-Not-Be-Named."

So through some bizarre husband/wife shared brainwaves, we both decided that work, i.e., Chicken Soup for the Soul, would be "He-Who-Must-Not-Be-Discussed," a bit like Voldemort. When either of us is sick of talking about work at home, we can "declare Voldemort," as we term it, and the other person is not allowed to talk about work at all. This usually happens on Friday nights and "Voldemort" remains in effect until Monday morning.

My husband is not even allowed to instant-message or text me a question about work when Voldemort is in effect, because texting is too much like talking. We can be sitting right next to each other at the kitchen table, working on our computers, but we have to e-mail each other our questions.

In addition to Voldemort, we have other little traditions that we use to take back ownership of at least a bit of our lives. On Sundays, we are adamant that we have a big fancy breakfast together, usually involving something with maple syrup, and we call those Sinful Sundays. Sinful Sunday is mandatory every week!

And we absolutely have to be on vacation for our wedding anniversary every November, no exceptions allowed. It doesn't matter what is happening in the business — this vacation is never cancelled or modified. We've gone to the Caribbean, Dubai, Hawaii, and even when we've taken a shorter trip, we have to be on vacation on our anniversary.

That's "couple time." Then there's "me time." No matter how tired I am, or how late I go to bed, I take ten or fifteen minutes every night to read a book that I have not edited.

Finally, and most importantly, there are the children, all grown, but still expecting full attention the rare times they seek it. I drop everything when one of them calls or texts. Work isn't taking that away from me, ever.

I may work seven days a week, but by carving out a few mandatory R&R opportunities that I can count on, it all works. I don't resent my job; I don't feel overwhelmed; and I can move from task to task knowing that my me time, my couple time, my kid time, and my anniversary trip WILL happen. They are guaranteed and inviolate. Those bits of time, those "carve outs" that I can count on, create the work-life balance that keeps me going.

~Amy Newmark

Meet Our
Contributors

Linda E. Allen is enjoying living happily ever after on the prairie of western Oklahoma. She writes about her family, pets and gardens, and volunteers her teaching experience to various groups. E-mail her at lindaeallen@pldi.net.

Lauren Ball studied nursing at Chamberlain College in Jacksonville, FL, worked as a Realtor and now has settled in to pair her experience in life with her love of writing. She is married to Tyrone Ball and has four children. She enjoys cooking, riding her horses, camping, fishing, homesteading and, most of all, writing.

Jacqueline (Jaki) Baskow came to Las Vegas in 1976 with $300 and created the largest and most successful talent, meetings and event company in Las Vegas. Discovery Channel named her "Queen of Las Vegas." She was named one of the top ten star brokers in the world. Jaki would like to thank Karie Millspaugh for co-writing the story with her.

Lola Bendana holds a degree in international relations and specialized in Latin American Studies, Interpreting and Translation. In 1997, she launched Multi-Languages Corporation, a multilingual translation service provider. Lola has served on several non-profit executive boards. She is passionate about psychology, life coaching and health.

Bonnie L. Beuth received her Bachelor of Science degree, with honors, in Computer Information Systems. She works in the legal industry as an Information Systems Trainer and Chair of an international non-profit. Bonnie enjoys time at the beach with her two dogs, reading and writing short stories.

Michele Boom turned in her teacher's chalkboard to be a stay-at-home mom. While juggling two toddlers and a traveling husband, she began to write. Her work appears in regional magazines in the U.S. and Canada. This is her fourth story to appear in the Chicken Soup for the Soul series. Visit her at mammatalk.blogspot.com.

Janet Newlan Bower is a retired professor of history teaching for over thirty years. Her publications include contributing a chapter to *Women in the Biological Sciences: A Bibliographic Sourcebook*, *Tigerpaper*, *National Parks and Conservation*, *The Explorer*, *Environment Southwest* and *Child Life*, among others. Read her historical blog at historyallaround.com.

Sage de Beixedon Breslin, PhD is a Licensed Psychologist and Intuitive Consultant. She is an accomplished author and screenwriter, generating material to inspire and touch those who have struggled with life's challenges. Her books, stories and chapters are available on her website at www.HealingHeartCenter.org. E-mail her at Sage@HealingHeartCenter.org.

Jill Burns lives in the mountains of West Virginia with her wonderful family. She's a retired piano teacher and performer. She enjoys writing, music, gardening, nature, and spending time with her grandchildren.

Courtney Campbell left the corporate world after twenty-five years to coach others in life and business. Her passion is helping others overcome adversity and achieve success as she has. She lives in Florida and enjoys sailing, traveling and spending quality time with her family.

Kay L. Campbell received her communication degree and paralegal certification from Florida Atlantic University. She currently works in education marketing. An avid reader, she also enjoys writing devotionals for *The Upper Room* and *The Secret Place*. Her hobbies include golf, tennis and Argentine tango.

Lorraine Cannistra is an author, speaker, blogger, wheelchair dancer and proud partner to her service dog, Leah. She enjoys using her writing to challenge negative perceptions some may have about those with disabilities. Follow her blog at healthonwheels.wordpress.com and contact her at lorrainecannistra.com.

Kathy Caprino, M.A. is an international career coach, writer, and speaker dedicated to the advancement of women in business. Author of *Breakdown, Breakthrough*, and Founder of Ellia Communications and The Amazing Career Project, Kathy is a *Forbes* and *The Huffington Post* contributor and top media expert on women's career success.

Katie Cash earned her Bachelor of Science degree, with honors, in Oceanography from the United States Naval Academy in 2011. She is a Surface Warfare Officer stationed in San Diego, CA, where she enjoys surfing, hiking, and triathlons. She is an aspiring novelist and loves to travel the world.

Marcia Castro-Rosenberg lives in Las Vegas, NV, with her awesome husband and amazing kids. She is a nurse, teacher, and strategic intervention coach. Her passion is helping people access internal resources and design the life and relationship of their dreams. She loves music, traveling, skydiving, dancing and thriving.

Lucy Lemay Cellucci is a dance educator in Ottawa, ON. She is the mother of two fantastic children and author of the young adult novel *True Colours*. Lucy is passionate about strong coffee, mellow wine and the elusive journey to becoming a real grown-up. E-mail Lucy at author@lucylcellucci.net.

Matt Chandler is the Director of Marketing and Business Development at Lippes Mathias Wexler Friedman LLP. He is the author of eleven books and two previous essays in the Chicken Soup for the Soul series. He also works as a freelance entertainment writer for *The Buffalo News*. Learn more at www.mattchandlerwriting.com.

Jane Choate has been telling stories to friends and family since she was a young girl. Now, a much older girl, she continues telling stories. Being part of the Chicken Soup for the Soul family is a dream come true.

Mike Conrad is a serial entrepreneur. He has been married for sixteen years and has two amazing kids. He loves to spend his free time with his family. To learn more about Zaycon Foods visit www.zayconfoods.com.

Lorri Danzig holds a master's degree in Jewish Studies. She teaches non-denominational programs for elders that approach aging as a journey of deepening wisdom and expanded possibilities. Her essays and poetry are published in journals and anthologies. Learn more at www.letitshinejourneys.com or e-mail her at lbdanzig@letitshinejourneys.com.

Barbara Davey is the Director of Community Relations at Crane's Mill, a retirement community in West Caldwell, NJ. She received her bachelor's degree in English and master's degree in education from Seton Hall University, and teaches business writing at Caldwell University. She and her husband live in Verona, NJ.

Shirley Deck is a retired Clinical Microbiologist living in the Pacific Northwest, where the rainy days inspire creativity. Shirley has a passion for reading, writing, drawing and engaging in outdoor activities. Her stories are most often centered around her priceless family, personal recollections and life's lessons.

Denise A. Dewald has been writing for nearly thirty years. Her work has been widely published and featured on radio. She has two grown sons and enjoys the outdoors, travel, reading and writing to uplift others. E-mail her at 83.kmgs@gmail.com.

Manpreet Dhillon is a freedom catalyst for women. Manpreet is a certified personal and business coach, Heal Your Money Story Certified Coach, and a certified human resources professional with a master's degree in Organizational Management.

Kristin Doney is a content writer and event consultant based in Southern California. In memory of her sister, Kristin founded Kate's Karts, a non-profit organization that delivers toys, books and gifts to hospital-bound children battling cancer. Kristin is a graduate of The Ohio State University and a proud Buckeye.

Chelsea DuHaime received her Bachelor of Arts degree in English literature at the University of California, Berkeley. She continues to explore her horizons in Los Angeles, CA, turning her dreams into a reality.

Sharon Earls received her bachelor's degree in Accounting from Tennessee Wesleyan College in 1990. She is the proud grandmother to Andrew, Ella, and Ava. She lives in Tennessee and is a small business owner. Sharon enjoys writing short stories and is currently revising her first romance novel.

Janet Perez Eckles is an international speaker and best-selling author. She dances the salsa of gratitude for the privilege of inspiring you, teaching you to conquer fear and helping you see the best of life. Learn more at www.janetperezeckles.com.

Terri Elders recently moved back to her beloved California. Her stories have appeared in over one hundred anthologies. She blogs at atouchoftarragon.blogspot.com. E-mail her at telders@hotmail.com.

Cindy L. Ely received her Bachelor of Arts degree, with honors, from Saint Mary-of-the-Woods College. Cindy is the retired mother of four children and grandmother to twelve. Cindy enjoys time with her family, latch hooking, reading, and water aerobics. She plans to write children's books and inspirational articles.

Pat Fish is a regular contributor to the Chicken Soup for the Soul series. She is also a blogger and writes often of local and national politics. Read Pat's blog at patfish.blogspot.com. Join her on Facebook at www.facebook.com/patricia.fish.5.

Heidi FitzGerald is a produced playwright, screenwriter and author. She lives with her eight-year-old twins in the Minneapolis area, where she is a freelance editor by day, creative writer by night. Learn more at www.heidifitzgerald.com.

Josephine Fitzpatrick lives in Southern California. She has been published in *Creative Nonfiction* magazine and the *California Prose Directory*. She co-facilitates a memoir writing class at the Osher Lifelong Learning Institutes located on the campus of California State University at Long Beach, CA.

Judith Fitzsimmons has been a freelance writer for twenty-plus years. Her newest book, *Not at Your Child's Expense*, published by Morgan James Publishing, is now available. Learn more at www.judithfitzsimmons. com. A certified aromatherapist, she lives in Franklin, TN, and enjoys teaching yoga.

Writing about exceptional events and wonderful people, **John Forrest** has had seventeen stories appear in the Chicken Soup for the Soul series. He has published the Christmas anthologies *Angels, Stars, and Trees* and *Home for Christmas*. He lives in Orillia, ON, with his wife Carol. E-mail him at johnforrest@rogers.com.

Cortney Fries is a freelance writer and Chicago mom of two. She believes in facing challenges head-on and focusing on the joys in life — family, love and adventure. Cortney writes about patience, gratitude and family fun. She loves crab legs and a good lip balm.

Sam Georges practiced law for seventeen years in Ohio and subsequently was the CEO/President and General Counsel of the Anthony Robbins Organization in San Diego, CA for twenty-two years. He served in the United States Air Force with the Strategic Air Command in the U.S. and Asia. He is now retired and lives in Las Vegas, NV.

Dianna Graveman is a former teacher, manuscript editor, college instructor, and training designer. She is co-author of four regional histories (and one forthcoming), co-editor of an anthology, and author of numerous articles and stories. Dianna owns 2 Rivers Editorial & Design, LLC.

Karen Gray-Keeler became addicted to the adventure and adrenaline buzz of bike trips. Since biking the Rockies, she has enjoyed exploring the world by bike with her husband and adult children. Her stories have also appeared in *Chicken Soup for the Soul: Runners* and *Chicken Soup for the Soul: Empty Nesters*.

Neha Gupta is the founder of Elite Private Tutors, a national company focused on making moms' lives easier. She is also the author of *The 4 Year Plan*, a guide to help get your child into college. A graduate of Rice University, Neha loves working with children and helping them find their passion at an early age.

Andrea Hadhazy is a full-time voiceover actress and singer who resides in Las Vegas, NV, with her dog Ruxin and her brother James — a nationally ranked competitive flair bartender. She voices national and local TV and radio commercials, video games, and corporate explainer and narration videos, living each day with gratitude.

Michelle Hauser is a former professional fundraiser turned humorist, newspaper columnist and freelance writer. She and her husband Mark live in Eastern Ontario, Canada with their son Joseph. Her work includes contributions to CBC Radio and numerous Canadian newspapers and magazines.

Mary Ann Hayhurst loves to write and read inspiring stories that lift the spirit. She loves to travel and spend time with her family.

Deirdre Higgins, a graduate of Columbia University's MFA program, has been writing since she could first hold a pencil. She's written for the stage as well as for the screen. She teaches writing at the American Language Center at UCLA. She has two children and is busy finishing up her first novel.

On Mondays, **Rebecca Hill** can often be found "socializing" (i.e., playing with) the cats at the Lange Foundation, searching thrift stores for a new dress or roaming the candy aisle of CVS looking for a special treat. She probably won't answer her phone on a Monday, but you can try e-mailing her at bohoembassy@verizon.net.

Ann Hoffman is a retired university lecturer of English and music. Her hobbies are choral singing, patchwork quilting and writing. She has five children, eleven grandchildren, and lives with her husband in the small coastal town of Port Elizabeth in Nelson Mandela Bay, South Africa.

Stephanie Jackson received her B.A. degree in Speech Communications and certification as a Health and Wellness Coach. She has a teenage daughter and lives in the Northwest. Stephanie enjoys being outdoors, traveling, music and being with friends and family. Her life's work is helping other women live a life of joy and meaning.

A graduate of California State University, Fullerton, with a bachelor's degree in Human Biology, **Linda M. Johnson** has held executive and leadership positions within hospitals, charities and other NGOs. Linda recently sold her California business, a full-service salon of twenty years, to move to Las Vegas, NV with her kitty, Scarlet.

Ericka Kahler has lived in eight states, each progressively farther north. She graduated from the University of West Florida with a B.A. degree in History in 1999. Ericka is now a web developer in Michigan, sharing her home with a husband and way too many dogs.

Sarah LM Klauda has been a full-time writer for four years and loves writing for young adults. She is an active volunteer with animal rescues in the Baltimore area. In her spare time, Sarah likes to camp, hike, fish, play video games, and read.

Ryan Kluftinger is a fiction and nonfiction writer from Montreal, QC. He studied physics and art history at McGill University, and still pursues these passions alongside his writing. Ryan is married to his high school sweetheart and loves exploring life's adventures with her.

Krystal Klumpp is a U.S. Army veteran who served in Afghanistan and currently resides in Japan. She began the site http://www.digtravelmagazine.com to help empower women to go out and explore the world. In her free time she enjoys photography, Netflix binges and trying out new and delicious food. E-mail her at krystal@digtravelmag.com.

April Knight's favorite thing to do is riding horses. Nothing comes closer to flying than galloping a horse on a windy day. April just finished writing a romance novel, *West of Nowhere*.

Ruth Knox has loved writing ever since she could first hold a pencil. She believes in the power of the written word to unite people. Born in Alberta, Ruth now lives in Idaho with her new husband and is working on her first novel. E-mail her at ruthknox@live.com.

Geetanjali Krishna is a journalist, children's book author and mother of two. She loves to read, travel the world and walk. This year, her resolution to have 365 really "good" mornings has meant that every day she listens to Bach, with a cup of tea in hand, for a slow, happy hour after waking.

Beth Levine is an award-winning writer whose work has been published in *O, Woman's Day* and many other national magazines. She was last seen on stage as Villager #6 in *Fiddler on the Roof*. Critics are still referencing her breakout performance (cough). Learn more at www.bethlevine.net or through twitter at @BethLevine75.

Anna Lucas is a real-deal Wellness Advisor and founder of Crave Yoga & Wellness LLC. She is a prolific writer, national speaker, an avid stunt kite flyer, a free-flowing yoga instructor, a pro-world traveler, and an expansive grinner. She hails from Wisconsin. E-mail her at craveyogawellness@gmail.com.

Rhonda Maller is a professional writer who writes blogs and social media and marketing copy for companies throughout the U.S. She is also a freelance inspirational writer/speaker. Rhonda enjoys reading, writing, crafting, traveling, and spending time with her family, including thirteen grandchildren, and friends.

Alana Marie once tipped the scales at 528 pounds. The addictions to food and alcohol wrapped their arms around her and held her captive for nearly twenty years. In 2012 she had an epiphany and changed her life. She stopped drinking, lost 250 pounds and began writing stories about her life for a book called *Pick a Struggle Cupcake*.

Denise Marks has a business administration degree and is CEO of a manufacturing company. Her stories appear in multiple Chicken Soup for the Soul books. In 2014 she published a children's book, *Remember the Rainbow*, to address bullying issues. Denise enjoys her three grandkids and writing for her devotional blog.

Judith Marks-White is an award-winning *Westport News* (CT) columnist of "In Other Words." She has authored two novels published by Random House/Ballantine Books: *Seducing Harry* and *Bachelor Degree*. Her work appears in magazines and anthologies. She teaches humor writing, lectures widely and is working on her third novel.

Alison P. Martinez lives with her husband Richard in sunny Tucson, AZ. She writes for magazines including *Woman's World*, *Purpose*, *Live*, and *Light*.

Australian-born **Buzz McCarthy**, a traveller since the age of twenty-one, has visited eighty-five countries and lived in several. She has a PhD in Psychoneurology and a large toolkit to help people transform their lives. Divorced with one son, she lives in London and enjoys summers in her beautiful villa in the hills of Tuscany, Italy.

Brianna Mears is a high school student from Austin, TX. She feels the most herself on the court with her tennis team and enjoys spending time with friends. Brianna has always enjoyed her academic courses, but has recently discovered her passion for English and writing.

Originally editor of an in-house magazine, **Marsha Warren Mittman** recently returned to writing. Numerous poems and short stories of hers have been published in anthologies, as well as a chapbook for use in meditation programs. A second chapbook, *Patriarchal Chronicles*, was just completed. She is the recipient of six writing awards.

Tamara Moran-Smith is a mom who enjoys reading (loads) and writing (of course), spending time with her family, music, dancing, travel, and being tugged around the neighborhood by her dog. She writes inspirational and humorous essays about life.

Marya Morin is a freelance writer. Her stories and poems have appeared in publications such as *Woman's World* and Hallmark. Marya also penned a weekly humorous column for an online newsletter and writes custom poetry on request. She lives in the country with her husband. E-mail her at Akushla514@hotmail.com.

Karen Coffee Nicholson is a graduate of the University of Washington and Western Washington University. She is a fifth grade teacher in Shoreline, WA. She loves books and sharing them with her students. Karen is the proud mother of an adult son and daughter. She loves to travel!

Emily Oman is currently working towards her Bachelor of Arts degree in English from Northeastern University in Boston. In addition to maintaining a 3.8 grade point average, she is also a stay-at-home mom to a twenty-month-old daughter and wife to her husband of seven years. She enjoys reading, drawing, hiking, and spending time outside.

Lisa Pawlak is a freelance writer, avid traveler and mother of two adventurous boys. A regular contributor to the Chicken Soup for the Soul series, *Carlsbad*, *Orange Coast Magazine*, and *San Diego Family* magazines, her personal essays can also be found in *Coping with Cancer* and *The Christian Science Monitor*.

Timothy Peterson is an award-winning marketing executive who received his B.A. degree from Yale in 1987. He and his partner of twenty-five years live on Long Island, NY, and spend much of their time together enjoying and collecting art.

Connie Pombo is a freelance writer, speaker, author of two books and contributor to numerous anthologies, including the Chicken Soup for the Soul series. When she's not writing or speaking, she enjoys traveling and divides her time between South America and California.

Connie Kaseweter Pullen received her Bachelor of Arts degree, *cum laude*, from the University of Portland in 2006, with a double major in Psychology and Sociology, at the age of sixty-three. She is the mother of five grown children and also a grandmother and a great-grandmother. Connie enjoys photography and writing.

Dr. Mitra Ray was born in Kolkata, India. She received her B.A. degree from Cornell University and her PhD from Stanford Medical School. Today she speaks around the world and has written several books—her latest: *Do You Have the Guts to Be Beautiful?* She resides in Washington with her husband and two daughters.

Denise Reich is an Italian-born, New York City–raised world traveler, writer, dancer, photographer, music fan and baseball aficionada. She contributes to the Canadian magazine *Shameless* and has written for publications in the U.S., Canada, Bermuda and elsewhere. Denise is very happy to be a repeat Chicken Soup for the Soul contributor.

Anjie Reynolds holds degrees in English from Western Washington University and teaches Writing at Rogue Community College. She is the recipient of an Oregon Literary Arts fellowship for Children's Literature and lives in Ashland, OR, with her husband and their two children. E-mail her at anjiereynolds@hotmail.com.

Sallie A. Rodman received her Certification in Professional Writing from California State University, Long Beach, where she currently teaches a class for seniors at the Osher Lifelong Learning Institute. Her work has appeared in many Chicken Soup for the Soul anthologies. E-mail her at sa.rodman@verizon.net.

Nicole Ross is a corporate marketer, freelance copywriter, aspiring novelist, recovering blogger, and chronic hobbyist who is equally at home on the back of a horse, inside the boxing ring, pounding away at her keyboard, or perched in downward dog atop her yoga mat. Learn more at nicolekristineross.com.

Stephen Rusiniak is a former police detective who specialized and lectured on juvenile/family matters. He now shares his thoughts through his writings and has appeared in various publications, including several Chicken Soup for the Soul books. Contact him via Facebook, on Twitter @StephenRusiniak, or e-mail him at StephenRusiniak@yahoo.com.

Beth Saadati is currently teaching high school writing classes, homeschooling her son and daughter, and drafting two narrative nonfiction books. In memory of her beloved daughter Jenna, she completed her second half marathon—this time without injury—366 days after her first. E-mail her at bethsaadati@gmail.com.

Sue Sanders' essays have appeared in *The New York Times*, *The Washington Post*, *Real Simple*, *Parents*, *Family Circle*, *Salon*, *Brain*, *Child* and others. She's the author of *Mom, I'm Not a Kid Anymore*.

Jenni Schaefer is a leading motivational writer and speaker, appearing on *Dr. Phil* and in *The New York Times*, at conferences and on college campuses nationwide. Her books include *Life Without Ed*; *Goodbye Ed, Hello Me*; and *Almost Anorexic*, written in collaboration with Harvard Medical School. Learn more at www.jennischaefer.com.

Edie Schmidt is a freelance writer and full-time mom, originally from Southeastern Kentucky. She earned her B.S. degree at University of the Cumberlands, Williamsburg, KY. She lives with her husband and two children by the sea, where she enjoys baking bread, coloring and going to the park.

Jennifer Simonetti-Bryan is the fourth woman in the U.S. to achieve the highest wine title in the world, Master of Wine. She is also an author, host and professor for *The Great Courses*, and partner in Wine Ring, a smart technology firm granted three U.S. patents that provides recommendations based on preference.

Paula Klendworth Skory received her B.S. and M.S. degree, *summa cum laude*, from the University of North Texas. She is a registered CPA and lives in Washington, IL, where she and her husband raised their three children. She is the youngest of ten children, and a breast cancer survivor. She tries to find the beauty in the little moments of life.

Sandi Staton is retired and enjoys creating digital designs. She makes piano recordings for family, friends, and nursing homes. She is married, has a son—four grandsons, one granddaughter, and one great grandson. She loves her family and the time she spends with them. She plans to write a book of poems and an inspirational devotional.

The more she concentrated on taking those five minutes, the more changes occurred. Remarkably, what was insurmountable was now do-able. **JC Sullivan** left Corporate America to backpack and is now happily (except for the cold) based in New York City, where she writes, acts and directs. E-mail her at PoetryByJC@yahoo.com.

Crystal Thieringer is blissfully retired yet busier than ever. She and her husband are the live-in people for two stubborn and rather opinionated cats. Her blog, *Muse & Meander*, also showcases her photography. It can be found at www.crystalthieringer.com. She is currently working on a contemporary series for young adults.

Elizabeth Titus has been an English teacher, journalist, advertising executive, and communications director (fifteen years at American Express). She has an M.A. degree in English and an MBA from the University of Pennsylvania. She is guardian in the U.S. to Sabira, now at Trinity College.

Ann Vitale lives in rural northeast Pennsylvania, has a University of Michigan degree in Microbiology, and worked in hospitals and research before joining her husband in their Ford dealership. She trained dogs and their owners for many years. She took the advice in her story and enrolled in beginning drawing and yoga classes.

Pat Wahler is a grant writer by day and award-winning writer of essays and short stories by night. She is proud to be a contributor to eight titles in the Chicken Soup for the Soul series. A lifelong animal lover, Pat ponders critters, writing, and life's little mysteries at www.critteralley.blogspot.com.

Kate Wan is an executive and leadership coach. When she isn't coaching, she's a passionate family woman who cares for her three children. She loves time with her husband, skiing, yoga, traveling, dining out and a glass of wine to bring a day to a close. Kate is always looking for a newfangled way to inspire the best in others.

Allyson Hawkins Ward is a motivational speaker, trainer and executive coach. She holds an MBA degree from the University of Michigan, a B.A. degree from Boston College and is an NLP Master Practitioner. She lives with her husband and daughters. Her passion is coaching career woman to balance love, life, career and parenting.

David Warren lives in Kettering, OH with his wife Angela and daughter Marissa. He is Vice President of Lutz Americas. David is the author of the children's book *Mealtime Guests*. He writes for *Dayton Parent* magazine and has now appeared in the Chicken Soup for the Soul series three times.

Benny Wasserman grew up in Detroit, MI. He was a former aerospace engineer and has been an Einstein impersonator since 1992. His book, *Presidents Were Teenagers Too* was published in 2007. Benny has been a journal writer since 1985, and has completed his autobiography. He is an avid reader and Ping-Pong player.

Sheila Wasserman has a science degree from York University in Toronto and a business degree from Keller Graduate School of Management in Chicago. When not traveling, she slips courses into her schedule at St. Petersburg College in Florida. Her husband and writing group, Women of the Round Table, encourage her written word.

Angela Wolthuis finds inspiration for her writing in everything around her and loves to share her stories as encouragements for others.

Berni Xiong is the author of *The Year of the Brave Bear: Speak Up. Stand Out. Change Your World.* She owns Brave Bear Media, a coaching and consulting firm serving entrepreneurs around the globe. She is a certified Weight Management Specialist, Reiki practitioner, speaker, and writing coach for change-making authors.

Meet Amy Newmark

Amy Newmark was a writer, speaker, Wall Street analyst and business executive in the worlds of finance and telecommunications for more than thirty years. Today she is publisher, editor-in-chief and coauthor of the Chicken Soup for the Soul book series. By curating and editing inspirational true stories from ordinary people who have had extraordinary experiences, Amy has kept the twenty-two-year-old Chicken Soup for the Soul brand fresh and relevant, and still part of the social zeitgeist.

Amy graduated *magna cum laude* from Harvard University where she majored in Portuguese and minored in French. She wrote her thesis about popular, spoken-word poetry in Brazil, which involved traveling throughout Brazil and meeting with poets and writers to collect their stories. She is delighted to have come full circle in her writing career — from collecting poetry "from the people" in Brazil as a twenty-year-old to, three decades later, collecting stories and poems "from the people" for Chicken Soup for the Soul.

Amy has a national syndicated newspaper column and is a frequent radio and TV guest, passing along the real-life lessons and useful tips she has picked up from reading and editing thousands of Chicken Soup for the Soul stories.

She and her husband are the proud parents of four grown children and in her limited spare time, Amy enjoys visiting them, hiking, and reading books that she did not have to edit.

Follow her on Twitter @amynewmark and @chickensoupsoul.

Meet
Loren Slocum Lahav

Loren Slocum Lahav is an international personal-development speaker, seminar leader, coach, author, philanthropist, entrepreneur, wife and mother. People tend to describe Loren as "the real deal." Loren has a very busy career as a keynote speaker and multi-day trainer for many companies around the world. She has had the remarkable experience of traveling the world to help people discover who they are at their core for the past twenty-five years.

As the International Crew Facilitator for over two decades for the recognized authority on the psychology of leadership and peak performance, Anthony Robbins, Loren has led and trained teams in cities around the world. For the past fourteen years, Loren has facilitated more than 160 five-day comprehensive programs for Anthony Robbins in the United States, Fiji, Puerto Rico and Europe that emphasize the power of living a balanced life.

Loren is the founder, chief executive officer, and president of Lobella International, an organization inspired to help women "stay true to who they are." She is also the author of *Life Tuneups* (2009) and *No Greater Love: Being an Extraordinary Mom* (1999), which was re-released in 2008 as *The Greatest Love*.

Loren lives with her husband Zohar Lahav and their four

children—Josua, Samantha, Quinn and Asher—in Las Vegas, Nevada. She is an active volunteer with her children's schools, and has been on the Las Vegas St. Jude Children's Research Hospital board for the past seven years. She also started Elevate and the SPIN campaign to help Las Vegas citizens in need.

Thank You

We owe huge thanks to all of our contributors. We know that you poured your hearts and souls into the thousands of stories that you shared with us. We appreciate your willingness to open up your lives to other Chicken Soup for the Soul readers and share your own experiences, no matter how personal. As we read and edited these truly awe-inspiring stories, we were excited by the potential of this book to inspire people.

We could only publish a small percentage of the stories that were submitted, but we read every single one and even the ones that do not appear in the book had an influence on us and on the final manuscript. We owe special thanks to senior editor Barbara LoMonaco, who read all the stories submitted for this book. She, along with assistant publisher D'ette Corona, editor Marti Davidson Sichel, and editor Ronelle Frankel, also helped us choose the final 101 stories. Marti and managing editor Kristiana Pastir helped edit and proofread the manuscript.

We also owe a very special thanks to our creative director and book producer, Brian Taylor at Pneuma Books, for his brilliant vision for our covers and interiors.

We at Chicken Soup for the Soul are also grateful to have had Loren join us in this project, and she wants to acknowledge the influence of several of her key mentors, including Anthony Robbins, Jeff Roberti, Keith Cunningham, and Bob Proctor.

~Amy Newmark and Loren Slocum Lahav

Sharing Happiness, Inspiration, and Wellness

Real people sharing real stories, every day, all over the world. In 2007, *USA Today* named *Chicken Soup for the Soul* one of the five most memorable books in the last quarter-century. With over 100 million books sold to date in the U.S. and Canada alone, more than 200 titles in print, and translations into more than forty languages, "chicken soup for the soul" is one of the world's best-known phrases.

Today, twenty-two years after we first began sharing happiness, inspiration and wellness through our books, we continue to delight our readers with new titles, but have also evolved beyond the bookstore, with super premium pet food, a line of high quality food to bring people together for healthy meals, and a variety of licensed products and digital offerings, all inspired by stories. Chicken Soup for the Soul has recently expanded into visual storytelling through movies and television. Chicken Soup for the Soul is "changing the world one story at a time®." Thanks for reading!

Share with Us

We all have had Chicken Soup for the Soul moments in our lives. If you would like to share your story or poem with millions of people around the world, go to chickensoup.com and click on "Submit Your Story." You may be able to help another reader, and become a published author at the same time. Some of our past contributors have launched writing and speaking careers from the publication of their stories in our books!

We only accept story submissions via our website. They are no longer accepted via mail or fax.

To contact us regarding other matters, please send us an e-mail through webmaster@chickensoupforthesoul.com, or fax or write us at:

Chicken Soup for the Soul
P.O. Box 700
Cos Cob, CT 06807-0700
Fax: 203-861-7194

One more note from your friends at Chicken Soup for the Soul: Occasionally, we receive an unsolicited book manuscript from one of our readers, and we would like to respectfully inform you that we do not accept unsolicited manuscripts and we must discard the ones that appear.

Chicken Soup for the Soul

For moments that become stories™

www.chickensoup.com